Time and Trauma in Analytical Psychology and Psychotherapy

I0092049

The Wisdom of Andean Shamanism

Deborah Bryon

R Routledge
Taylor & Francis Group

LONDON AND NEW YORK

Designed cover image: Ecstasy by Deborah Bryon

First published 2024
by Routledge
4 Park Square, Milton Park, Abingdon, Oxon OX14 4RN

and by Routledge
605 Third Avenue, New York, NY 10158

Routledge is an imprint of the Taylor & Francis Group, an informa business

© 2024 Deborah Bryon

British Library Cataloguing-in-Publication Data
A catalogue record for this book is available from the British Library

Library of Congress Cataloging-in-Publication Data
Names: Bryon, Deborah, author.
Title: Time and trauma in analytical psychology and psychotherapy : the wisdom of Andean Shamanism / Deborah Bryon.
Description: Abingdon, Oxon ; New York, NY : Routledge, 2024. |
Includes bibliographical references and index. |
Identifiers: LCCN 2023050234 (print) | LCCN 2023050235 (ebook) |
ISBN 9781032411385 (hardback) | ISBN 9781032411378 (paperback) |
ISBN 9781003356448 (ebook)
Subjects: LCSH: Time—Psychological aspects. | Jungian psychology. |
Shamanism—Andes Region.
Classification: LCC BF468 .B77 2024 (print) |
LCC BF468 (ebook) | DDC 153.7/53—dc23/eng/20240209
LC record available at https://lccn.loc.gov/2023050234
LC ebook record available at https://lccn.loc.gov/2023050235

ISBN: 978-1-032-41138-5 (hbk)
ISBN: 978-1-032-41137-8 (pbk)
ISBN: 978-1-003-35644-8 (ebk)

DOI: 10.4324/9781003356448

Typeset in Times New Roman
by Newgen Publishing UK

Dr. Bryon's bold weaving together of interpersonal and Jungian analytic perspectives, informed by indigenous Andean shamanism, and contemporary scientific understanding of time invites the reader into an expansive, enriched vision of the world. Her personal descent to deep layers of unconscious phenomena is shown to bring an enhanced awareness of reality with profound healing effects. The wisdom and integrative power of a syncretic approach to recovering from trauma shines through the text and will open doors for all who enter.

Joe Cambray, Ph.D., IAAP, Past-President-CEO, Pacifica
Graduate Institute.

Jungian analyst and psychologist Deborah Bryon offers Andean shamanic wisdom as it dovetails with concepts from contemporary relational psychoanalysis. After being adopted and inducted by Peruvian paqos, Bryon seamlessly combines her personal experience with theoretical concepts to highlight practices of connection and compassion. This is a one of a kind, can't-put-down book, a roadmap for connecting states of light, energy, joy, and wholeness with processes of healing.

Terry Marks-Tarlow, Ph.D., author of *Psyche's Veil, Clinical Intuition
in Psychotherapy, Awakening Clinical Intuition, Play & Creativity in
Psychotherapy*, and A *Fractal Epistemology for a Scientific Psychology*.

Deborah Bryon presents a novel view of the roots of trauma based on her own transformative, spiritual experiences in Peru, combined with her clinical encounters as a Jungian analyst. What emerges is a fascinating insight into how trauma gets stuck in time, quite literally frozen in an atemporal, unconscious realm, supplemented with an understanding on how it might then be released by bringing it back into time, switching between the two viewpoints. Using a wide range of examples, from psychology to poetry to physics, Bryon skillfully navigates the two worlds like a shaman.

Professor Dean Rickles, Ph.D. - Faculty of Science, University of
Sydney, Co-Director, Centre for Time, co-author of *Dual-Aspect
Monism and the Deep Structure of Meaning*.

Deborah Bryon's *Time and Trauma in Analytical Psychology and Psychotherapy* provides a wide-ranging perspective on experiences central to contemporary depth psychology – i.e., the subjective experience of time and trauma. In this refreshingly integrative volume, she draws extensively on her experiences as a psychologist and Jungian psychoanalyst as well as her extensive immersion in Andean shamanistic practice. She utilizes the conceptual framework of quantum theory to reveal underlying links between mystical and clinical experience, expanding the reader's understanding of both experiential domains. The book also provides the reader with an in-depth introduction to Andean medicine practices. *Time and Trauma* is scholarly, insightful, and experientially grounded. Recommended for any reader seeking a fresh lens for understanding subjective experience across a variety of settings.

Mark Winborn, PhD, NCPsyA - clinical psychologist and Jungian psychoanalyst, author of *Jungian Psychoanalysis* and *Interpretation in Jungian Analysis*.

A masterful journey through Andean medicine to offer a new, valuable perspective on Jung's unconscious and its atemporal vastness. This is accomplished by bringing us on a journey through the eyes and mind of an Andean shaman (*paqo*), its secrets passed on to her orally and elucidated here by thorough scholarship, making this a unique and significant contribution to the dimensions of transcendent experiences, the energy and nature of psyche, Jung's notion of individuation and why psychoanalysis and the Andean tradition weave so smoothly with Quantum physics.

Professor Leslie Stein, Ph.D. - Jungian Analyst, author of *Working with Mystical Experiences in Psychoanalysis*.

Time and Trauma in Analytical Psychology and Psychotherapy

This book explores the experience of time in psychoanalysis and Andean shamanism. It plots ways to work through unresolved trauma by expanding how we conceptualize both implicit and nonverbal atemporal experience, drawing from the rituals, narratives, and medicine of Andean shamans and quantum theory.

Shifting between subjective states in time is fundamental in trauma work and psychoanalysis. Integrating traumatic experiences that have become split off and held in "timeless" unconscious states of implicit memory is an essential aspect of psychic healing. Becoming familiar with the Andean shamans' understanding of atemporal experience, as well as learning about their ways of "grounding" the experience consciously, can offer a route through which psychoanalysis and therapy may deepen the therapeutic process and open new states of consciousness. Theories developed in quantum physics are included to parallel the shamans' experience and for describing the analytic process.

Written by a noted expert in this field, this insightful volume will interest trainee and practitioner analytical psychologists, as well as any professional interested in the resolution of trauma within a psychotherapeutic setting.

Deborah Bryon is a graduate of UCLA and the University of Denver. She has previously published two books and several articles on Andean shamanism and psychoanalysis and is a frequent lecturer in the international Jungian analytic community. In addition to teaching and private practice, Deborah exhibits her paintings at Spark Gallery in Denver.

Time and Trauma in Analytical Psychology and Psychotherapy

In loving memory of my sweet son Colin, who has walked in other realms.

Contents

Introduction

Our subjective experience of the interaction of time with space in any given moment defines our perception of reality in the present and in our dreams, in how we remember the past, and in our projection of potential future trajectories. I remember studying painting and hearing my favorite professor comment that musicians control experience through manipulating tempo and rhythm in the fourth dimension, while visual artists slow a viewer down by creating interest in the first three dimensions, through the expression of color and composition by using space.

When I was about six or seven years old, I had the impression that time was an abstract structure existing outside of me that could not be altered. I remember periods of longing for time to pass. Time seemed to move much slower when counting the days until my grandmother came to visit us, or waiting for Christmas morning, or trick or treating on Halloween. In grade school, waiting for recess during a boring lesson could feel like an eternity, while Friday afternoon art classes seemed to fly by much faster. At that age, things that were happening in the world seemed larger—both in size and figuratively. In childhood states of reverie during the summer months—taking time during play to lie down in a field of grass to watch the clouds, the days seemed longer than they do now. Perhaps this is because there was no schedule to conform to. In the summer, I didn't experience life as a habitual routine—every experience was new. As I've grown older, sitting in my consulting room with my analysands, I often hear them commenting that they feel time is speeding up and passing them by more quickly.

Although the sense of time passing is subjective, these experiences exist within the context of time and space, in consensual reality. There are other psychic states that do not conform to temporal experience, which have shaped my understanding and interest in the phenomenon of time.

More than a couple of decades ago, while building a private practice and entering analytic training with the Inter-Regional Society of Jungian Analysts (IRSJA), I began to travel to Peru to study with the Q'ero paqos (shamans) in the Andes.[1]

This is when I became acutely aware of the existence of atemporal reality. In my training to become a *yachacheq* (a paqo who works with the mind), I began receiving *karpay* rites in initiation ceremonies from the paqos, when the "lineage" from their *misa* (medicine bundle) was energetically transmitted into mine. During

DOI: 10.4324/9781003356448-1

these rituals, I found myself dropping into atemporal states that to me seemed to be in an undifferentiated energetic realm beyond form and words, where everything was connected. These experiences, which took place over several years, sparked my interest in atemporal time. I began to see connections between the shamanic states of ecstasy I was experiencing, the oceanic experience of oneness in infancy that Freud (1930) described, and the atemporal states of implicit memory that often develop in response to trauma. This was the impetus in my writing this book.

My descriptions of shamanic experience that I will be drawing from in this writing are based upon my study with the Q'ero shamans living in the Andes of Peru. I am a psychologist and a psychoanalyst—not an anthropologist. The information presented is based upon my own experience and what was passed on to me orally by the paqos (Andean shamans). For this reason, I will be unable to provide research references when describing Andean shamanic practices, although I will be referencing psychoanalytic literature, as well as other scientific references regarding time. Because my training has been with the paqos in the Andes specifically, this is the method and cosmology I will be working from. Although there may be overlap between Andean medicine (shamanism), and other forms of shamanism, because there are cultural differences and so forth my descriptions of Andean practices may not necessarily apply to other types of shamanism.

Temporality and Atemporality in Andean Medicine

While undergoing experiential training that often involved deep meditative states in ceremony and initiatory rituals, I often felt my sense of linear time dropping away. Although I could not put words to it, in a deeply calm state I often had the sense of being outside of time, and that the past, present, and future were accessible simultaneously because everything was one. When I attempted to put words to the experience and describe it, I was immediately back in a temporal state and outside of the experience.

This is when I discovered that when I tried to describe the experience—using words—language exists in a state of temporality. I came to understand that temporal reality requires context, anchored in experiencing the outer world of physical reality, sequentially, while atemporal or extra-temporal reality was not necessarily a linear experience. In addition, deep atemporal meditative states, a sense of separation between one's self, others, and the world drops away and everything is experienced as being connected. This is frequently described as a state of ecstasy and a felt sense of "coming home." I learned through the initiations I was experiencing that the deeper one "drops into" a state of connected experience of oneness, the less differentiated the experience becomes and it can feel as though multiple points in time are accessible at the same time and can be experienced simultaneously.

Atemporal states are not bracketed in a past, present, and future. Because there is no temporal sequencing and no experience of separation, these experiences cannot be referenced by language. Consensual reality—a shared sense of a physical and symbolic world between one's self and others—is understood within the constructs of temporality. Life unfolds on a timeline with a beginning, a middle, and an end, and a sense of then and now that can be reflected upon and described through language.

Liminal States between Temporal and Atemporal Experience

In temporal reality, sequential timelines exist, which enable the formation of narratives that can organize experience within the context of consensual, physical existence. I discovered that in psychic states bordering on ego-consciousness, such as the imaginal realm of dreams and reverie, "everything" is not necessarily happening at once. In these liminal states, time can bend, and is not inescapably bound to an order of past, present, and future. Jumps are often made back and forth between a "then and now" and an imagined future.

I've observed in my own analytic work with my analysands that in dreamscapes, and "working through" and reliving past trauma, reality is frequently experienced in spaces of psychic "borderlands"—somewhere beyond ego-consciousness—where the experience or re-experiencing of events often does not comply with the parameters governing a linear time and space paradigm. The experience of time is often inconsistent. In dream states, a long span of time may be occurring only in minutes in the "real-time" of physical reality. In *The Lion, The Witch, and the Wardrobe* (Lewis, 1950) decades could pass in the land of Narnia that took place in a few minutes in the outer physical world.

In Peru, some of the gifted coca leaf trackers I have worked with have an uncanny sense of the future. By throwing coca leaves and reading the pattern formations that the leaves land in they can interpret current events and what will follow. They have told me that "seeing" the occurrence of a future event is much easier than forecasting when the event will take place in time. Predicting the actual time an event will occur is a greater challenge because it requires accessing information in an atemporal realm and then transferring it and translating it within the context of temporal reality and these different realms do not correspond to each other in a predictable way.

Temporality and Atemporality in Psychoanalysis

As mentioned earlier, while returning from trips to Peru my interest in the subjective experience of time in my work as an analyst also grew stronger. I became increasingly aware that some of the nonverbal shamanic energetic states I was experiencing seemed to correspond with early states of regression that analysands were entering into while working through past trauma, with the healing process involved moving between then and now.

Sitting with analysands in sessions who were processing previously undifferentiated trauma from the past, I observed that the psychic healing process followed a progression that was not linear. I noticed that often they had difficulty accessing their feelings, and often became disconnected from forming a cohesive personal narrative of the past. There appeared to be toggling back and forth between atemporal memory states where past trauma was being held and the temporality of ego-consciousness in the present.

In sessions with some analysands with traumatic histories, who had become attached to the personal stories they had constructed about their past, sometimes it became possible to move beyond the preconceived narratives by encouraging them to shift their attention to tracking less familiar nonverbal somatic states. If these states started to become too intense, the analysand would often begin to dissociate, indicated by their description of having a lack of feeling or a sense of numbness. In these atemporal states, time became frozen. In these cases, I would encourage the analysand to focus their attention on coming back to an awareness of being with me, in the room. In this process, we shifted between atemporal and temporal experiential states together. I became increasingly aware that the unmetabolized implicit memories of trauma that were beginning to surface for analysands during sessions, which had been previously stored in the unconscious, usually didn't emerge into their awareness on a linear sequential timeline. In fact, the more traumatic an event had been for them, the more disjointed the timeline became.

Some analysands could only access feeling states linked to fragmented memories previously frozen by noticing the feelings they were having in their bodies. The phenomenon of not having a sense of time often seemed to be linked to previously repressed emotional states, often combined with the sensation of feeling frozen in a traumatic past event that felt stuck.

Analysands with trauma histories frequently had gaps in the timelines of their lives that they could not remember. I discovered that the memory gaps indicated times that were too overwhelming to hold in consciousness. Other analysands were stuck in reliving periods of the past that they said they could not get out of their minds while in both waking states and in their dreams. They had become stuck in a memory time loop of the past that repeated itself that they felt they couldn't escape from. Often, they reported also finding themselves compulsively continuing to repeat destructive patterns of behavior. I am not the first analyst to observe this reaction to trauma with their analysands. I am providing an overview here and will reference the work of other theorists and analysts in subsequent chapters that coincide with these observations.

As I have described, there is a switching back and forth that happens between selfstates when moving between temporal and atemporal experiences. Temporal states are cognitive because they require the use of language, while atemporal states are experienced and held in the body. Atemporal somatic experience in shamanism and the tendency for unprocessed trauma to be held as implicit memory outside of ego-consciousness in the body also share commonalities with preverbal, nontemporal somatic states during infancy. Traumatic memories that become fragmented and locked away in implicit memory, shamanic states of ecstasy, and preverbal infancy states all exist outside of linear time.

Note

1   The Quechua word *paqo* translates as "doorway", in reference to being a conduit to the spirit world.

References

Freud, S. (1930) *Civilization and Its Discontents* (Standard Edition, vol. 21).
Lewis, C. S. (1950) *The Lion, The Witch, and the Wardrobe*, New York, NY: MacMillan Publishing CO.

Part I

Overview and Andean Medicine

Chapter 1

An Overview of the Origins of the Conceptualization of Time in Psychoanalysis and Depth Psychology

Temporal versus Atemporal Experience of Time

While the importance has been recognized of the effects of the experience of time on the psyche, many psychoanalysts, starting with Freud (1930), have voiced aggravation regarding the intangible qualities of time's intrinsic ambiguities and have acknowledged a struggle in comprehending time (Namnum, 1972; Loewald, 1972; Eissler, 1955). Freud (1937, p. 34) has written, "There is nothing in the id that corresponds to the idea of time; there is no recognition of the passage of time and—a thing that is most remarkable and waits consideration in philosophical thought—no alteration in its mental process is bent in the passage of time."

Freud's (1923–1925) concept of the beginning of awareness of time is based upon the perceptions of need or drives that the psyche experiences, first somatically, then eventually through imagining, conceptualizing a narrative. In the somatic state, the feelings of need that the psyche experience, or "instances," become "points of perception" (Freud, 1925, p. 291). Modern neuropsychology has theorized that the summation of these points of experience in time as intervals is a way of bracketing human experience (Benedetti, 1969).

Freud (1925) proposed that the existence of both a preconsciousness and a consciousness provides a means of separating from and defending against being absorbed in the experience of stimuli from the outside world. Freud has written that the capacity to contextualize time in an awareness of temporal reality occurs through ego-consciousness. "It creates a sense of 'me' and other, with the potential for establishing a historical narrative and a means of differentiating between the past and the present. Differentiation, necessary for reflection between one's experience and the external world, requires a way of delineating between then, now, and what may come to be" (Freud, 1915, p. 187).

Freud's (1915) description of time as a function of consciousness aligns with Einstein's (1954) theory that time and space are relative and variable. This "relativism" is the basis for understanding the experience of being of time itself: relativity and interdependence between what we have been and what we are becoming. Freud told his friend Marie Bonaparte (1940) that once consciousness develops, the perception of the internal experience then becomes projected

DOI: 10.4324/9781003356448-3

onto the outside world. Bonaparte (1940) expanded on Freud's ideas and associated a sense of time mindfulness of inner perceptions of the passing of life. With
the development of consciousness, this inner perception is projected outward and
referred to as time.

While consciousness is contextualized in time, Freud proposed that the unconscious was "timeless" (1915, p. 187) because there is "no reference to time at all
in the unconscious" (1915, p. 187). The unconscious exists without language and
is not organized sequentially. Rather than referencing psychic material within the
framework of a temporal reality, the feeling charge associated with psychic experience dictates how the psychic material is arranged and stored. This is evident in
dreams, where the unconscious emotional response associated with the memory of
the experience determines how it will emerge into consciousness, rather than being
regulated by the constructs of consensual reality in the external world.

Similar to Jung's (1954a, p. 12, par. 15) concept of the collective unconscious,
which he described as "a collecting place where all psychic life originates", Freud
(1940) believed that deeper layers of the unconscious contain our ancestry. The fluctuating accumulation of experience is contained and stored in a psychic depository,
where new experience continues to be absorbed. While experience may become
consciously assimilated and integrated into an explicit organizational framework
of how the world is perceived through a functioning ego, in the deeper layers of
the unconscious, structure dissipates into a reality of timelessness. This has been
referred to as oceanic experience (Saarinen, 2012).

Atemporality Time and Oceanic Experience

The oceanic feeling state can be described as a timelessness sense of oneness with
the universe (Saarinen, 2012) and has been portrayed in many Eastern and Western
disciplines, including artistic creativity and aesthetics (Stokes, 1978; Milner,
1987; Fuller, 1980; Newton, 2001, 2008), literature (Rooney, 2007), religion and
mysticism (Masson, 1980; Kakar, 1991; Merkur, 1999, 2010; Ostow, 2007), and
altered states of consciousness (Epstein, 1990) similar to the paqos' experience of
ecstasy (Bryon, 2012). In addition to denoting feelings of oneness with the universe, oceanic experience is also linked to what Jung would refer to as archetypal
experience often associated with mania, or "mana" (1954a). Jung viewed mana as:

> a universal medicinal or healing power which renders men, animals, and plants
> fruitful and endows chieftain and medicine-man with magical strength. Mana
> ... is identified with anything "extraordinarily potent," or simple with anything
> impressive. On the primitive level anything impressive is therefore medicine.
> (Jung, 1954a, p. 6)

Saarinen (2012) has used the metaphor of a diver and an ocean to describe
oceanic experience, insisting that a pairing must exist in oceanic states. The diver
would involve a temporal state of ego-consciousness while oceanic experiences

are atemporal. Freud (1930) also conceptualized the oceanic state as including two modes of functioning—although different, with an established autonomous ego and a younger narcissistic ego, which were both dependent upon development.

Psychoanalytic Discussions on Oceanic Experience

Saarinen (2012) has written that in psychoanalysis there are three descriptions of oceanic states, which are the metaphysical one (Rolland, 1929), the developmental one (Freud, 1930), and the cognitive-perceptual one (Ehrenzweig, 1967). Rolland's understanding was based upon his experience, Ehrenzweig's writing is founded in theory and experience, and Freud's conceptualization, never having experienced it directly, was based solely in theory (Saarinen, 2012). Because each of these conceptualizations share the general theoretical premise that oceanic experience occurs outside of ego-consciousness in undifferentiated psychic states, each of these theories would agree that these states exist in atemporal psychic spaces.

In *Civilization and Its Discontents* Freud (1930) first described oceanic feeling, or nondual states of being experience. In *The Future of an Illusion* Freud (1927) said that religion was a form of wish fulfillment, a fantasy arising out of the oldest, most powerful, and crucial yearning of humanity.

The concept of oceanic experience was explored further in communication between Sigmund Freud and Romain Rolland (Masson, 1980). Responding to Freud's writings, from 1923 to 1936 Rolland wrote to Freud about a sense of an eternal "oceanic" primary religious experience (Masson, 1980, pp. 36–44). Rolland (1947) was interested in deepening an understanding of the importance of establishing meaning to a universal oceanic experience. Like the paqos, Rolland's ability to maintain a connection with mystical states of oceanic experience was the result of his dedication to understanding and deepening his relationship to these experiences over his lifetime. For Rolland (1947), because a mature ego has developed firm boundaries, it could at times descend into oceanic experience without decompensating.

Rolland wrote that he lived two lives simultaneously: one in the physical reality, grounded in space and time, and another that he described as spiritual, an "infinite self of formless being, nameless, homeless, timeless, the very substance and breath of all life". Rolland pronounced the mature state he had come to enjoy as an "immediate communion with universal life" (1947, p. 10). He has written:

> *Now of all rivers the most sacred is that which gushes out eternally from the depths of the soul ... From the source to the sea, from the sea to the source, everything consists of the same Energy, of the Being without beginning and without end ... Unity, living and not abstract, is the essence of it all.* (Rolland, 1929, p. xvii)

Freud (1930, p. 66) recognized that ego boundaries were not constant and could be disrupted in the experience of being in love, in a state of psychopathology—and even in mystical oceanic states, which did not always involve a narcissistic regression. In a letter to Rolland, Freud wrote:

> *We seem to diverge rather far in the role we assign to intuition. Your mystics rely on it to teach them how to solve the riddle of the universe; we believe that it cannot reveal to us anything but primitive, instinctual impulses and attitudes—highly valuable for an embryology* [sic] *of the soul when correctly interpreted, but worthless for orientation in the alien, external world.* (Freud, 1960, pp. 392–3)

For Rolland (1930), Freud's psychoanalytic conceptualization was a disappointment and missed the true core of oceanic experience. He disapprovingly wrote:

> *You, doctors of the unconscious, instead of making yourselves citizens of this boundless empire and possessing yourselves of it, do you ever enter it except as foreigners, imbued with the preconceived idea of the superiority of your own country and incapable of ridding yourselves of the need, which itself deforms your vision, of reducing whatever you catch a glimpse of in this unknown.* (Rolland, 1930, pp.282– 3)

Because Freud (1930) was less convinced of the value of oceanic experience he was less interested in accessing oceanic primordial states. Unlike Freud who was more aligned with the paqos, Rolland focused on achieving the ability to fluidly move between ego states and oceanic experience. A primary goal in his life was spiritual consciousness, which did not alter the way he engaged with the external world (Rolland, 1929). Ehrenzweig also was a proponent of engagement with oceanic experience, to "maintain a relationship with a creative source of imagery" (1967, p. 177). Andean paqos would most likely agree with Rolland and Ehrenzweig, based on their belief that it is "important to grow corn" with mystical experience—in other words, bring back into consciousness and integrate mystical experience in states of ecstasy (Bryon, 2012).

Ehrenzweig analyzed artistic creativity and arrived at the premise that symbol formation emerged out of oceanic experience and was necessary for the "creative process in accumulation of imaginal material" (1967, pp. 32–46). Ehrenzweig described undifferentiated oceanic perception as a kind of "unlimited inter-merging between imagery and ideas enabling inner and outer realms to join and merge, with the limitations of space and time to drop away" (pp. 103, 120, 192). Based on this, Ehrenzweig (1967) proposed that a separate oceanic space of undifferentiated creativity was the source of new symbology. Ehrenzweig has written:

> *It is now widely realized that any—not only religious—creative experience can produce an oceanic state, which artists can access for creative expression.* (Ehrenzweig, 1967, p. 294)

Both Rolland and Ehrenzweig, like the paqos, viewed this kind of atemporal experience as important—a means of connecting with the "essential truth of one's being in connection with the state of universal oneness" (Rolland, 1930, p. 184).

The Shadow Side of Oceanic Experience

While oceanic experience is often described as a state of ecstasy, it can also bring up fear associated with a lack of control, and death. Saarinen's (2012, p. 14) description of oceanic experience includes concepts of unity, timelessness, boundlessness, and the potential feeling of terror. He wrote, "The ocean is structurally repressed unconscious form in its most unfathomable state" (Saarinen, 2012, p. 14). Ehrenzweig acknowledged that oceanic states could be anxiety-provoking in the beginning but argued that when more profound levels of oceanic experience were entered into an "elated sense of mania could potentially occur" (1967, p. 294).

In *Civilization and Its Discontents*, Freud (1930) resisted engaging with an "oceanic experience of connection." He stated, it is "a sensation of 'eternity', a feeling as of something limitless, unbounded—as it were, 'oceanic'" (p. 64). He continues:

> *We cannot fall out of this world ... it is a feeling of an indissoluble bond, of being one with the external world as a whole ... "I cannot discover this 'oceanic' feeling in myself ... It is not easy to deal scientifically with feelings. One can attempt to describe their physiological signs. Where this is not possible—and I am afraid that the oceanic feeling too will defy this kind of characterization—nothing remains but to fall back on the ideational content which is most readily associated with the feeling".* (Freud, 1930, p. 65)

Freud was fearful of the loss of control, which perhaps he associated with death. Roiphe has written (2016, pp. 83–4) about Freud's attitude toward his own death: "He would not allow himself the luxury of rage, or the loosening of control; he would not allow himself any kind of outspoken rebellion against the hard facts of mortality.... he talked openly about his fear of death which he referred to as his 'death deliria.'" His friend Ernest Jones wrote about Freud's early obsession to a neurotic horror of old age and death:

> *Freud interpreted the primordial feeling of oceanic connectedness as a regression into infancy, into the mother-infant bond. He believed the experience to be pathological because it resists death in its attachment to immortality. Initially, he stated that these states could exist within adult consciousness but later retracted the statement arguing that there was no validation that these feelings were linked to the need for religious experience.* (Roiphe, 2016, p. 84)

Freud perceived oceanic experience—or the experience of being in a state of "oneness" —as a regression, with a breakdown occurring between the boundaries of the ego and the external world. (Freud, 1930). It should be noted, however, that while Rolland understood the importance of oceanic experience, like Freud, he also believed that these kinds of experiences could lead to dysfunctional psychic states involving catatonia, delirium, a manic identification with deities—as well as episodes of unconsciousness. He recognized that the experience associated with oceanic states covered a broad spectrum of reactions, which included "compassion, ecstasy, terror, as well as sensations of engulfment, suffocation, flooding, dizziness, and timelessness" (Rolland, 1929, p. 17).

Jung's View of Oceanic Experience in Contrast to Freud

Many psychoanalytic writers have tried to formulate theories that include a mystical aspect of the psyche. Parsons has described Erikson's "unborn core of creation," Bion's "O", and Lacan's "Real" as examples of this (1999, p. 134). Jung (1954a) agreed with Freud (1930) that it was possible to experience atemporal oceanic states in deeper layers of the unconscious. Jung's view of oceanic experience was more closely aligned with Rolland's perception that oceanic experience involves spiritual connection and explored the existence of a "soul-complex" (Jung, 1953a, par. 302). He later wrote about the archetype of the Self (Jung, 1954b, par. 378). "The Self as such is timeless and existed before any birth." This difference of opinion may have contributed to the split between Jung and Freud. Freud was reductive in his approach, while Jung was intuitive with a prospective orientation, imagining wholeness. Ackerman (2017) has written:

> No doubt one impetus to Freud's wish to clear away the oceanic is to be found in his conflictual relationship with Jung, with whom he had broken in 1912. Jung was then importing spiritual and oceanic conceptions into his theory of analytic therapy, moving farther and farther from the metapsychology Freud had established, and the latter might have needed to keep a distance from his erstwhile ally. (Ackerman, 2017, p. 10)

Oceanic experience of non-differentiation is atemporal and although Freud (1930) understood the unconscious to be timeless, it was from a temporal vantage point, an ego perspective existing outside of the experience. Freud (1923) felt that psychoanalysis was largely a way of becoming aware of id experiences so as not to be overtaken by them—becoming conscious to control. Freud was willing to interpret atemporal experience as outside observer; he apparently felt too threatened to relinquish control and allow himself to experience it directly, which for Freud would have been a regression. Jung's approach, on the other hand, involved a willingness to be swept away and informed by the experience of atemporality. Jung believed in the numinosity of the Self and that surrendering to the experience wasn't a regressive reaction of defense, but rather part of the individuation process of moving toward wholeness (Jung, 1954b). For Jung (1958), the act of "surrendering" was a means of transcending into numinous experience that was spiritual, and greater than ego-consciousness. He allowed himself to drop into the experience with his analysands, trusting the wisdom of the unconscious, which Freud never acknowledged.

The Paqos' Perception and Oceanic Experience

The understanding of oceanic experience has been controversial. Even before Freud's writing on the topic, Herbert Silberer (1917) proposed that mystical experience was potentially therapeutic, while Paul Federn (1932) saw it as a regression into a primitive state.[1] Rolland's statement, "Unity, living and not abstract, is the essence of it all" corresponds most closely with the paqos' attitude (1929, p. xvii). Paqos maintain that moving deeper into oceanic experience (energetic states of oneness) involves profound connection with *apu kuna* (the collective of the mountain spirits, or winged beings), *Pachamama* (Mother Earth), and *Inti Tayta* (Father Sun). For paqos, entering states of ecstasy is the result of connecting deeply with the natural world.

Unlike Freud, paqos don't perceive oceanic experience to be a shift away from ego-consciousness, as they do not view psychic organization to be a composite of separate distinct parts, determined by conscious and unconscious. Current psychoanalytic thought, such as complexity theory (Galatzer-Levy, 1978; Sashin and Callahan, 1990; Spruiell, 1993; Thelen and Smith, 1994; Stolorow, 1997; Ghent, 2002; Coburn, 2002; Sander, 2002; Seligman, 2005) has moved away from conceptualizing conscious and unconscious as separate, rather viewing them as inter-related.

Jung did not believe the psyche was organized in discrete parts either. He believed that there wasn't a clear distinction between the conscious and unconscious and understood the psyche to be a "conscious-unconscious whole" (Pauli, 1994). Contemporary psychoanalyst Zeddies (2002) has argued that integration of a network of unexpressed and unspoken meanings allows for the development of new articulated meaning. Donnel Stern (2002) has agreed with Timothy Zeddies and has written about the interplay between the conscious and unconscious:

It is true, of course, that without the continuous infusion of the nonverbal and the vitality of the unconscious, language would be a dead thing. But it is just as true that without language, there would be no meaning at all, since even the nonverbal is defined by the possibility of speech and thought ... The unformulated, nonverbal background that accompanies explicit verbal meanings is part of the patterning or emotional atmosphere that underlies the ongoing sense we have of what relationships "feel like" to us ... And the meaning of these unconscious relational patterns shifts slightly when, from within them, we find our way to a meaning they would not previously have accommodated. Explicit conscious meanings and unconscious relational patterns continuously influence one another. (Stern, 2002, p. 520)

Expanding the Conceptualization of the Analytic Third and a Co-Created Field in Analysis

Bion conceptualized a "caesura," a form of primitive unrepressed unconscious that Bergstein (2013, p. 621) has written "serves as a model for bridging seemingly unbridgeable states of mind." Shapiro and Marks-Tarlow (2021a, p. 505) have challenged Stern (2002) and Bion (Bergstein, 2013)—and the concept of field theory in general, because it illustrates the frequent accepted problematic psychoanalytic supposition that intersubjectively shared states are composed of "energy" and signify an "information exchange". According to the laws of physics, energy fields have a "carrier and degrade" with the square of distance in space, whereas conscious processes and uncanny "extraordinary knowing" do not. Shapiro and Marks-Tarlow (2021a, p. 505) have encouraged making a shift from perceiving clinical metaphor as an information exchange happening within an intersubjective field, to viewing it as informational sharing within an intersubjective matrix of the analyst and patient. In the model they are proposing, a flow of fractal, or repetitive patterning exists which become channels that carry meaning of resonance between states of temporality existing in physical reality that are predictable, to states that are atemporal, unpredictable quantum domains.

Rather than doing away with the conceptualization of a field theory completely, expanding on the notion of a field that is co-created as an inter-subjective third in the analytic encounter further may address some of the issues raised by Shapiro and Marks-Tarlow (2021a). A more extensive definition of the analytic energy field needs to be established—inclusive of the intersubjective matrix Shapiro and Marks-Tarlow (2021a) are proposing that can be broadened to incorporate transpersonal experience, transcending constraints associated with a reality limited to a temporal time and space paradigm. This energetic field, according to paqos and Einstein (1954), is the essence of everything, and includes a fractal dimensionality (Mandelbrot, 1967) with a complexity that changes based upon the scale from which it is perceived and experienced in the moment. In the environment of the analytic encounter, this field becomes a fluid process that is happening simultaneously, in a system continually experiencing and re-experiencing itself.

In its totality, this conceptualization of an energic field being applied to the analytic encounter is subsumed in the paqos' experience of the energetic collective (Bryon, 2012), explained on page 22 of this text.

In his exploration of synchronicity in relation to time and space, Jung has written:

Under certain conditions space and time can be reduced to almost zero, causality disappears along with them because causality is bound up with the existence of space and time and physical changes, and consists essentially in the succession of cause and effect. For this reason, synchronistic phenomena cannot in principle be associated with any conceptions of causality. (Jung, 1960b, pp. 29–30)

Applied to the potential energy field in the analytic encounter, this opens up possibilities beyond what is happening contextually in the dyad to a much wider range of what can emerge.

This is consistent with Einstein's space-time theory that every particle in temporal reality exists on an unchanging timeline from past to future and theory of relativity that mass and energy are the same physical entity and can be changed into each other. In Einstein's theory, matter and energy are expressions of an integrated reality that can be combined differently in different frames of reference—or levels. Einstein's theory of relativity corresponds with the paqos' perception that the ego isn't the only way to experience consciousness. Paqos understand the capacity to shift into a state of oneness (which Freud considered to be an unconscious oceanic state) to be the result of developing the ability to move into states of somatic awareness, not delineated by ego-consciousness. Paqos believe in the existence of a somatic consciousness that expands beyond cognition and ego functioning that is fluid and dynamic.[2] Although Jung maintained the premise that consciousness was a function of the ego, in his later writing he acknowledged the probability that matter (physical reality—or soma) and psyche (a type of energy) were different states of the same material. He has written:

Since psyche and matter are contained in one and the same world, and moreover are in continuous contact with one another and ultimately rest on irrepresentable, transcendental factors, it is not only possible but fairly probable, even, that psyche and matter are two different aspects of one and the same thing. (Jung, 1970, p. 5)

This statement indicates that here Jung viewed matter and psyche as changeable and not constant. This supports the theory that they can exist in different states that are flexible rather than fixed as distinct parts, which implies that there are different ways of interacting in the world, depending upon the state at a given point in time. Jung also wrote:

But this much we do know beyond all doubt, that empirical reality has a transcendental background. (Jung, 1970, p. 8)

Psyche and matter exist in one and the same world, and each partakes of the other, otherwise any reciprocal action would be impossible. If research could only advance far enough, therefore, we would arrive at an ultimate agreement between physical and psychological concepts. (Jung, 1951, p. 261)

Both statements by Jung point toward supporting the paqos experience of multiple levels of psychic engagement. Jung's conceptualization of the existence of a psychic continuum becomes established in his discussion of the unconscious psychoidal realm.[3] What is significant here is the consideration that this continuum could potentially extend into consciousness awareness, which for paqos is through somatic awareness. In *The Psychology of Kundalini Yoga* Jung has written:

> *[T]he gods are asleep: the linga is a mere germ, and the Kundalini, the sleeping beauty, is the possibility of a world which has yet to come off. So, that indicates a condition in which man seems to be the only active power, and the gods, or the impersonal, non-ego powers, are inefficient and doing practically nothing. And that is very much the situation of our modern European consciousness... For it is the something that is within our body, whereas we had reached the conclusion that it was without—that is, our conscious world. That the Hindu commentaries put the conscious world inside the body is to us a very astonishing fact.* (Jung, 1996, p. 23)

Although acknowledging the possibility for consciousness to occur potentially as a non-ego state happening in the body, this was not a primary focus in his work. Jung (1968) admitted to the limitations of the conceptualization of the domain of consciousness as it exists today in the Western paradigm. He has written, "The area of the unconscious is enormous and always continuous, while the area of consciousness is a restricted field of momentary vision" (Jung, 1968, p. 8).

Jung's colleague Marie-Louise von Franz (1992, p. 253) wrote about physicist David Bohm's work on unifying psyche and matter:

> *David Bohm also presupposes the existence of an "ocean of energy" as the background of the universe, a background that is neither material nor psychic, but altogether transcendent ... Ultimately, it corresponds exactly to what Jung calls the* unus mundus, *which is situated beyond the objective psyche and matter which also is situated outside space-time.* (von Franz, 1992, p. 253)

Bohm has written:

> *The essential feature of this idea was that the whole universe is in some way enfolded in everything and that each thing is enfolded in the whole ... there is a great deal of relative independence of things ... this enfoldment relationship is not merely passive or superficial. Rather, it is active and essential to what each thing is. It follows that each thing is internally related to the whole, and therefore, to everything else.* (Bohm, 1990, pp. 271–86)

Bohm (1980) has described an implicate order including both psyche and matter, which adds further support to levels of engagement—and that it is more accurate to view the psyche as a conscious/unconscious whole without clear distinctions.

We are suggesting that the implicate order applies both to matter ... and to consciousness, and that it can therefore make possible an understanding of the general relationship of these two, from which we may be able to come to some notion of a common ground of both. (Bohm, 1980, p. 196)

Bohm (1980) has argued that the tendency to view reality in a state of separation with an explicate order is the result of language and creating narratives or, as he puts it, "the activation of memory recordings whose content is mainly that which is recurrent, stable, and separable" (1980, p. 206). This supports the paqos' premise that atemporal experience is nonverbal.

Jung (1970) agreed:

Of course, there is little or no hope that the unitary Being can ever be conceived since our powers of thought and language permit only of antinomian statements. But this much we do know beyond all doubt, that empirical reality has a transcendental background. (Jung, 1970, p. 8)

Bohm (1980) acknowledges that there is a tendency to consciously orient oneself. Through explicit easily accessible surface material in the external world it is possible to become conscious of implicit levels of reality. He has reasoned that it is not accurate to maintain a rigid separation between the transcendent and the empirical because explicit and implicit experience is interwoven and essentially integrated.

Shapiro and Marks-Tarlow's (2021a, p. 508) "fractal psychophysical perspective", which proposes that mind and matter are two sides of the same thing, parallels Jung's conceptualization of the psychoidal relationship between soma and psyche. A fractal conceptualization describes a structure that can account for synchronistic, atemporal experience.

The state of oneness described within the context of oceanic experience within the context of a conscious/unconscious continuum manifests in other ways as well. It can occur through relationships in the external world, in the context of the phenomenon of *participation mystique.*

Oceanic Experience and Participation Mystique

While oceanic experience has been described as an individual intrapsychic, a state of oneness in the inner world, *participation mystique* is an interpsychic experience that involves merging with the external world. There are many examples of participation mystique, the existence of states of connectivity in group experience, in our world today. In Egypt, I had the opportunity to watch whirling dervishes perform and enter a state of ecstasy. Sitting in the room during a ceremony, I witnessed a vibrational shift in the entire energetic field of more than 100 people! Chanting, drumming rituals and tribal dancing are illustrations of similar phenomena. The power of a group creating an energetic field is well known, practiced in meditation circles and monasteries around the world. Pentecostal churches with members of a congregation speaking in tongues, the emotional charge created by a group of gospel singers, and modern "raves" are examples seen in current Western culture.

While the phenomenon of participation mystique is seen in current culture, the occurrence is ancient, dating back to early mankind. Primordial man lived in an animistic state with the belief that everything in nature is alive, and that thoughts could take on a life of their own as "thought forms". Because of this, clairsentience, the psychic ability to gather information through feeling, was accepted. This belief, still held in Andean medicine and other forms of shamanism today, corresponds to the phenomenon described by Jung (1964, pp. 64–5, par. 132) that he referred to as participation mystique—a term derived from Lévy-Bruhl.

Jung has described the phenomenon of participation mystique: "Projection is one of the commonest psychic phenomena. It is the same as participation mystique" (1964, pp. 64–5, par. 132). He goes on to say, "In the archaic world everything has soul—the soul of man, or let us say mankind, the collective unconscious for the individual yet has no soul of his own" (p. 7, par. 136).

Even though Jung (1960a, par. 218) stated that he was not "implying any kind of value judgment" on primitive man (primitive because they lived in an undifferentiated state of oneness with the natural world), Jung considered primitive man to be the original primordial man in a state of *prima materia*[4] before undergoing the process of transformation through civilizing experience.

Jung (1959, par. 226) also described participation mystique as "nothing other than an unconscious identity," and pointed out that the primitive man was less mentally developed, operating from a "prelogical state of mind." He also said that they "were simpler and more childlike," and "unpsychological," implying that experiences were unintegrated—remaining externalized and concretized.

In *Shared Realities: Participation mystique and beyond*, Mark Winborn has written:

> These inferences about primitive thinking underlie Jung's central notion of participation mystique—namely that in participation mystique experiences there is a blurring of psychological boundaries between individuals, between individuals and their environment, and in some instance between individuals and objects. For example, if an indigenous group believed that a tree was also a dwelling for a spirit that provided protection for a nearby village. (Winborn, 2014, p.3)

Mark Winborn (2014) quotes Marcus West as describing Jung's relationship with participation mystique as:

> There could be powerful experiences of affect, numinous feelings, the boundaries between one person and another become dissolved, and the phenomenon of participation mystique predominates—the individual has the experience of union and oneness with others (or the universe). There can be feelings of timelessness, eternity (feelings go on forever as there is no I to mark time)…

universality and what Freud called oceanic feelings. Feelings experienced on this level have a sense of certainty, trueness, and rightness that appears to follow from the immediacy, power and the "fullness" of the experience. (Winborn, 2014, p. 7)

Jung appears to have had faith in the value of the experience of *participation mystique* when it occurs between an individual and the greater cosmos (*Wira Cocha*) in a practice that corresponds to what paqos call *supan haipay*.[5] In this instance, the experience of merging is an individual rather than a group experience, which Jung seemed to have a more favorable view of. Conceivably, the difference in attitude between Jung's view of oceanic experience and participation mystique in general may be that while oceanic states are atemporal intrapsychic states of oneness, the phenomenon of participation mystique is more often experienced collectively in a group. Jung had less trust in the outcome of group experience.

Jung has written:

A group experience takes place on a lower level of consciousness than the experience of an individual. This is due to the fact that, when many people gather together to share one common emotion, the total psyche emerging from the group is below the level of the individual psyche. If it is a very large group, the collective psyche will be more like the psyche of an animal, which is the reason why the ethical attitude of large organizations is always doubtful. The psychology of a large crowd inevitably sinks to the level of mob psychology. If, therefore, I have a so-called collective experience as a member of a group, it takes place on a lower level of consciousness than if I had the experience by myself alone. (Jung, 1959, par. 225)

Paqos would be less inclined to make the distinction that favored individual over group process—in fact, quite the opposite. Perhaps they place high value in community activity because they are a culture that has survived through communal support. Paqos also believe that psychic engagement[6] takes place on multiple levels—from physical to energetic, which is how they orient themselves in their actions so they would not view participation mystique as a limited way of understanding the world.

Perhaps because Jung was introverted rather than extraverted, and suspect of groups, he emphasized individual psychological development through the "individuation" process. He viewed it conceptually as more differentiated and less reified. He has written,

Individuation is a heroic and often tragic task, the most difficult of all, it involves suffering, a passion of the ego: the ordinary empirical man we once were is burdened with the fate of losing himself in a greater dimension and being robbed of his fancied freedom of will. He suffers, so to speak, from the violence done to him by the self. (Jung, 1942, par. 233)

Jung later wrote that it was "only experienced by those who have gone through the wearisome but indispensable business of coming to terms with the unconscious components of the personality" (1954, par. 430). Jung's individuation process of establishing connection with the Self resembles the paqos' initiation process and acquiring the ability to enter profound states of oneness through cultivating availability, necessary for moving into states of ecstasy.[7] Paqos believe that states of oneness happen through developing the capacity for availability, by becoming open to connection with the living cosmos, *Wira Cocha*. According to paqos, being available requires being anchored in physical reality—like a tree, requiring a solid root base for stability in soil that provides nourishment before growing branches that reach high into the sky.

L'evy-Bruhl (Segal, 2007) had a more favorable view of participation mystique, different from Jung's perspective, because, as an anthropologist, he interpreted primitive from within the context of indigenous experience—not through the eyes of civilization. He understood primitive to mean everything is considered the same, while somehow still distinct (Segal, 2007). This is different from Jung's (1970) Western cultural viewpoint that "primitive" implied living in an unconscious state before the development of a differentiated ego structure had been sufficiently formed.

Jung (1970) believed that unintegrated archetypal projections from the collective unconscious could never be fully incorporated into ego-consciousness even though he did believe in the importance of archetypal material from the collective unconscious and the psychoidal realm becoming conscious through symbols and images. He felt that a relationship with this aspect of the unconscious was necessary to find meaning in life. Jung also shared Freud's view of the importance of making the unconscious conscious in service of mental well-being. He (Jung, 1959, par. 620) wrote, "Anyone who overlooks the instincts will be ambuscaded by them." Jung proposed that emerging and separating from an unconscious undifferentiated state of fusion created a vantage point to reflect upon the experience, from an ego perspective. While, as described previously, Freud viewed oceanic experience as a regression, Jung viewed participation mystique as a lack of differentiation. Both believed it was necessary to separate from the unconscious through developing a healthy ego to avoid being ambushed by the instincts.

Paqos have a somewhat different view. From an Andean perspective, moving into a state of ecstasy, or an experience of oneness, comes through connecting with the living cosmos of *kausay pacha* by "being in right relationship" (*ayni*). This is neither a regression nor lack of differentiation as it can only occur after reaching a state of consciousness after a healthy ego has been established, and when previously existing trauma that has caused psychic blockage has been cleared.

Jung's Concept of the Numinous and the Self

As described earlier, while Jung believed in the numinosity of oceanic experience in adulthood, he thought that consciousness was experienced through the ego, and experience occurring outside of the ego was unconscious. Although Jung believed in the numinosity and intelligence of the unconscious, and that the unconscious "fed" consciousness, like Freud, he didn't think it was possible to move beyond ego-consciousness—consciously (Jung, 1954a). Rather than identifying oceanic experience solely as a unitary numinous state, Jung's understanding of oceanic experience was interrelated to his understanding of the organization of the psyche, specifically in relation to the importance of the Self and the soul.

Shamdasani (Jung, 2020, p. 99) has described the Self as "a construct that attempts to define an ultimately nondefinable god-like force; an archetype of wholeness that permeates and unites all sets of polarities including inner and outer, consciousness and the unconscious."

Jung has written:

The autonomy of a soul complex naturally lends support to the notion of an invisible, personal entity that apparently lives in a world very different from ours. Consequently, once the soul is felt to be that of an autonomous entity having no ties with our mortal substance, it is but a step to imagine that this entity must lead an entirely independent existence, perhaps in a world of invisible things. (Jung, 1953a, par. 912)

By introducing the concepts of the Self and the soul, Jung implied the potential for psychic differentiation existing in the unconscious, more evolved than Freud's concept of an id. Von Franz (1978) and Jung (1958) both described a state of union through the Self. Von Franz wrote, "Whereas relations based merely on projection are characterized by fascination and magical dependence, this kind of relationship by way of the Self has something strictly objective, strangely transpersonal about it. It gives rise to a feeling of immediate, timelessness, being together" (1978, p. 177). Lionel Corbett has also written about a *glutinum mundi,* or "glue of the world, that is secretion of the Self" (1997, p. 164).

Jung (1958, par. 912) stated, "Objective cognition lies behind the attraction of emotional relationship; it seems to be the central secret ... In this world created by the Self, we meet all those many to whom we belong, whose hearts we touch; here there is no distance but immediate presence," and described a "life force, —uniting body and soul." These kinds of ecstatic spiritual experiences of connecting with the *numinous* transcend time and space, and as a result transcend temporality.

Stanislav Grof (2006) has proposed that the universe was created and is permeated by a superior creative intelligence, which Jung has referred to as an *anima mundi,* of which we—and all living things—are an integral part. In her description of the objective psyche, Von Franz (1978, p. 84) has written, "As this central unified area of the unconscious is approached, time and space are increasingly revitalized. That deepest area of the unconscious that is simply a unit or the center may be therefore understood as omnipresent continuum omnipresence without extension."

The Psychoidal Realm and the Paqos' Energetic Collective

Jung (1973) described the objective psyche, which he said was the unit or layer existing underneath the sum of the archetypal structures. For Jung, archetypes were the link between the physical world and the psychic reality. As deeper movement into the archetypal psyche occurs—away from subjective experience, the psyche becomes increasingly objective and universal. Jung believed that the essential nature of the archetype could never be made fully conscious because it is transcendent and psychoidal, an atemporal universal state of being.

Jung believed that the archetypes function as a bridge between physical and psychic reality, anchored in the psychoidal realm. This aligns with the paqos' description of psychic levels of engagement that transition from physical reality to the imaginal realm, to the mythic or archetypal domain, and finally arrive into an energetic collective where everything exists in a state of oneness.

Jung has written:

> *We have to distinguish between a personal unconscious and an impersonal or transpersonal unconscious. We speak of the latter also as the collective unconscious, because it is detached from anything personal and is common to all men, since its contents can be found everywhere, which is naturally not the case with the personal contents ... The collective unconscious stands for the objective psyche, the personal unconscious for the subjective psyche ... As progression continues along this continuum, archetypes of the objective psyche, or the collective unconscious, eventually crossover into the realm of matter referred to as the psychoidal realm.* (Jung, 1966, p. 66)

This description of a transpersonal unconscious in the psychoidal realm aligns with the energetic realm where everything is connected in Andean medicine. Like paqos, Jung understood the psychoidal realm to be the central ground of empirical being, existing beyond time and space. The difference is, however, that more advanced paqos develop conscious awareness of these transpersonal conscious states. Jung has written, "Where instinct predominates, psychoid processes set in which pertain to the sphere of the unconscious as elements incapable of consciousness. The psychoid process is not the unconscious as such, for this has a far greater extension" (Jung, 1973, par. 380). For paqos, levels also exist within the realm of the energetic collective that are only accessed by advanced paqos who have acquired significant power, which for paqos refers to the capacity to hold energy.[8]

Anthropos and *Wira Cocha*

Both Jung (1968, par. 931) and von Franz (1978, p. 85) have described the existence of an *anthropos,* "the ancient idea of an all-extensive world-soul, a kind of cosmic subtle body". This corresponds to the paqos' description of *Wira Cocha.*[9]

Jung has also referred to this as the *unus mundus*, or "one world," which is a "composite universal Self" existing in the deepest level of the collective unconscious in what he called "the psychoidal realm," the central ground of empirical being, existing beyond time and space. This is the atemporal psychoidal realm of the objective psyche where matter and psyche merge into one. Jung considered the *unus mundus* to be an ultimate unity of physical and psychic energy. Emphasis is on the functional relationship between things rather than on the things themselves, and on the relationship of the relationship. At the deepest regions of the unconscious, the *unus mundus* consists of psychoidal structures that transcend the distinction between psyche and matter. Marie-Louise von Franz has written:

> *The unexpected parallelisms of ideas in psychology and physics suggest, as Jung pointed out, a possible ultimate oneness of both fields of reality that physics and psychology study. The concept of a unitarian idea of reality (was called by Jung the unus mundus, the one world, within which matter and psyche and are not yet discriminated or separately actualized) … As this central unified area of the unconscious is approached, time and space are increasingly revitalized. That deepest area of the unconscious that is simply a unit or the center may be therefore understood as omnipresent continuum omnipresence without extension.* (von Franz, 1964, p. 384)

Karl Pribram (1982, p. 27) expanded upon the concept of an *unus mundus*. He has written, "In the holographic domain, each organism represents in some manner the universe, and each portion of the universe represents some manner the organism within it." Ulanov (2017, p. 24) has written, "We are changed by moments of aperture to the one wholeness of the whole *(unus mundus)*. Such experiences of ecstatic transcendence are known to mystics, artists, lovers, sages, and anyone acting creatively. Experience of the psychoid level of the unconscious plants a seed of the larger circumference of reality." Jung's concept of the *unus mundus* is a way of understanding the collective consistent with the paqos' understanding of *Wira Cocha*, the living Andean cosmos. In both the *unus mundus* and *Wira Cocha* emphasis is on the functional relationship between things—and on the relationship of the relationship, rather than on the cosmos being made up of separate isolated objects. Paqos move into a state of connectivity with the collective cosmos—by experiencing the connection through their own individual energy body,[10] which becomes the conduit into experiencing on a much greater, collective scale. The states of oneness, or oceanic experience, occur at the deepest level of the collective unconscious where soma and psyche meet—the link between the physical and the psychic world. This collective subtle body is the template that carries past personal memory, the totality of ancestral lineage, and the blueprint of wholeness. The connection with *Wira Cocha* is the medium of shifting into the experience of collectivity, from an individual to the universal state of the *unus mundi*. A collective representation of an aspect of *Wira Cocha* is an energetic expression of the unlimited depository of man's universal psychic heritage in the psychoidal realm.

The Individual Energy Body: The Subtle Body and the *Manos Wasi*

In addition to describing the presence of a collective universal energy body, the *unus mundus*, Jung described the existence of an individual subtle body that expands beyond the individual psyche, into the collective psychoid. Jung's view of the *unus mundus* and the subtle body corresponds with the Andean view of *Wira Cocha* and the energy body that paqos refer to as the *manos wasi*.

The subtle body is both the veil and the container that lies between and holds individual consciousness and the collective unconscious, which Jung described as the "totality of all psychic processes, conscious as well as unconscious" (Jung, 1921, par. 797). This energetic expression separately defines and holds all aspects of the conscious and unconscious psyche. It is the blueprint—the urn that holds the totality of psychic experience—the collective lineage of one's ancestors.

Like Jung's definition of the archetype, Grof (2006, p. 349) has described an atemporal *transpersonal* state existing within the psyche, consisting of "ancestral, racial collective and phylogenic memories, karmic experiences, and archetypal dynamics". Grof (2006) has added the addition of "perinatal domain" to the subtle body map to include the memory of the birth trauma experience—held in the individual energetic field. The subtle body is both the energetic expression of individual archetypal experience, as well as a collective expression that occurs through the psychoidal experience of the *unus mundus*. Von Franz (1978) wrote that psychic healing occurs through numinous archetypal experience contained within the subtle body.

Jungian analyst Nathan Schwartz-Salant (1989, p. 73) has called the subtle body a "garment of the soul," the necessary container for inner life that is neither spirit, nor physical body, but a place in between. He viewed the subtle body as both temporal and atemporal. It is both the veil and the container that lies between and holds individual consciousness and the collective unconscious. This energetic expression separately defines and holds all aspects of conscious and unconscious psyche. It is the composite of lived and unlived collective experience—the urn that holds the totality of psychic experience, the collective lineage of one's ancestors.

In summary, the subtle body or *manos wasi* of the individual is connected to all living things through an energetic field. The energetic field that holds the *manos wasi* and subtle body is temporal and atemporal and includes all aspects of the individual experience—conscious and unconscious, in waking and dream states, in past and present, as well as being a blueprint for the future.

States of Reverie and Implicit Sharing through the Subtle Body in the Analytic Third

In past decades in psychoanalysis, the existence of an energetic field existing in the analytic encounter has become widely accepted. In analytic work, this is often conceptualized as an intersubjective exchange—co-created within the analytic relationship. Ogden (1994, 1999) and others (Schwartz-Salant, 1998; Spiegelman, 1996, Cwik, 2006) have referred to a shared state of imaginal reverie as the "analytic third." Jungian analyst Gus Cwik (2011, p. 19) has expanded on the notion of the analytic third in which "all material arising from the analytic encounter is more or less co-created." He has described this as a kind of shared active imagination involving both the psychological "metaphorical language" found in Jungian psychology as well as sensate body awareness of body language, and unconscious autonomic indicators.

Like what Sidoli (2000) has described, Cwik (2011) has proposed that, in this process, the therapist enters into a receptive altered state of reverie through which information emerges from the analytic third. This can be conceptualized as a dyadic subtle body experience. Cwik (2011) and Schwartz-Salant (1988) have each tied an analytic third, created jointly by the analysand and analyst—stimulated by the process of active imagination—back to the emergence of the transcendent function occurring within the context of the analytic relationship.

Shapiro and Marks-Tarlow (2021b) have proposed a model of "fractal dynamics" compatible with the notion of an analytic third and entering an altered state of reverie. While they have acknowledged that Stern's (2002) focus on development within the interpersonal field is a worthy effort toward conceptualizing implicit relational engagement and sharing, they argue the field metaphor itself is limiting because it suggests a physical medium of information exchange, which cannot hold in "nonlocal" knowing (Shapiro and Marks-Tarlow, 2021a).

Nonlocal knowing refers to the concept of entanglement theory in quantum systems,[11] in which elements within a system are influenced by other parts regardless of the distance between them. They are proposing a paradigm that involves "information sharing" because it is more inclusive of nonlocal phenomena, which can account for greater psychophysical dimensions. According to Gisin (2009, p. 1358) entanglement is fundamental to quantum theory, a state in which time and space become irrelevant. Because no explanation in the space–time continuum of temporality exists on how nonlocal correlations happen, they emerge atemporally outside of a space–time paradigm.

There are many approaches toward working with the subtle body within the analytic frame—both inter and intersubjectively that involve "information sharing". Recapitulating memories of dreams and experience from both the inner and outer worlds in a state of reverie—which Jung referred to as active imagination—is another way of accessing feelings and images *energetically* that are not normally reachable from a conscious ego state (Raff, 2002, p. 30). Jungian analyst Arnie Mindell (1985, p. 61) has suggested that the subtle body is a "felt sense" rather than a mental idea or construct, that is accessed through processes of active imagination—like entering states of reverie. He has written about the subtle body as a "field experience", and as "a gaseous apparition deviating from and threatening reality". Consistent with Jung, Mindell has stated that the only way the unconscious can be experienced by the conscious is through retrospective reflection or through the experience of "nonverbalizable" feelings. Mindell refers to these kinds of feelings as sentient awareness. "Signals" from the realm of the subtle body often manifest as "body phenomenon lying just at the border of awareness" (Hoerni et al., 2019, p. 260). While Mindell (1985) and Cwik (2011) have conceptualized and worked with the imaginal realm, by holding an openly receptive attitude, Whitmont (1993) has emphasized the importance of focusing one's intent on the process of active imagination in the clinical setting. The imaginal realm he is referring to can range from the ordinary imagination to that of the psychoidal realm existing beyond the psyche, depending on the individual's ability to direct their intent. Like Mindell and a bio-energetic approach, Whitmont (1993, p. 173) has described using a form of active imagination as a way of discovering "intents" of physical symptomology. In working with clients, Whitmont has used this technique to help them feel what is lodged in the body psychologically.

The Paqos' Perspective

If we give merit to the reality that we are all part of a living energetic system surrounding us, then, like the paqos, we begin to live in relationship with atemporality. What has existed before is still alive in the field indefinitely until the energy of the field changes. If we consider the energy field to be real and palpable then thoughts are alive, and intention has power. This coincides with the concept of participation mystique and aligns with the paqos' perspective.

Paqos believe that what exists in the living energy field is directly linked to an ancestral way of relating to the world in which perception becomes passed down and incorporated into a current belief system in patterns of relating and knowing. This becomes a template for how we experience the world and conversely how we affect the world in an interdependent relationship. Mentalizing, as a function of clairscience, enables the potential of seeing different experiences from different perspectives simultaneously.

The patterns that influence our perspective affect the kinds of trauma we carry and incorporate into our *manos wasi,* and as a result project out into the world in a bidirectional relationship. An example of this is the phenomenon of shame. Psychoanalysts and other psychotherapists (Deyoung, 2022) recognize that shame is contagious (and intergenerational) when it is carried in the field. When shame remains unconscious it may become introjected and then passed on as a projection.

Jung said (1959, p. 171, par. 126) that when the individual remains undivided, and does not become conscious of his inner opposite, the world must act out the conflict and be torn into opposing halves. This becomes the lineage that is passed down and becomes intergenerational trauma until it is resolved. According to paqos, as well as other shamans, this energetic configuration can begin to take on a life of its own and with the potential to become imprinted as familial lineage or as a collective identity signature. Paqos refer to the act of full disclosure of one's essential nature, including shadow material, as *tupay*. This process, which enables paqos to become more connected and open to the living world around them entails confrontation and may involve conflict as all parts are made conscious and available.

Notes

1 Federn (1932) later shifted his opinion toward Rolland's stance when Ehrenzweig (1967) and later Milner (1987) expanded upon Rolland's theory.
2 See p. 73 for a description of somatic awareness.
3 Explained in greater detail on pp. 21–5 of this text.
4 In alchemy, *prima materia* refers to the fundamental, undifferentiated state of base materials before they are transformed into something of greater value through the various processes associated with alchemy.
5 The practice of *supan haipay* is described on p. 64.
6 Psychic engagement is described on pp. 41–54.
7 See Chapter 2 for descriptions of initiation rituals.
8 See description on p. 33 of the most advanced paqos, *hatun misayoqs*.
9 *Wira Cocha* is a universal state of all worlds and all aspects of time.
10 Jung referred to the energy body as the subtle body and paqos refer to it as the *manos wasi*.
11 See Chapter 10, p. 126, for a more detailed explanation.

References

Ackerman, S. (2017) 'Exploring Freud's resistance to the oceanic feeling', *Journal of the American Psychoanalytic Association* 65: 9–31.
Benedetti, G. (1969) *Neuropsicologia*, Milan: Feltrinelli.
Bergstein, A. (2013) 'Transcending the caesura: Reverie, dreaming and counter-dreaming', *The International Journal of Psychoanalysis* 94(4): 621–44.
Bohm, David (1980) *Wholeness and the Implicate Order*, New York, NY: Routledge & nan Paul.
Bohm, David (1990) 'A new theory of the relationship of mind and matter', *Philosophical Psychology* 3(2): 271–86.
Bonaparte, M. (1940) 'Time and the unconscious', *Int. J. Psycho-Anal.* 21: 427–68.
Bryon, D. (2012) *Lessons of the Inca Shamans, Part I: Piercing the veil*, Enumclaw, WA: Pine Winds Press.
Coburn, W. J. (2002) 'A world of systems: The role of systemic patterns of experience in the therapeutic process', *Psychoanal. Inq.* 22: 655–77.
Corbett, L. (1997) 'Seduction, psychotherapy, and the alchemical *glutinum mundi*', in S. Marlan (ed.) *Fire in the Stone: The alchemy of desire*, Wilmette, IL: Chiron Publications, pp. 125–59.
Cwik, A. J. (2006) 'The art of the tincture: Analytical supervision', *Journal of Analytical Psychology* 51: 209–25.
Cwik, A. J. (2011) 'Associative dreaming: Reverie and active imagination', *Journal of Analytical Psychology* 56: 14–36.
Deyoung, P. (2022) *Understanding and Treating Chronic Shame*, New York, NY: Routledge.
Ehrenzweig, A. (1967) *The Hidden Order of Art: A study in the psychology of artistic perception*, London: Phoenix Press.
Einstein, A. (1954) *Relativity: The special and general theory*, London: Methuen & Co. Ltd.
Eissler, K. (1955) *The Psychiatrist and the Dying Patient*, New York, NY: International Universities Press.
Epstein, M. (1990) 'Beyond the oceanic feeling: Psychoanalytic study of Buddhist meditation', *International Review of Psychoanalysis* 17: 159–65.

Federn. P. (1932) 'The reality of the death instinct, especially in melancholia: Remarks on Freud's book: "Civilization and Its Discontents" ', *Psychoanal Rev* 19: 129–51.

Freud, E., ed. (1960) *Letters of Sigmund Freud, 1873–1939*, trans T. Stern and J. Stern, London: The Hogarth Press.

Freud, S. (1915) *The Unconscious* (Standard Edition, vol. 14).

Freud, S. (1923) *The Ego and the Id* (Standard Edition, vol. 19).

Freud, S. (1923–5) *The Ego and the Id and Other Works* (Standard Edition, vol. 19).

Freud, S. (1925a) *A Note Upon the 'Mystic Writing-Pad'* (Standard Edition, vol. 19).

Freud, S. (1927) *The Future of an Illusion* (Standard Edition, vol. 21).

Freud, S. (1930) *Civilization and Its Discontents* (Standard Edition, vol. 21).

Freud, S. (1937) *Analysis Terminable and Interminable* (Standard Edition, vol. 21).

Freud, S. (1940) *An Outline of Psycho-analysis* (Standard Edition, vol. 21).

Fuller, P. (1980) *Art and Psychoanalysis*, London: Writers and Readers.

Galatzer-Levy, R. M. (1978) 'Qualitative change from quantitative change: Mathematical catastrophe theory in relation to psychoanalysis', *Journal of the American Psychoanalytic Association* 26: 921–35.

Ghent, E. (2002) 'Wish, need, drive: Motive in the light of dynamic systems theory and Edelman's selectionist theory', *Psychoanal. Dial.* 12: 763–808.

Gisin, N. (2009) 'Quantum nonlocality: How does nature do it?' *Science*, 326(5958), 1357–1358.

Grof, S. (2006) *When the Impossible Happens*, Boulder, CO: Sounds True.

Hoerni, Ulrich, Fischer, Thomas, and Kaufmann, Bettina, eds (2019) *The Art of C.G. Jung*, New York, NY and London: W. W. Norton & Company.

Jung, C. G. (1942) *A Psychological Approach to the Trinity* (Collected Works, vol. 11).

Jung, C. G. (1951) *Aion* (Collected Works, vol. 9, part 2).

Jung, C. G. (1953a) *The Relations between the Ego and the Unconscious* (Collected Works, vol. 7).

Jung, C. G. (1953b) *Two Essays in Analytical Psychology* (Collected Works, vol. 7).

Jung, C. G. (1954a) *On the Nature of the Psyche* (Collected Works, vol. 8).

Jung, C. G. (1954b) *The Practice of Psychotherapy* (Collected Works, vol. 16).

Jung, C. G. (1958) *Psychology and Religion* (Collected Works, vol. 18).

Jung, C. G. (1959) *The Archetypes and the Collective Unconscious* (Collected Works, vol. 9).

Jung, C. G. (1960a) *Structure & Dynamics of the Psyche* (Collected Works, vol. 8).

Jung, C.G. (1960b) 'Synchronicity: An acausal connecting principal' (Collected Works, vol. 8), in *The Structure and Dynamics of the Psyche Princeton*, Princeton, NJ: Princeton University Press.

Jung, C. G. (1964) *Archaic Man* (Collected Works, vol. 10).

Jung, C. G. (1966) *Two Essays on Analytic Psychology*, Princeton, NJ: Princeton University Press.

Jung, C. G. (1968) *Analytic Psychology: Its theory and practice*, New York, NY: Random House.

Jung, C. G. (1970) *Psychological Reflections*, Princeton, NJ: Princeton University Press.

Jung, C. G. (1973) *On the Nature of the Psyche*, Princeton, NJ: Princeton University Press.

Jung, C. G. (1996) *The Psychology of Kundalini Yoga*, Princeton, NJ: Princeton University Press.

Jung, C. G. (2020) *The Black Books, 1913–1932: Notebooks of transformation*, series ed. Sonu Shamdasani, series trans Sonu Shamdasani, Martin Leibscher and John Peck, New York, NY: W.W. Norton and Company.

Kakar, S. (1991) *The Analyst and the Mystic: Psychoanalytic reflections on religion and mysticism*, Chicago, IL: The University of Chicago Press.

Loewald, H. W. (1972) 'The experience of time', *Psychoanalytic Study of the Child* 27: 401–10.

Mandelbrot, B. (1967) 'How long is the coast of Britain? Statistical self-similarity and fractional dimension', *Science* 156(3775): 636–8.

Masson, J. M. (1980) *The Oceanic Feeling: The origins of religious sentiment in India*, Dordrecht: Reidel.

Merkur, D. (1999) *Mystical Moments and Unitive Thinking*, New York, NY: State University of New York Press.

Merkur, D. (2010) *Explorations of the Psychoanalytic Mystics*, Amsterdam and New York, NY: Rodolpi.

Milner, M. (1987) *The Suppressed Madness of Sane Men: Forty-four years of exploring psychoanalysis*, London: Tavistock.

Mindell, A. (1985) *Working with the Dream Body*, Boston, MA: Routledge.

Namnum, A. (1972) 'Time in psychoanalytic technique', *J. Am. psychoanal. Ass.* 20: 736–50.

Newton, S. (2008) *Art and Ritual: A painter's journey*, London: Ziggurat.

Newton, S. J. (2001) *Painting, Psychoanalysis, and Spirituality*, Cambridge: Cambridge University Press.

Ogden, T. H. (1994) 'The analytic third: Working with intersubjective clinical facts', *International Journal of Psycho-Analysis* 75: 3–19.

Ogden, T. H. (1999) 'The analytic third: an overview', in S. Mitchell and L. Aron (eds) *Relational Perspectives in Psychoanalysis: The emergence of a tradition*, Hillsdale, NJ: Analytic Press, pp. 487–92.

Ostow, M. (2007) *Spirit, Mind, and Brain: A psychoanalytic examination of spirituality and religion*, New York, NY: Columbia University Press.

Parsons, W. B. (1999) *The Enigma of the Oceanic Feeling: Revisioning the psychoanalytic theory of mysticism*, New York, NY: Oxford University Press.

Pauli, W. (1994) *Writings on Physics and Philosophy*, Berlin: Springer-Verlag.

Pribram, K. (1982) 'What the fuss is all about', in K. Wilber (ed.) *The Holographic Paradigm and Other Paradoxes*, Boulder, CO: Shambala, pp. 24–34.

Raff, J. (2002) *Jung and the Alchemical Imagination*, Newburyport, MA: Nicolas-Hays.

Roiphe, K. (2016) *The Violet Hour: Great writers at the end*, New York, NY: Random House.

Rolland, R. (1929) *The Life of Ramakrishna* [Essai sur la mystique et l'action de l'Inde vivante. La vie de Ramakrishna], 20th edn, trans. E. F. Malcolm-Smith, Kolkata: Swami Bodhasarananda.

Rolland, R. (1930) *The Life of Vivekananda and the Universal Gospel* [Essai sur la mystique et l'action de l'Inde vivante. La vie de Vivekananda et l'Evangile universel, tomes I et II], 25th edn, trans. E. F. Malcolm-Smith, Kolkata: Swami Bodhasarananda.

Rolland, R. (1947) *Journey Within* [Le voyage interieur], trans. E. Pell, New York, NY: Philosophical Library.

Rooney, C. (2007) 'What is the oceanic?', *Angelaki—Journal of the theoretical humanities* 12: 19–32.

Saarinen, J. A. (2012) 'The oceanic state: A conceptual elucidation in terms of modal contact', *Int J Psychoanal* 93: 939–61.

Sander, L. (2002) 'Thinking differently: Principles of process in living systems and the specificity of being known', *Psychoanal. Dial.* 12: 11–42.

Sashin, J. I. and Callahan, J. (1990) 'A model of affect using dynamical systems', *Annual of Psychoanalysis* 18: 213–31.

Schwartz-Salant, N. (1989) *The Borderline Personality: Vision and healing*, Wilmette, IL: Chiron Publications.

Schwartz-Salant, N. (1998) *The Mystery of Human Relationship*, New York, NY: Routledge.

Segal, R. A. (2007) 'Jung and L'evy-Bruhl', *Journal of Analytical Psychology 52:* 635–58.

Seligman, S. (2005) 'Dynamic systems theories as a metaframework for psychoanalysis', *Psychoanalytic Dialogues* 15(2): 285–319.

Shapiro, Y. and Marks-Tarlow, T (2021a) 'Bridging the unbridgeable: Toward a meta-reductive science of experience: Response to Harris and Cartwright commentaries', *Psychoanalytic Dialogues* 31(4): 503–10.

Shapiro, Y. and Marks-Tarlow, T. (2021b) 'Varieties of clinical intuition: Implicit, explicit and nonlocal neurodynamics', *Psychoanalytic Dialogues* 31(3): 262–81.

Sidoli, M. (2000) *When the Body Speaks: The archetypes in the body*, ed. P. Blakemore, Hove: Brunner-Routledge.

Spiegelman, M. J. (1996) *Psychotherapy as Mutual Process*, Tempe, AZ: New Falcon.

Spruiell, V. (1993) 'Deterministic chaos and the sciences of complexity: Psychoanalysis in the midst of a general scientific revolution', *J. Amer. Psychoanal. Assn.* 41: 3–44.

Stern, D. B. (2002) 'Language and the nonverbal as a unity: Discussion of "where is the action in the 'Talking Cure'?" ', *Contemporary Psychoanalysis* 38: 515–25.

Stokes, A. (1978) *The Critical Writings of Adrian Stokes, Vol. III, 1955–1967*, London: Thames and Hudson.

Stolorow, R. D. (1997) 'Dynamic, dyadic, intersubjective systems: An evolving paradigm for psychoanalysis', *Psychoanal. Psychol.* 14: 337–64.

Thelen, E. and Smith, L. (1994) *A Dynamic Systems Approach to the Development of Cognition and Action*, Cambridge, MA: MIT Press.

Ulanov, A.B. (2017) *The Psychoid, Soul and Psyche: Piercing Space/Time Barriers*, Einsiedeln, Switzerland: Daimon.

von Franz, M-L. (1964) 'Science and the unconscious', in C. G. Jung (ed.) *Man and his Symbols*, New York, NY: Dell Publishing Co., Inc.

von Franz, M-L. (1978) *Projection and Recollection in Jungian Psychology*, La Salle, IL: Open Court.

von Franz, M-L. (1992) *Psyche and Matter,* Boston, MA: Shambhala.

West, Marcus (2014) 'Identity, narcissism, and the emotional core', in Mark Winborn (ed.) *Shared Realities: Participation mystique and beyond*, Skiatook, OK: Fisher King Press.

Whitmont, E. C. (1993) *The Alchemy of Healing*, Berkeley, CA: North Atlantic Books.

Winborn, Mark (2014) *Shared Realities: Participation mystique and beyond*, Skiatook, OK: Fisher King Press.

Zeddies, T. (2002) 'More than just words: A hermeneutic view of language in psycho-analysis', *Psychoanalytic Psychology* 19: 3–23.

Chapter 2

Temporal and Atemporal Experience in Andean Medicine

While many psychoanalysts are resistant to exploring atemporal, oceanic experiences outside of ego-consciousness, many are interested in the subjective experience of time (Loewald, 1972; Seton, 1974; Pollock, 1971). Here are many parallels between Andean shamanism, depth psychology, and other schools of psychoanalytic thought in the understanding of temporal and atemporal states. There are also many differences. Although they each acknowledge a form of atemporal, nonverbal "oceanic experience" in their own way, a major distinction is that in Andean medicine, conscious awareness can exist in non-ego, somatically based states. This is because the ego is not the only organizer of conscious experience. Paqos believe that conscious expands beyond cognitive comprehension into somatic states of awareness that are often atemporal and nonverbal. Although depth psychologists acknowledge the role of the subtle body, like what paqos refer to as the *manos wasi,* it is viewed as a container for individual experience rather than as an "metabolizer" that can hold consciousness through the energy centers and energetic field surrounding the physical body that are part of the *manos wasi.*

Eliade (1964) characterized shamanism as a technique of ecstasy. Michael Harner (1980) described shamanism as "a great mental and emotional adventure" and wrote, "Ultimately shamanic knowledge can only be acquired through individual experience."

The energetic felt sensation of "being" part of the cosmos contrasts with a psychic framework where discrete boundaries of separation are experienced between the oneself and others, which is a function of the ego. In psychoanalytic thought (Freud, 1915) a functional ego is needed for explicit understanding, through the capacity to reflect between "then" and "now" in temporal reality, enabling the capacity to create a narrative of experience using language.

In the Andean culture, community is valued over the individual, perhaps as a survival mechanism. They believe that living in a culture based upon separation, where emphasis is placed on the individual with a focus on personal orientation, creates a sense of scarcity and loneliness that can create blockage in the *manos wasi.*

For paqos, entering a state of spiritual connection with the cosmos, the conscious, atemporal experience is very different. Instead of differentiating between oneself and others—necessary in healthy ego development from a psychoanalytic

DOI: 10.4324/9781003356448-4

perspective—being in a "felt sense" of energetic atemporal connection involves "dropping into" the immediate process of letting go and surrendering. In these states, no sense of context exists beyond being alertly aware of being part of something much greater, without a sense of past and future. Once paqos make the decision to enter these states, the mental framework shifts to the side, and the paqos' focus is directed toward first attending, then merging into the constancy of the energetic experience itself—with a felt sense of expansion through energetic body awareness.

In Andean medicine, there are levels of psychic engagement, ranging from temporal experience in a physical reality, to atemporal, energetic states of oneness. The paqos' experience of time will be explored in relation to their conceptualization of levels of psychic engagement. In addition to explaining the interpsychic structure of the ways in which paqos conceptualize temporal and atemporal experience, their strong connection with nature will be described.

Paqos live in a psychically active relational bond with their environment, dependent upon an energetic connection with their *manos wasi,* or energy body that is essential to their survival, and the way they experience consciousness. Their affiliation with the Andean cosmos and connection to *Pachamama,* or Mother Earth, will be described. The types and qualities of energetic interaction will also be considered, fundamental to the way they experience consciousness, and atemporality.

The Function of the *Manos Wasi*

A memory of a healed state of wholeness existing within a state of collective connectivity is held within the *manos wasi,* or energy body. In addition to holding the energetic memories from the past, and ancestral lineage, the luminous body carries the visions we create for our future. Paqos believe that all experience is held in the *manos wasi,* which holds the template that encodes energetic material in the substance of our physical bodies.

All knowledge regardless of the sensory channel is experienced through the *manos wasi.* The experience can be kinesthetic, or can happen through hearing sound, smelling—or as an "inner knowing." Through awareness in the *manos wasi,* the experience of being in connection and seeing occurs at the same time. In this experience, time becomes atemporal.

In *Quechua,* the word *poq'po* refers to the energy body, the bubble of light infusing and surrounding the physical body. Paqos refer to the luminous body, an aspect of the *manos wasi,* as *runa kurku k'anchay,* which translates as "luminous light body." The *ruphay* or "inner sun," part of the *runa kurku k'anchay,* located in the solar plexus, is responsible for forming a connection to everything that exists in the cosmos. In profound meditative states, paqos experience the living world as being connected energetically in a web of light, without physical form. The Quechua word *ch'ulla,* refers to the phenomenon that everything is connected through energy lines, or *ceke* lines.

The *manos wasi* is the bridge between seeing and being in consciousness—and for more advanced paqos, allows both to be experienced simultaneously. Seeing through the *manos wasi* using a "felt sense" is not limited to vision. In this expanded state of awareness, the experience of a universal link to every living thing occurs through the energetic field. For paqos, this is the basis of spiritual connection, with states of ecstasy. At this level, a deeper, more direct connection occurs, bypassing words, which is where paqos believe that the soul, or essence of one's being, sources and expresses itself. In this realm the soul taps into a universal meta language in the collective that is timeless, endless, at a higher level of consciousness.

Putting a description of the sensation of energetic connection into words is never exact because there are no words in the English language that portray the properties associated with the subjective experience. While the Quechua language has descriptive words that pertain to different types of energetic connections, there are no words involved when sourcing from direct experience. This is also because atemporal experience cannot be explained accurately in words.

Cognitively comprehending this occurrence requires creating a bridge between energetic experience and analytic thought, that occurs as a function of the *manos wasi*. The transfer of memory of energetic experience begins as a formless feeling state in the body that gradually takes on form through imagery in reverie or dreams. From these metaphors, images can then be shaped into words and conceptual narratives may then develop. Symbols and language provide a sense of identity and provide a temporal context in the current pacha of physical reality. After the pathway of the transfer of the memory of energetic experience to stories that validate the experience in physical reality has been established through the *manos wasi*, in a mental configuration that is applicable, paqos use their intention to return to an energetic state of connection with the cosmos again through the *manos wasi*. The *manos wasi* becomes the mechanism to re-enact the return to a state of oneness without resorting to language.

The Andean Paqos' Understanding of Time

Connection and Atemporality

Experiencing atemporal time is different from conceptualizing and referencing explicit details of experience as if it has already happened. Describing an experience is a cognitive action that necessitates mentally separating from it, reflecting on it, and imagining it taking place. This involves stepping outside of the flow of experiencing/being in the experience. In deep states of energetic "oneness" there is no demarcation between past, present, and future, nor awareness of beginning, duration, ending, or anticipated ending—only being. In psychic states closer to ego-consciousness, such as in dream states, the past, present, and future may be experienced as multilayered—permeating one another simultaneously, as fluid states without discrete boundaries. In liminal spaces between deeper levels of the unconscious and ego-consciousness, such as dream states, sequences of events often do not conform with the parameters of physical time and space. For example, a span of time taking place in a dream state may only be occurring in minutes in the "real-time" of physical reality.

Pachas: *Time and Space*

In the Quechua language, the word *pacha* refers to an allocation of energy at a point in time and space. According to paqos, a *pacha* is an Inca map of consciousness referring to a temporal structure that contains *kausay*, or life force. *Kausay* is the energy of creation that is often experienced in the body as a vibration, or in the heart as a feeling of universal love toward everyone and everything. *Kausay* may also be seen as an intense light or experienced as clarity or a sense of all-knowing wisdom, which often takes place during an altered state of *numinous* experience in "nonordinary reality."

In Andean cosmology, the veil between the worlds of *kay pacha* (ordinary reality) and *kausay pacha* (the energetic realm), is a boundary between temporal reality—an intersection in time and space—and an atemporal fluid state of energy. In Andean medicine, cosmology refers to a map of understanding of energy fields and belief systems brought together.

In each person's life there are significant events, which occur at specific times in space, that influence personal fate and destiny. These are times when the veil "thins" and *kausay* moves into a *pacha*, infusing it with energetic life force. These pivotal points on one's life journey possess greater amounts of *kausay*. Recapitulating memories of these events can alter the conscious awareness of the *pacha*, providing an opportunity to break free from old patterns and wounds from the past often tied to a person's lineage. In a conversation with the *altomisayoq* (high shaman), Dona Alahandrina, which took place more than two decades ago, she stated:

> *Linage enables us to gain balance… As we serve lineage, we need to be creators of tradition, re-enacting presences before and after. Bodies of custom and knowledge. As we undergo our journey, although the person is important, collective identity occurs through the lineage of our becoming—and the ones after us—our children. We carry our traditions, our past, in our bodies. Clearly, the civilizations that once flourished here have a rich knowledge. We, as humans, carry our past realities. Mountains also have such knowledge of the past. The moment is who you are. It is what we are right now that matters. Even if beliefs are forgotten, the primordial identity is remembered. Our identity resides in reawakening our lineage.* (Dona Alahandrina, May 7, 2011, Cusco Peru)

For paqos, lineage is atemporal and lives in the individual energy body—or *manos wasi*. Lineage also carries the templates of collective "blueprints." In Quechua, the word *kanay* describes the process of remembering one's collective cultural identity through accessing an awareness of ancestral lineage. There are Andean codes and organizing principles that define and support this process. Engaging in the process of *kanay* provides a means of working through karma—the principle governing moral causation. Andean medicine is a practice of channeling the energy, or *kallpa,* associated with lineage through building *hap'ichiy* connection with the collective memory of the Andean cosmos.

According to Dona Alahandrina, initially there were 42 *ceke* lines, or lines of energetic connection, between 42 *wakas* (places of power) that contained 12 different ancestral lineages of medicine people. Over time, the lineage of the sacred ancestry died out, and now there are only three lines of lineage remaining in Peru today. The *Q'ero* paqos, living in the Andes, are in the process of losing their connection to their sacred lineage and soon there will only be two—located in the sacred areas of *Bilkabamba* and *Salcantay*.

References

Alahandrina, Dona (2011) personal correspondence, Cusco Peru, 7 May.

Eliade, M. (1964) *Shamanism: Archaic techniques of ecstasy*, Bollington Series LXXVI, Princeton, NJ: Princeton University Press.

Freud, S. (1915) *The Unconscious* (Standard Edition, vol. 14).

Harner, M. (1980) *The Way of the Shaman*, New York, NY: HarperCollins Publishers.

Loewald, H. W. (1972) 'The experience of time', *Psychoanalytic Study of the Child* 27: 401–10.

Pollock, G. H. (1971) 'On time, death, and immortality', *Psychoanalytic Quarterly* 40: 435–46.

Seton, P. H. (1974) 'The psychotemporal adaptation of late adolescence', *Journal of the American Psychoanalytic Association* 22: 795–819.

Chapter 3

Power

The Capacity to Hold Energy

The Paqos

Allpa kamasqa means "life-giving earth energy" in Quechua. Paqos derive energy from this depository of *kausay* energy in service of their communities and the collective. I have heard paqos say that they "source" from "the land because people come and go but the mountains and *Pachamama* of the Andean cosmos are always there."

In Quechua, the term *Wira Cocha* describes all worlds existing in the Andean cosmos, both temporal and atemporal, including the land in addition to the celestial realms. *Wira Cocha* is a universal state of all worlds and all aspects of time. The paqos' practice of sourcing from *Wira Cocha* is called *qaway kuy*. *Qaway kuy* refers to the practice of entering into a state of intentional receptivity and connecting with the Andean cosmos, or *Wira Cocha*, through the individual energy body of the *manos wasi*.

Pampamesayoqs

As students on the spiritual path of Andean medicine grow through the practice of *kallpa* and their ability to work with *pacha-wan kausay*,[1] their connection to the Incan codes, which paqos refer to as "the technology," or laws of the universe (*Wira Cocha*) increases, and they may become *pampamesyayoq* healers. *Misayoq* means "master." The duties of *pampamesayoqs* primarily focus on healing and tending to *Pachamama*, and members of their community. They often use herbs in healing and soul retrieval.

Pampamesayoqs have different specialties and use different elements in their healing practices to heal ailments of members of their community by developing ways to "track" illness or issues due to misalignment, as well as tracking the future. Ways of tracking include *akarituq*, the process of using guinea pig droppings to track illnesses. *Ninapirikuq* involves the ancient practice of forecasting by placing staff and rod instruments made of silver and gold in burning coals. *Chiampuq* is the practice of using small stones to diagnose illness. These are only a

DOI: 10.4324/9781003356448-5

few descriptions. Other healing methods involve using coins, breath, llama fat, and body postures as divination instruments.

Yachacheq

Yachacheq paqos work specifically with *y'anchay*, the mind, and approach healing in two different ways. The first, like psychoanalysis, involves revisiting the past and dying to the old ways of being so that a new vision for the future can emerge.

The second approach to healing is to move into visionary experiential states of connection with the cosmos, which in depth psychology would be a prospective orientation of surrendering to the Self. In Andean medicine the hero figure does not exist because the hero is attached to upholding an ego position, having to do with personal identity. Paqos believe that being aligned with "causes" creates reactivity, which prevents moving into a fluid state of awareness, or availability toward the cosmos. In psychoanalysis this is sometimes referred to as "beginner's mind." Like depth psychology when the ego yields to the Self, in Andean medicine psychic movement is made from a personal perspective to a collective orientation. A difference between paqos and Jungian analysts is that paqos say they serve the experience in *munay*, while in depth psychology, particularly in dream interpretation, meaning is made from the experience.[2]

Altomesayoqs

Alto translates from Quechua to "high." There are only about eight *altomesayoqs* living in Peru today. Many *altomesayoqs* begin their shamanic path by first becoming *pampamesayoqs*. A paqo becomes an *altomesyoq* through an extremely arduous initiation ceremony often after being struck by a bolt of lightning (*kaq'lla*) in the mountains. During the ceremony, if they can survive the initiatory process, they receive an *apu* benefactor who gifts them a *q'ollona misa*.[3] *Misas* are a collection of stones, or *q'uiyas,* that become a paqo's medicine body. The *apu* benefactor becomes the director of the *altomesayoq's q'ollona misa*, serving as a bridge between the physical and spirit world. The *apu* director becomes a conduit for other *apu* mountain spirits to enter the *misa* and physical reality. *Kurak akulliq*s are the highest level of *altomesayoqs* who have mastered physical manifestation in *pachas* in temporal reality, and who have allegedly become shapeshifters.

Q'ollana misas are the highest level of *misas*, as they have transcended beyond a personal orientation and are a direct essential expression of collective creation. The *altomesayoq's q'ollona misa* is made up of *q'uiyas* resonating at an extremely high vibrational level that are rooted in atemporal dimensions. With the assistance of the *apu* director, and through their capacity to hold power with tremendous amounts of energy, *q'ollona misas* have the capacity to serve as channels between worlds, enabling other *apus* (collective mountain spirits also referred to as "winged beings") and *santa tierras* (collective earth spirits) to *literally* speak during ceremony. The *apu* personalities that manifest during ceremony through an *altomesayoq's misa* are an expression of an aspect of the *apu* mountain collective (not the *apu* in totality).

In ceremony, when the *apus* are called by an *altomesyoq*, the spirits' arrival is often marked by the sounds of flapping wings and accompanied with stomping sounds across the altar that has been placed at the front of the room. During ceremonies with the *apus*, arrangements of colorful flowers, large quartz crystals, burning incense (often San Paulo wood), offerings of bottles of Incan soda pop (*apus* are said to like the sweet flavor), along with the *altomesayoq's misa* and the *misas* of other people present in the ceremony are placed on the altar.[4]

During ceremonies all electronic devices are removed, including cell phones and watches. Prior to a ceremony they are said to interfere with the *apus'* transmission. Ceremonies with the *apus* and *santa tierras* are held in pitch black rooms, with thick wool blankets covering all the windows. In the dark sometimes light emissions can be seen and heard from clicking crystals being rubbed together by the *apus* present in the ceremony. Sometimes the tops of the bottles of soda popping off can also be heard, and some people present in the room experience being touched gently by wings on the shoulders, heads, and backs of their physical bodies.

The voices of the different *apus* are heard in Quechua, each with their own unique timbre. The *altomesyoq* serves as the channel and remains silent after calling the spirits. Other people in the room—primarily other paqos—converse with the *apus* and the *apus* are sometimes open to receiving questions with the people present. Usually, another *paqo* will serve as a translator.

Apus and *santa tierras* have different personalities, as well as distinct voices. The manifestation of the aspect of the collective mountain spirit of an *apu* that appears during ceremony is influenced by the personal qualities of the *altomesyoq* serving as the channel.

Some *apus* have deep serious voices while others are playful and have a sense of humor. Some *apus* sound like wise old men, while the voices of the san*ta tierras* are feminine, usually in a very high youthful pitch.

In addition to serving as a gateway between the physical world and the spirit world, with the assistance of other paqos, *altomesayoqs* create *despachos*, or fire offerings, for their *apu* benefactors, *apu kuna* (the Andean *apu* collective) and *Pachamama* in service of the Andean cosmos to facilitate connection between the cosmos and their community. *Altomesayoqs* also function as healers and track the future using coca leaves.

Hatunmesayoqs

Hatunmesayoqs are reported to be even more evolved than *altomesayoqs* and are legendary (I have never heard of one or met one, although I have met four different *altomesayoqs*).[5] Potentially, *altomesayoqs* can advance into becoming a *hatunmesayoq*.[6] *Misayoq* means "master" and the translation of the Quechua word *hatun* means "multi-dimensional." Unlike *altomesayoqs*, the realms of the *hatunmesayoq* do not exist on a linear continuum ranging between high and lower levels of energy frequency and power, or the capacity to hold energy. *Hatunmesayoqs* are said to exist in a temporal dimension of reality that cannot be conceptualized in a paradigm understood using cognitive constructs, so they are impossible to describe. Like *altomesayoqs, hatunmesayoqs* are said to possess the capability to psychically meet one another in deep meditative states, in ceremony and dream time, energetic realms existing in atemporal reality.

The Hierarchy of the *Apus* and *Santa Tierras* in Andean Cosmology

The *apus,* or "winged beings," the collective mountain spirits of the Andean cosmos, exist in a fluid state of connectivity moving between atemporal and temporal reality in the energetic and physical realms respectively. Like everything else in the Andean cosmos, the *apus* are in relationship that exists as a hierarchy based upon power, or the amount of energy they hold—and their capacity to connect and influence the more highly evolved celestial realms that expand far beyond human comprehension. In Andean cosmology, the functions and positions of the apus vary.

Apu Everest is the light of the world, a sacred mountain that keeps the light of the world.

Suyu apus such as *Ausangate* and *Salkantay* watch over entire regions. *Apu Salkantay* is the most powerful of the *apus* in the Andean cosmos based upon its capacity to hold energy, and the *apu* responsible for deciding the *misas* of *altomesayoqs*. The Quechua word *salqa* means "wild and untamed" and refers to energetic potential that is formless and unmanifested. Paqos consider *Apu Salkantay* to be a sacred place in tune with all realities—temporal and atemporal. Paqos return to *Apu Salkantay* for inspiration and for vision in multiple realities.

Umantay is the feminine counterpart to *Apu Salkantay.*

Apu Ausangate is the second most powerful *apu* in the Andes, and one that paqos frequently make pilgrimages to call and call upon in ceremonies.

Apu Walki Wilka means sacred tear and is the provider of *misas*. Walki Wilka is where *altomesayoqs* go to renew their vows after a complex process of preparation that takes about two to three years.

Apu C'ollorit'i (which means snow star) is another *apu* that chosen village (or *ayllu)* members make pilgrimages to atone for the sins of the *ayllu* and for purification and is also a destination to renew spiritual commitment, as well as for vision to anticipate change.

Apu Pachatusan is the backbone or architect running through the Andes and is the axis of all local and collective *pachas.*

Apu Kaylash is an *apu* of initiation.

Apu Wyanakari instills morality and discipline.

Apu Pitasiway and *Apu Sawasiray* are a pair of *apu* spirits in *yanantin* that are multi-dimensional and balance dimensions in the Andean cosmos. *Apu Sawasiray* embodies the power of dreaming or eternal youth.

Apu Alangoma is the keeper of the eagle's nest and is a guardian in the celestial realm of *Hanaq Pacha*.

Quelque Punqo (golden door) serves as a portal into other dimensions. These *apu* mountain spirits are often named when calling sacred space and are destinations for sacred pilgrimages, made for purification and initiation ceremonies.

Some *apu*s have specific functions. For example, some of the roles of the *apus* around the city of Cusco are as follows: *Apu Sacsayhuaman Cabildo* is the guardian of knowledge and wisdom. *Apu Picol* is the shepherd watching over people. *Apu Senq'a* is the keeper of water in Cusco who rules all rainwater, lagoons, and rivers. *Apu Calque* is the accountant in charge of records of all births, deaths, and residents of Cusco. *Apu Pukeen* is the *apu* associated with housing construction. *Apu Mama Simona*, one of the female *apus*, is related to fertility and gives the power of healing. *Llaqta apus*, such as *PachaTuscon* and *Haunacuari*, are medium-sized village *apus,* that have authority over a specific geographical area. *Ayllu apus* influence the smallest villages and are often considered to be the guardian *apus* of specific communities.

In Andean cosmology, the *santa tierras* are the feminine spirits who are collective expressions of *Pachamama* residing in the earth. At the core of the earth there are three *santa tierras* that function as the glue that keeps the earth together. At the next level, the middle layer, there are seven other *santa tierras*—each with specific purposes. One *santa tierra* governs water; another *santa tierra* oversees plants, trees, animals, minerals, and land formations. On the earth's surface, there are thousands of *santa tierras* that are keepers of all seeds and fertility, bringing seeds to life.

Codes in Incan Technology

All paqos, regardless of their level of power, work with energetic codes, sometimes referred to as "Incan technology." Through entering a state of connection with *Wira Cocha,* through *qaway kuy,* the Andean medicine people can access these ancient Incan "codes," referred to as *pacha-wan kausay*. These are inherent essential properties of the universe in *Wira Cocha* that transcend everything that exists—both physically and energetically—temporally and atemporally. The codes of *pacha-wan kausay* are universal and apply to all living things, pertaining specifically to the properties of the manifestations, or expressions of *kausay* energy. A paqo's capacity to work with *pacha-wan kausay* is a function of their capacity to hold energy with knowledge and wisdom, which is a paqo's definition of power. The power that is acquired through spiritual sourcing is called *kallpa*.

The Code of Correspondence

The Quechua word *remolino* describes the law of correspondence in Andean medicine. It literally refers to an energetic essence in the form of a "spiritual whirlpool," existing in atemporal dimensions that comes into being in temporal reality through the energetic vortex, often manifesting as something new in psychic development. *Puyqo* is the word that describes energy in space before it comes into form. *Muyuq unu* refers to whirlpools of water living in the physical world of *Kay Pacha,* which is a way that *remolino* is expressed in the physical world. Through the code of *remolino,* "as above so below," *puyqo* becomes *muyu unu.*

The Relationship between Masculine and Feminine Principles

In addition to *remolino* there are other types of energetic relationships bringing a transition from spirit into matter. Each of the spirit beings in the Andean cosmos have a gender. *Pachamama* (Mother Earth), the *Santa Tierras* (earth spirits), *Mama Qocha* (Mother of the Lagoons) and *Mama Qilla* (Grandmother Moon) are all feminine cosmic beings, while (most) of the *apus,*[7]as well as *Inti Tayta* (Father Sun), are masculine.

Kamakuy refers to the process of energy coming into physical manifestation through the relationship between masculine and feminine forces. The term *yanantin* refers to the attraction between masculine and feminine energy coming together. Paqos refer to the joining of opposites, considered to be an act of creation, as *tinku.* The phrase *paqarichly* means to "be born" or "give life." Through this unification, the emergence of something new, like the transcendent function in depth psychology (Jung, 1976, par. 1554), is referred to as *sawa* in Quechua.

The paqos' experience of intentionally entering an atemporal state of oneness through the principle of *yanantin* is based upon the relationship between masculine and feminine energy, or an attraction between opposites (Jung, 1954). In a relationship of *yanantin,* intent is the masculine force that gives form to the feminine principle of creativity, bringing energy into temporality by creating context within a temporal time and space paradigm. Similar to alchemy, in Andean medicine the masculine principle applies to a linear force of penetration with direction while the feminine principle pertains to a being state of holding, inclusion.

In addition to moving from spirit into matter, a process referred to as *coagulatio* in alchemy (Edinger, 1985), the reverse is also true. Temporal experience may also transcend from matter into atemporal realms of spirit, a process referred to as *sublimatio* in alchemy (Edinger, 1985). The energetic relationship of *yanantin* creates a structure that then becomes a doorway and container that can be moved through or "dropped into" to merge into an oceanic relationship, based upon the masculine supporting the feminine principle. This state of surrender is the transition from temporal to atemporal experience. The engagement of the feminine and masculine principles in this way leads to a state of ecstasy or blending and merging.

Like *yanantin, masantin* is also an energetic relationship based upon masculine and feminine principles. *Masantin* is the relationship between like energies or beings of the same sex, which might be the dynamic between a father and son, mother and daughter, brothers, sisters, and so on. It is a supportive connection that amplifies the shared essential nature of both beings.

Repulsion and Attraction

In addition to energies having an affinity that are masculine or feminine in a relationship of *masantin*, energies vibrating at similar vibrational frequencies also have an affinity for one another based upon attraction, operating under the principle "like attracts like." According to paqos, energetic vibrational frequencies that have the same wave lengths create form. In addition to the law of attraction, there is also the energetic law of repulsion. *Sami,* a very pure energy of light vibrating at a high frequency, is associated with healing and is repelled by *hucha* (dense energy causing blockage) and *layka* (evil energy associated with sorcery). *Hucha* and *layka* are associated with trauma states and live in *llanthu* (the shadow). With an increase in *sami, hucha* and *layka* decrease and healing moves toward a state of *sonqoyqui,* ever flowing joy and abundance.

Like the Jungian conceptualization that archetypes have both light and dark aspects (Jung., 1979) all energetic beings in the Andean cosmos have a shadow, and this is true for the *apus* as well. Paqos develop power as a capacity to hold energy in service of the light while *brujas*, or sorcerers, acquire *layka* for personal power. As is true for everything in the Andean cosmos, the paqos and brujas live in their own communities in the sacred mountains together, with each group working with the aspects of their *apu* benefactors that they have an affinity for.

While light and dark forces always exist together as integral parts of the cosmos, in times when the light becomes overpowered by dark forces, a phenomenon referred to as a *pacha cuti* occurs. The phrase *pacha cuti* describes the collective experience of a cataclysmic event that takes place when a world is out of alignment, or *ayni,* for too long.

According to the Andean prophecies, the world is currently in a time of a *pacha cuti*. When the dense energy of *hucha,* or the evil intent of *layka* overpowers the clear light energy of *sami,* a *pacha cuti* occurs, turning the world upside down. This results in the death of a collective persona, creating a retreat or regression of energy.

Pacha callari pava describes the collective experience of a new beginning for our planet in an archetypal death and rebirth process when the old perception of reality changes. *A pacha callari pava* occurs when there is not a re-identification with the past collective complex involving a participation mystique to belong. Instead, a transcendent shift is made into a new age of an archetypal rebirth, where there is a letting go of attachment to the old ways, into a new incarnation with a collective vision of alignment in *ayni* for the future—experienced in the present.

The Code of Collectivity

In Andean medicine emphasis is focused on moving toward connection with the collective away from the limitations of an individual perspective. A collective perspective is intersubjective and does not pertain specifically to people and community. Instead, it is a spiritual focus aimed toward the experience of oneness as a part of the greater cosmos, which, according to paqos, is essentially made up of an endless source of energy—through light, life, and fertility. *Kausay* is the life force, the vital resonance of spirit or soul as it manifests at different vibrations. In healing ceremonies, paqos transfer *kausay* from an energetic state of collectivity into a conscious physical reality.

Everything living in the cosmos holds a memory of a healed state of wholeness existing within a state of collective connectivity. Personal healing and development coming from a collective perspective that informs the creation of an individual sense of self leads to a more profound understanding of one's true nature in relation to the cosmos.

By honoring the connection between all living things, paqos uphold the harmonic balance of being in *ayni,* or right relationship. Paqos serve relationships in the Andean cosmos, through the whole being of their *manos wasi* that is not only mental. Cultivating an energetic connection with the Andean collective is the crux of healing.

Trauma is the result of becoming disconnected from the collective life force of *kausay,* often the result of a stagnant belief system that is blocked and stuck in the past. Healing occurs through regaining a balance of being in *ayni* with the collective. Andean medicine starts from a collective orientation and from the collective heals the personal.

This is different from a psychoanalytic approach, where psychic healing begins through focusing on and understanding personal experience that then informs the relationship with the outside world. In Andean medicine, psychic healing occurs in an atemporal non-personal energetic state, which involves moving beyond personal circumstances and transcends into remembering the universal experience of belonging in the Andean cosmos.

Organizing Principles in Andean Medicine

In addition to codes, which pertain to properties of energetic relationships, in Andean medicine there are seven organizing principles in the cosmos. These principles further define qualities of energetic engagement in the natural world that transcend temporality and atemporality. Together, these organizing principles provide order in the way the cosmos functions and evolves.

Munay

Munay is a state of unconditional love, connection between all living things, and a way of being. The definition of *munay* in Andean medicine is different from personal attachment. It is an attitude of openness experienced in the heart center that applies to the collective, which transcends individual relationships. Paqos believe that abuse is misguided love, aggression is confused love, and that *munay* is necessary to achieve higher states of consciousness. *Munay* also refers to the capacity to create affinities, or vibrations of a similar wavelength, which create form through attraction. If the parameters of the affinities or vibrations change and no longer support an attraction or repulsion there is potential for transformation away from old patterns and greater capacity for creation. These changes often occur when receiving *karpay* rites.

Nuna

Nuna refers to the phenomenon that everything in the Andean cosmos is alive and an expression of spirit—or "God." Because everything is alive there is capacity for relationship and connection between all living things, with no separation. *Nuna* is the embodiment of knowledge and how the universe lives in a fluid state within us.

Chekak

Chekak is the inherent truth in the natural order of things that informs our belief systems as the lens of our perception. *Chekak* refers to relative truth, an aspect of resonance in the cosmos that facilitates navigation, and absolute truth as empowerment. As living things evolve, they become more aligned with the essential truth of who and what they are through the process of mapping the belief systems of their guiding mythology to determine where their true identities reside, and to avoid becoming attached to a position, imposing limitations on perception. Conversely when one is open and involved as an active participant, they find balance and ultimate truth, which creates personal and collective meaning.

Yuya

Yuya refers to wisdom of knowing through observation that organizes the energy of the cosmos. By being fully present and available to everything as it exists in the living world, deeper understanding is developed. Power is knowledge, which is information gathered in a way that it can be applied.

   At more advanced levels of *yuya*, the awakening process of *siwar q'enti* (the royal hummingbird archetype) refers specifically to a very high level of shamanic journeying, or learning directly from collective knowledge beyond the lens of a personal framework that is a way of acquiring power in service of the cosmos. There is an Andean myth that *siwar q'enti* was the only animal being that looked directly into the eyes of the creator.

Ch'ulla

Ch'ulla pertains to the energetic connection that exists between all living things through *ceke* lines. *Ceke* lines are the energetic threads that form the web of light that makes up the universe. There are three types of *ceke* lines, determined by the quality of energy they hold. They include the basic level of *kayau*, the intermediate level of *payan,* which is more evolved than *kayau* and carries lineage, and the highest level of *q'ollona*, which is the essential level of creation. These three different levels of energy appear throughout the cosmos, in manifestations of *kausay*, or life force.

Ch'ulla also refers to the energetic state of oneness and communion in connection. In a natural state, everything in the universe moves toward harmonious union, anchoring one's identity in the *pacha* they are living in (allocation of energy at a point in time in space) with the capacity for reflection in relationship. The reflection that is possible in states of *ch'ulla* brings a more differentiated understanding of experience as expressions of consciousness in temporality and atemporality. This process, referred to as *reqsequiy*, offers a means of recapitulating memories of destructive patterns, freeing up "stuck" energy from the past. *Qaway kusaq* refers to the process of deciding which thoughts and behaviors are positive and which are negative and then deciding to eradicate the ones that are not beneficial to one's spiritual path. The practice of *reqsequiy* and *qaway kusaq* lead to restoring a state of *kallari*.

Kallari

Kallari is the state of dynamic flow and changing movement that occurs in the universe. To engage in progressive states of evolution it is necessary to be part of the flow. Staying attached to the past creates stagnation and blocks *ch'ulla*.

Muki

Muki is the organizing principle in the lower world of *Uku Pacha* connected to the "belly" or source in *Pachamama* (mother earth). Paqos teach that experiencing through the belly enables one to enter a state of *fluidity*, a state of no separation with *Pachamama*.

Notes

1   See p. 35 of this text for a more detailed explanation of *pacha-wan kausay*.
2   Paqos tend to interpret dreams as messages from the spirit world, often involving the *apus*, while analysts tend to focus on the symbolism.
3   A *misa* is a paqo's medicine body made up of a group of stones or *q'uiyas*.
4   The *misas* of people attending the ceremony are placed on the altar for blessings.
5   *Alto* distinguishes between high and low whereas *hatun* refers to multi-dimensional space.
6   *Hatunmesayoqs* are legendary. I have never heard of the existence of a *hatunmesayoq* in the present day.
7   *Umantay*, *Mama Simone*, and *Siwasiray*, are collective feminine *apu* mountain spirits.

References

Edinger, E. F. (1985) *Anatomy of the Psyche: Alchemical symbolism in psychotherapy*, Peru, IL: Open Court Publishing.

Jung, C. G. (1954) *The Practice of Psychotherapy* (Collected Works, vol. 16).

Jung, C. G. (1976) *The Symbolic Life: Miscellaneous writing* (Collected Works, vol. 18).

Jung, C. G. (1979) *Collected Works of C.G. Jung, Volume 9 (Part 2)*, eds Gerhard Adler and R. F. C. Hull, Princeton, NJ: Princeton University Press.

Chapter 4

Psychic States in Andean Medicine

The Paqos' Levels of Psychic Engagement: Between Physical and Energetic Reality

There are different levels of perception and interaction existing on a range of levels between matter and spirit, or temporality and atemporality in the Andean cosmos. Depth psychology and other schools of psychoanalysis view temporal experience as a function of ego-consciousness, with explicit understanding being the outcome of ego processing, and atemporal oceanic experience occurring at deeper layers of the unconscious psyche. Paqos do not conceptualize "ego functioning" as a way of delineating between consciousness and the unconscious, and temporal and atemporal experience, but share some commonality with aspects of psychoanalytic theory regarding the transition between ego-consciousness and oceanic experience.

Paqos experience consciousness not only as a cognitive ego function. At deeper levels of atemporal consciousness, they perceive a shift from relying on cognition to experiencing the cosmos through what might be described as a somatic state of awareness. There are not words that describe this state in English because it is atemporal and lacks discrete form. Even though I am referring to this phenomenon as somatic awareness, the paqos' experience of "somatic awareness" is more than a cognizance of body sensation because it extends beyond the physical body into the *manos wasi* or subtle body, and even further into a connection with the cosmos both physically and energetically. Through this timeless connection, paqos can "feel into" the sentient presence of the *apus, Pachamama*, and other beings that have an energetic presence with an essential identity without physical form. Experiencing this way happens through the energetic field that connects everything in the cosmos, and registers in the *munay*, or heart, and the five senses. Often this connection occurs through a vibration in the body, overwhelming experience of love in the heart, and seeing different colors and levels of intensity of light, sound, and even smell. (I have never experienced a connection through smell but one *altomesayoq* told me that it often has the fragrance of flowers.)

Paqos experience distinctive kinds of energetic presence at different levels of psychic engagement and move between levels of psychic engagement and temporal and atemporal states through meditative practices, which each have names in

DOI: 10.4324/9781003356448-6

Quechua, the language of the paqos. The individual meditative practices are linked to the levels of psychic engagement. These meditative practices will be described in relation to each of the levels of psychic engagement.

Developing a basic Quechua vocabulary helped me to develop a better under-standing of Andean cosmology and to appreciate subtle differences in the states they were describing. I discovered that there are many words in Quechua that can-not be translated into English or Spanish. This is because in Quechua there are more words for implicit energetic experience that clarify qualities and processes associated with these kinds of experiences and connections in Andean medicine. References will be made to Quechua terminology in describing practices and medi-tative states in Andean medicine, and how they apply to the different levels of psychic engagement.

In Andean medicine there are four levels of psychic engagement or states of perception, which I am referring to as the literal, symbolic, mythic, and essen-tial levels. These levels of psychic engagement correspond to a transition from ego-consciousness into deeper states that depth psychologists have associated with the collective unconscious and the psychoidal realm. These states reflect shifts between temporal and atemporal experience, as well as moving from a personal to a collective focus—which, for paqos, is a transition between physical and energetic realms.

The Literal Level of Engagement

The literal or first level is a concrete awareness of the physical world—of everyday, out-in-the-world "ordinary" reality. The literal level is ego-based, oriented from a personal perspective. Because of this, the literal state is temporal and a function of the ego taking in and organizing information from the outside world. As mentioned earlier, the term *kausay pacha* refers to energy existing within the context of time and space, which provides form and matter in the present. According to paqos, perceiving physical reality occurs in the immediacy of the present as a function of one of the three energy centers located in the body, related to one of the three major mythic animal figures in Andean cosmology.

Although each of these energy centers, *y'ankay, munay,* and *y'anchay*, are rooted in the physical body and pertain to perceiving at the literal level of engagement, they are also linked energetically to the greater cosmos through the *manos wasi*. Through the link that exists between the physical and energy body, in addition to receiving information within the context of temporal experience, perception also occurs in atemporal dimensions, providing a bridge, or *chacana*, between the lev-els of engagement.

While perceiving from the literal level, time is experienced sequentially. Reality is based upon the narrative derived from the cognitive organization of perception. There is a natural order of cause and effect that determines practical engagement in the world. For paqos, after a spiritual experience the question, "Can you grow corn with it?" is asked—meaning is the experience useful in helping one's self or community in some way? Mystical experiences that happen "on the mountain" are valuable if they are practical; if they can be brought back "to the village," or *ayllu*, in service that is beneficial to oneself or others.

Haipay *Rituals*

The daily ritual *haipay* is an Andean practice that is often rooted in physical reality, and although there is a relationship of correspondence at the other levels of psychic engagement, *haipay* begins as an engagement at the literal level. *Hai* means opening or reaching and *pay* translates as "knocking on a door for connection."

Yupachay, a form of *haipay,* is the practice of honoring and worshipping *Inti Tayta, Pachamama,* and the *apus* with gratitude and is part of the process of opening oneself, through one's heart center (*munay*), to the Andean spirit world. The phrase *chaskichiwaychis* is part of an Andean prayer, which translates as, "Receive us, welcome us, embrace us with your love."

There are many different *haipay* rituals practiced by paqos daily. *Haipay* involves using breath to blow prayers into *k'intus* (coca leaf offerings made of three leaves grouped together), with the purpose of giving the *k'intu kausay* (life energy) through the practice of *mikuchiy* in an act of devotedness. *Phukey* refers to the ritual act of blowing an intention into the leaves of a *k'intu.* I have heard some paqos say that they feed one another through *haipay* and that the ritual of *haipay* is how they remember their collective identity.

Through the physical act of *haipay,* paqos set the intention of connecting their bodies to the earth and cosmos. The practice of *haipay* is done repeatedly on hiking pilgrimages to sacred mountains (*paq'o wachu*) to gain strength from *Pachamama* and the *apus* during an uphill journey. The action of *haipay* prepares paqos for moving into symbolic and energetic levels of engagement. *Antimachulaq* refers to the practice of making a pilgrimage to the Andean spirits, often to a specific *apu* mountain.

During the *antimachulaq,* in a process of a "spirit dance" referred to as *puriynin*—walking slowly in connection with the spirits using breath, *k'intu* offerings are carried, expressing feelings of love and gratitude to *Pachamama* and the *apus. K'intus* are always a very important component of *antimachulaq.* Eventually, during *antimachulaq,* the *k'intus* are presented and placed along the path as a gift through the practice referred to as *reqsichiy.* Besides leaving *k'intus* as gifts in the act of *reqsichiy,* for *Pachamama* and the *apus,* sometimes other *k'intus* are chewed slightly and held in the upper left or right side of the mouth for strength, protection, and connection during the *puriynin.* This practice of chewing and holding *k'intus* in one's mouth is referred to as *chacchar.*

Reqsequiy

The practice of *reqsequiy* is another Andean practice that occurs at the literal level of psychic engagement that involves self-reflection. Through reviewing their experience, paqos form a narrative about who they are in relation to their personal past that determines how they understand themselves in the present. *Reqsequiy* involves delving into feeling reactions, interpretations, and actions in response to past life events and relationships in the present. The phrase *taripachikuy* refers to the process of rediscovering or finding oneself.

By examining reactions and relationships with different situations, paqos can identify reoccurring themes in their emotional responses and behaviour, and then set an intention to eradicate them. This act of recapitulation serves to free up psychic energy that may be stuck in the past, to stop projecting the unresolved response patterns into the future. The practice of *reqsequiy* provides paqos with more psychic availability to respond to situations in the present with immediacy, and to remove potential blocks that could prevent them from entering more profound psychic spaces of energetic connection. *Reqsequiy* is a process of mentation, which also occurs in psychoanalysis.

The Symbolic Level of Engagement

The second level, which pertains to the imaginal and creative realms, is called the symbolic level. It also involves a personal perspective and is accessed through dreams, metaphors, and imagery—in states of reverie. Winnicott (1971) has described this as a transitional psychological space existing between fantasy and reality. It is the realm of play, a liminal space between the unconscious and conscious, and temporal and atemporal reality. As mentioned earlier, as is often the case with dream content, this liminal state is not necessarily limited to a sequential order of past, present, and future. The symbolic realm can be both temporal and atemporal and is the intermediary between the unconscious and conscious. Jungians have described this as the imaginal realm where inner dialogue using the technique of "active imagination" can occur (Hoerni et al., 2019).

Stan Marlan (2005) has said that it is not the resolution of dissimilarities between images but the recognition that each image is an independent entity on to itself. This premise describes operating at the symbolic level of the psyche. While being metaphorical rather than physical, concepts and imagery at the symbolic level are often delineated by discrete boundaries and are often imagined as existing in a realm with physical properties defined by form.

When the level of psychic engagement moves further away from ego-consciousness the distinction between images becomes less important and eventually ceases to exist the further one moves toward the atemporal energetic realms of the objective psyche. The expression of energy moves away from consciously perceiving through orienting using symbols, form, and imagery toward a fluid state of connectivity, where experiencing through separation is less important. The mythic level of engagement functions as a bridge between these states.

Jung's concept of "active imagination" is an example of a symbolic level process that bridges deeper levels of the unconscious psyche with ego-consciousness. In the active imagination technique, while awake, the dream setting would be re-entered and the conscious mind would allow internal imagery from a dream to emerge and the scene to develop without directing it, to enable the unconscious to express itself without influence.Jung was insistent that some form of active participation in active imagination was essential: "You yourself must enter into the process with your personal reactions: ... as if the drama being enacted before your eyes were real" (Jung, 1963 [1955], par. 753).

Creative expression and exploring imagination in states of reverie can also be symbolic level processes used to access and work with deeper layers of atemporal unconscious material in temporal psychic spaces. For an artistic act to become meaningful to the creator, it must be an expression of an urge that wants to be made conscious. Jung (1921) believed that libidinal drives were not only sexual in nature and believed that they could manifest as a need to create as well.

The expression of a creative urge for artists is similar in some ways to the release of pent-up sexual energy in that it reduces tension. However, the difference in creative expression is that energy is not merely dissipated—it is made conscious and shifts from atemporal to temporal experience. Artistic creativity expressed through the medium of writing or visual arts usually happens using symbols. Symbols arising from our own imagination tend to hold the most psychic energy, coming from the unconscious. Some people work with collective religious motifs in rituals that have taken on meaning through personal associations with a temporal conscious context.

Despacho Offerings

A *despacho* is an offering usually for the *apus* and *Pachamama*, given through the fire or buried in the earth (see Figure 4.1). It is a circular arrangement of *k'intus* (cocoa leaves are used in Peru while bay leaves are frequently used—symbolic of coca leaves—in the United States), resembling a mandala. There are about 365 different types of *despachos* created for special ceremonies, entities, and so forth. An *ayni despacho* is often created before initiation ceremonies as a way of "coming together with the land and mountain spirits." Most *despachos* are gifts to *Pachamama* and the *apus*, although some are for releasing *hucha*, or misaligned energy from trauma. The process of preparing an offering for *Pachamama* for payment or atonement is called *q'onyay.* Other *despachos* are created to ask for strength, protection, and/or clarity, and for the *apus* blessings before an initiation ceremony.

K'intus are a fundamental component of all *despachos,* regardless of their purpose. Preparing *k'intus* is the first step in building a *despacho.* After carefully creating *k'intus* by separating coca leaves into groups of three, the paqo transfers intent into the *k'intus* using breath through the ritual act of *phukey.* Each group of leaves takes on a specific prayer or pattern to be let go of and given to the fire based upon the specific intention of the prayer. Blowing into the leaves of *k'intu* in creating *despachos* also establishes an energetic connection linking the three worlds. In *despachos* shaped like mandalas, the *k'intus* are often placed in a

Figure 4.1 A *Despacho* ceremonial offering, a grouping of stones arranged on an Andean mastana cloth.

circular pattern, like rays emanating from the sun, surrounding a central symbolic object determined by the type and purpose of *despacho*.

Next the *despacho* is embellished with grains, candy, and other colorful objects that symbolize gifts to the upper, lower, and middle worlds. Different materials are used for gifts to each of the worlds, For the lower world of *Uku Pacha*, grains and seeds are used. For the middle world of *Kay Pacha,* the world of physical reality, colorful candies are often added. Small silver-colored figures of homes, cars, or couples may be used when requesting help with security, mobility, relationships, and so on. For the upper celestial world of *Hanaq Pacha*, silver threads (*qolilazo*) connecting the feminine energy of *Mama Qilla* (Grandmother Moon) and gold threads (*qorilazo*) connecting the energy of *Inti Tayta* (Father Sun) are used to bring integration and clarity. When crafted by an advanced paqo (even when constructed on a mountain on a windy day) *despachos* become beautiful works of art, created to honor, and please the deities of the spirit world.

The paqo then brings the completed *despacho* upright to the fire after wrapping it carefully in tissue or gift paper. In fire ceremony, before the *despacho* is brought to the fire, a paqo helps the fire to become "alive" by calling sacred space. First, the paqo takes Florida water into their mouth and blows it forcefully using sweeping hand movements. Florida water is a combination of alcohol and flower essences and is used frequently at the beginning of most ceremonies for purification before calling sacred space. Paqos call sacred space by calling the *apus* and *Pachamama* through prayers and invocation individually. *Takis* or songs are often sung when the fire ceremony is taking place with a group, or *ayllu*.

Before placing the *despacho* offering on the fire, it is customary for paqos and other group members to individually approach the fire from four sides, from each of the four directions to "clean" the three energy centers in their body (*y'anchay, munay, y'anchay*) and personal *misas* (medicine bundles made up of *q'uiyas* of stones imbued with meaning and energy for the paqo). Cleansing the energy centers occurs by making circular movements with both arms over each of the three chakras. Next, with intention, the paqo draws the fire into each of their three energy centers with gestural movements using their hands. First, counterclockwise movements open the three chakras. Next, the fire is "pulled" by reaching into the fire (but not touching it) and "packing" each energy center with the fire's spirit energy, followed with circular clockwise motions that then close the chakras. Finally, the paqo holds their medicine bundle or *misa* over the fire for cleansing. At the end of the ceremony, the paqo places the *despacho* on the fire, turns their back, and walks away from the fire. The shaman does not look at the *despacho* after placing it on the fire to avoid reversing the effect.[1]

The Mythic Level of Engagement

The third level of psychic engagement in Andean medicine is the mythic realm. It is atemporal, existing outside of the constructs of linear time, and is the dimension where synchronicities connect. Corbett (1996) proposed that shamanism and depth psychology are similar because both acknowledge the realms of the psyche and the archetype—which refers to the mythic level of perceiving. For Jung, the archetypes were primordial universal themes existing in the collective unconscious, the deepest layer of the individual psyche, not defined or limited by time and space in temporal reality (Jung, 1959).

In both depth psychology and Andean medicine, the mythic realm is the psychic space in the collective unconscious that functions as a veil between the individual psyche and the objective psyche (that is, the *unus mundus* in depth psychology and for paqos, the spirit dimension of the cosmos). In describing the veil, Jung has written, "As well as being an archetype in its own right, it is at the same time a dynamism which makes itself felt in the numinosity and fascinating power or an archetypal image" (1960, p. 121, par. 414). Here, Jung is referring to the liminal space that exists between spirit and matter, which can be represented conceptually or as an experiential state. Jung (1960a) said that archetypes have a dual nature that is transgressive, existing in the realm of both psyche and matter. Jung has written:

If the position of the archetype would be located beyond the psychic sphere, analogous to the position of physiological instinct, which is immediately rooted in the stuff of the organism and, with its psychoidal nature, forms the bridge

to matter in general. In archetypal conceptions and instinctual perceptions, spirit and matter confront one another on the psychic plane. Matter and spirit both appear in the psychic realm as distinctive qualities of conscious contents. The ultimate nature of both is transcendental, that is irrepresentable since the psyche and its contents are the only reality that is given us without a medium.
(Jung, 1960a, p. 216, par. 420)

Paqos view the mythic level as the gateway between the personal and the collective, and temporal and atemporal. In Andean cosmology in this realm, there are collective mythic beings that represent the realms of the three worlds, *Uku Pacha* (Lower World), *Kay Pacha* (Middle World), and *Hanaq Pacha* (Upper World), as well as possessing an animal form. These mythic animal beings symbolize certain desirable qualities or abilities linked to specific modes of perception, in addition to representing spaces associated with the three worlds.[2] Paqos refer to high vibrational beings as *killki.*

The Mythic Beings of *Amaru, Chocachinchi,* and *Apucheen*

In Andean cosmology, the three major mythic beings are *Amaru,* the serpent form of *Pachamama, Chocachinchi,* the jaguar that is the spirit of the jungle, and *Apucheen,* the great condor that soars overhead and is associated with the realm of the collective mountain spirits. In Andean cosmology, these mythic beings represent guiding principles and are multidimensional, taking on the properties of the environment they are associated with. Like the archetypes in Jungian depth psychology, each of these mythic beings possess a numinosity, which paqos sometimes encounter while in deep meditative states. In addition to being atemporal energetic emanations that are interpsychic, in Andean medicine they exist with their own autonomy in the cosmos.

While rooted in the mythic realm, these beings have physical and symbolic forms that through the law of correspondence (*so above, so below),* also exist in the literal and symbolic level of psychic engagement. These beings often appear in dreams for people connected to Andean cosmology. The paqos use the word *musquchay* to describe the phenomenon of appearing in another's dream. Over the course of a decade when I first began working with the Andean medicine people, *Amaru, Chocachinchi,* and *Apucheen,* have each appeared to me in dream states in a dream narrative applicable to my life at the time. I will share an example of this from my personal experience.

Apucheen

In Quechua the spirit of *Apucheen* is referred to as *mallku.* It was one of the three mythic figures associated with vision states and the upper world of *Hanaq Pacha* and with the energy center *Y'anchay,* in the mind.

Wamani refers to the archetype of the upper world of *Hanaq Pacha*. *Wanakuna* refers to the collective bird spirit of *Hanaq Pacha*. For me, seeing this figure first in a dream and then later having it pointed out in a painting by Adolfo was powerfully synchronistic. This occurred at a time when I was first beginning to work with the *apus* in my inner world. I begin working with the dream figure in imaginal states and created many paintings of it to keep the connection with *mallku* alive in my mind.

Chocachinchi

The energetic connection associated with the mythic rainbow jaguar, *Chocochinchi*, is based in the heart center, or *munay*. Through the heart center, *Chocochinchi* brings connection and a sense of aliveness experiencing through all the senses. As the spirit of the jungle, *Chocochinchi* appeared and became my protector during an *ayawausqa* ceremony when due to unforeseen circumstances, the *ayawausqero*, the shaman responsible for facilitating the ceremony, had left. For hours, I experienced being held safely in the powerful yet loving arms of *Chocochinchi* until dawn.

Amaru

Although the mythic serpent *Amaru* is generally associated with the lower world of *Uku Pacha*, as an image of creativity, fertility, and manifestation *Amaru* also has to do with moving from a state of atemporal fluidity, into form and matter in the present.

Amaru is the energetic organizing code of manifestation existing in all dimensions. *Wayramama* is the aspect of *Amaru* associated with air in the upper sky realms. *Sach'amama* is the serpent *Amaru* of the jungle that often emerges in the form of an anaconda in *ayahuasca* ceremonies. *Yakumama* is the two-headed serpent who is the mother of the living waters. *Amaruina* is the serpent of fire, which is considered by paqos to be the lineage from eons ago, belonging to Incan wizards who had special visions.

In addition to *Pachamama* and the individual *apus,* or collective mountain spirits of the sacred mountains of the Andes, *Mama Qilla* (grandmother spirit of the moon), *Inti Tayta* (father spirit of the sun, who is the most powerful being in Incan cosmology), *Yukumama* (mother spirit of water), *Mama Qocha* (mother spirit of the lagoons in the Andes), and *Sochimama* (mother of the jungle) are a few of the other spirit beings in the Andean cosmos.

The Energy Centers of Y'ankay, Munay, and Y'anchay

As mentioned earlier, the mythic beings *Amaru, Chocochinchi,* and *Apucheen* are each associated with one of the three major energy centers in Andean medicine—the belly (*y'ankay*), the heart (*munay*), and the mind (*y'anchay*), respectively, with certain properties. *Y'ankay* is in the first two *chakras* (base of the spine and belly) and is associated with fertility and manifestation in *Kay Pacha* (the physical world we live in) through its connection with *Pachamama*. *Y'ankay* has the function of actively participating in the physical mechanics of doing and is the center of creation, bringing into form what has been formless.

Munay is in the heart and throat *chakra* and is the center of exchange and state of universal love and connection. *Munay* is where we relate with the experience of the fullness of all our senses through the mastery of love. *Munay* also has to do with the mechanics of membership with the cosmos, which is how paqos acquire and hold energy.

Y'anchay is the energy center located in the third eye and crown chakras and is associated with vision states. While *y'ankay* is associated with creation and survival, and *munay* is associated with being in relationship with the cosmos through the heart, *y'anchay* has to do with seeing objectively through the mind. Everything that has form is moving to an energetic state of formlessness that can be envisioned—from matter into spirit, which becomes freedom from limited defined by the past.

Vision States Related to the Mythic Beings

According to *paqos,* there are three main energy centers in the human body— *y'ankay* (the belly), *munay* (the heart), and *y'anchay* (the mind). Each of these energy centers are linked with a collective mythic being associated with an animal form. These beings are guiding principles, as well as ways of perceiving, which manifest as emanations of the spirit world that govern the energy centers in the body. *Amaru*, the great snake of creation, resides in the lower world of *Uku Pacha*, and is associated with the Belly energy center in the body. *Chocachinchi* is the powerful jaguar spirit of the Amazon that resides over the middle world of *Kay Pacha*, in the Heart. *Apucheen* is the commanding condor of wisdom and vision in the celestial realm of *Hanaq Pacha*, in the Mind. According to paqos, perceiving reality occurs in the immediacy of the present as a function of one of the three energy centers located in the body, related to one of the three major mythic animal figures in Andean cosmology.

Snake Vision

The *literal* or first level is a concrete awareness or gut feeling of the physical world in everyday, out-in-the-world "ordinary" reality. As mentioned earlier, the term *kausay pacha* refers to energy existing within the time and space paradigm of physical reality. Snake vision is associated with the serpent *Amaru* and is linked with survival response in the autonomic nervous system, and the energy center located in the belly (*y'ankay*). Like the snake who moves with its belly on the ground—the world is experienced as immediate and binary. There is no psychic space for reflection because this is somatic, a reactive "gut" response to what one encounters.

Snake vision is the most elementary vision—used in reaction to traumatic situations requiring a flight-or-flight reaction.

From the perspective of *Amaru*, everything exists in a primary, volatile state between spirit and matter. Although primitive, it is the realm of creation and manifestation, a place of no separation—where anything is possible. Operating Being in connection through *y'ankay* corresponds with the Taoists' idea of being in balance with the energy and world around us.

Accessing memories in states of heightened awareness begins with "swallowing the energetic experience whole"—in other words, instead of analyzing the experience, dropping into it by merging with it somatically. Through *y'ankay*, the belly becomes the vessel that holds the experience while it is metabolized into a form that can be worked with and assimilated—and then translated into cognitive understanding.

The process of anchoring through *y'ankay* is like the digestion process of snakes. Snakes ingest their prey completely, in one piece, and then become inactive as digestive enzymes dissolve the nutrients in their prey. The process of absorption happens as the threshold of what is referred to as "the energy barrier" is crossed, producing a reaction. Like snakes digesting their food, by surrendering into the somatic experience through the *y'ankay* the threshold of the energetic wall between ordinary and nonordinary reality is crossed. Paqos refer to this as merging with mythic snake, which in Andean cosmology is the manifestation of *Pachamama*, or mother earth. Paqos believe that experiencing energetically through our bodies is how we become aware of being connected.

Jaguar Vision

"Jaguar vision," associated with the jaguar *Chocachinchi*, relates to the heart center (*munay*), or universal love, the hub of connectivity through experiencing using acute sensing. *Munay* is the ability to love unconditionally, beyond personal experience and limitation. For paqos, this is different from love attached to a specific individual, with a need for reciprocation.

Chocachinchi presides over the middle world of *Kay Pacha* and is the forceful jaguar, the spirit of the Amazon, as the master of all relations in *ayni*. The jaguar has a heightened awareness and lives in a present state of alert. The jaguar is oriented toward tracking the outside world—using its five senses to navigate. In a state of jaguar vision, the world is experienced as sensual and alive. In Andean cosmology, *Chocachinchi* takes on a broader significance, as a universal motif symbolizing all animals with the capability to manifest in any physical form in *Kay Pacha*. The jaguar is mystical, sometimes symbolized as a rainbow or *k'uychi*, the representation of completeness in Andean cosmology. Through the *manos wasi*, *munay* is felt energetically as a sense of belonging or coming home that goes beyond words. It is the vehicle of relatedness—where paqos experience being in a state of union through connecting with *Pachamama*.

Condor Vision

The third kind of perception in Andean cosmology has to do with the vision state of condor vision, or *anka*, meaning "bird spirit," associated with the great condor *Apucheen*. Condor vision is post-sensorial, seeing beyond words. In Andean medicine the word vision describes creation coming into—and out of—form or shifting between spirit and matter, and atemporality and temporality respectively. Condor vision comes from the energy center of the mind (*y'anchay*). Activities of the mind are associated with the organizing principle of *yuya*, linked to wisdom and vision states where perception shifts from subjective experience into an objective and inclusive perspective. From the perspective of *yuya*, it is possible to view things from a "big picture," bird's eye view of what is happening in the present and avoid becoming bogged down in unimportant details.

According to paqos, our experience of the reality of the past and future are independent from one moment to the next but are woven together and linked in the *kausay pacha*, and can influence each other, because although they may appear fixed in consensual reality, they are fluid and ever-changing.

Using condor vision, what paqos refer to as *anka*, it is possible to reflect upon the past or envision the future with *yuya*, and to see the relationship or intersection between the worlds, or *pachas*, of *qepe* (the past), *kunan* (the present), and *nawpay* (the future). Because *anka* is transpersonal and atemporal, time is symmetrical, with the potential for both *hysteron proteron*, things moving in backwards order, and retro-causality when the future influences the past. In *anka* there is complete clarity. Time is symmetrical because consciousness in *yuya* remains fluid and impersonal with perception that is simple and precise, unclouded and unfiltered.

In *anka*, when assuming a *pacha*, a specific point in time and space, in each moment of *kunan* the *pachas* of *qepe* and *nawpay* are independent from the last moment and the next moment. The *pacha* of each moment has the potential for a unique past and future onto itself with an unlimited range of possibilities, objectively transpersonal and unattached to the outcome. Because of this *anka* is clear and nonbiased, free from assumptions based upon subjective context.

When operating in *anka*, an active state of conscious and presence with no distraction, there is greater availability to perceive, imagine, and create. The action of crafting a vision or forming a plan that becomes constructed with energy for manifestation is called *kamay*. In *anka*, *kamay* occurs after clear intent has been established in a state of energetic alignment, with no affiliations. Through this process of dreaming while asleep or imagining with intention while awake, through being in a state of connection and sourcing from the Andean cosmos, paqos engage in *kamay* to interpret what is being seen in a vision state using metaphors that can hold the energy, as symbols hold archetypal energy.

Maintaining a position of availability in the current *pacha* in physical reality, *kausay pacha* is remaining open to what is emerging and unfolding. From a *y'anchay* perspective of *anka,* paqos can use their minds to straddle between temporal and atemporal dimensions, with the capacity to hold awareness in both simultaneously.

The Essential Level of Psychic Engagement

The fourth level is the essential or energetic level of universal spirit that occurs in an atemporal realm, which paqos refer to as *teqsi muyu.* Although *teqsi muyu* refers to the consciousness of the universe on a collective level, experientially from the personal perspective of the individual, the essential level also shares a timelessness sense of oneness with the universe described in psychoanalysis (Saarinen, 2012). Eliade (1964) has written in-depth about shamanic practice, stating that the shaman's role and primary function involves the techniques of ecstasy in which he or she enters a trance state to connect with the spirit world. This corresponds with the paqos' experience of *tukay.* In Andean medicine, the word *tukay* means "complete, total, each, any—everything and everyone." This description of *tukay* applies to the essential level of engagement.

In Quechua, the phrase *"tukay llank ayni yoq"* translates as "the state we manifest and co-create in the abundance of the cosmos, as experience." This atemporal energetic level of universal connection is what Jung referred to as the objective psyche, which he said was the primordial unconscious layer existing underneath the sum of the archetypal structures (Whitmont, 1993). In these kinds of atemporal states, the experience of separation between self and "other" doesn't happen. The cognitive construct of language as means of delineating between the past, present, and future does not exist, and the phenomenon of time does not occur.

All experience at the essential level is atemporal because it is energetic, existing beyond the temporal parameters defined by time and space. Temporality is a compartmentalizing structure, separating the totality of the energetic collective into discrete events existing in space, in defined time intervals. This creates the "space" in ordinary reality to work with the energetic experience by differentiating and understanding it through symbolic representation in discriminate images, with words. Linear time provides a snapshot of the totality of an energetic experience, like the way in representational art an object can only be seen from one vantage point at a time (unless looking at a cubist painting). In Quechua, the word *k'anchay* refers to celestial light energy, which requires a *pacha,* an allocation of energy at a point in time and space to exist in temporal reality.

Outside the temporal laws of physical reality, limitations drop away, and everything is experienced in the present at once. By shifting beyond the constraints of time and space, the perception of the essence of the object—and its connection to everything around it in the energetic collective—happens completely and simultaneously. Conceptualizing the energetic collective is challenging because it exists outside of a temporal space and time paradigm and therefore cannot accurately be described in words.

The controversial anthropologist Carlos Castaneda (1981), who taught at the University of California, Los Angeles (UCLA) in the 1970s, wrote,

The richness of our perception on the left side was a post-facto realization.

Our interaction appeared to be rich in the light of our capacity to remember

it. We became cognizant then that in these states of heightened awareness we had perceived everything in one big clump, one bulky mass of inextricable detail. We called this ability to perceive everything at once intensity. For years, we had found it impossible to examine the separate constituent parts of these chunks of experience; we had been unable to synthesize those parts into a sequence that would make sense to the intellect. Since we were incapable of those syntheses, we could not remember. Our incapacity to remember was in reality an incapacity to put the memory of our perception on a linear

experiences flat, so to speak and arrange them in a sequential order. The experiences were available to us, but at the same time they were impossible to retrieve, for they were blocked by a wall of intensity. (Castaneda, 1981, p. 167)

In *A Practical Guide to Qabalistic Symbolism*, Gareth Knight (1993) has written:

The teaching of the mysteries, in that many of them are religious truths, is beyond the human mind. To the logical mental processes, which so many people insist on operating entirely, they may well appear nonsensical. The Mystery of the Holy Trinity for example, is a religious truth beyond the reach of the mind. Most have to take it on faith, but for the few, the mystics of the church, it can be a great reality, a profound experience that cannot subsequently adequately be described in words. But words are the data upon which the rational mind works and the only means of communication of such things in words is by analogy, allegory, and symbol. (Knight, 1993, p. 5)

Knight's passage is applicable to understanding properties of the *energetic collective*. A leap into the atemporal realm of the *collective* requires creating and facilitating a shift in conscious awareness—moving beyond understanding through the mind into felt nonverbal experience accessed through the body.

There are no suppositions in somatic experiencing because it is not a cognitive operation. Thinking about something always requires being outside of the experience to reflect on it, which requires whatever is being thought about to be in the past. Because of this, a shift from cognitive understanding to a greater sense of somatic experiencing occurs as movement is made toward the essential level of engagement. For paqos, a deeper felt awareness comes through attuning to direct experience in energetic states of connection that they "source," or derive power from—existing outside of contextual time and space.

Members of native cultures, such as the Andean medicine people in Peru, grow up learning about atemporal connection with the energetic collective through sensing it in their bodies. The essential level of psychic engagement occurs as a type of somatic spiritual experience, in feeling deep connection in the *manos wasi* energy body in conjunction with the collective of the land. Paqos believe that because experiential memory involving all atemporal and temporal states of consciousness is stored in the *manos wasi*, moving beyond ordinary reality occurs through being energetically anchored in the subtle body.

Anthropologist Castaneda (1998) has written about the energetic appearance of the subtle body from a sorcerer's perspective, and stated:

> *When they are seen as fields of energy, human beings appear to be like fibers of light, like white cobwebs, very fine threads that circulate from the head to the toes. Thus, to the eye of a seer, a man looks like an egg of circulating fibers ... The seer sees that every man is in touch with everything else, not through his hands, but through a bunch of long fibers that shoot out in all directions from the center of his abdomen. These fibers join a man to his surroundings: they keep his balance; they give him stability.* (Castaneda, 1998, pp. 31–2)

Castaneda is describing *seeing* the luminous or subtle body at the *energetic* level. In this state of awareness, a sense of a universal link to all living things is experienced because it occurs through the *energetic* field. In Quechua this is referred to as *runa kurku k'anchay*, which translates in English to "person body light." Through awareness in the *manos wasi,* one experiences *being* in the connection and *seeing* it at the same time. It is the bridge between seeing and being—which allows both to be experienced simultaneously.

In an *energetic collective* state, everything is fluid and interconnected energetically in the organizing principles of *kallari* and *ch'ulla* respectively. Paqos experience connection with the *collective* of "the land"—or *energetic collective*—through the *manos wasi,* which becomes the conduit into experiencing on a much greater, collective scale. The land is the medium used in shifting into *collectivity,* from an individual to the universal state as the unlimited reservoir of man's universal psychic heritage. In Andean medicine, the collective of the land is in some ways like the collective unconscious in the psyche, although broader. While the collective unconscious is the culmination of all ancestral experience universal to mankind, the collective of the land is the depository of all experience in nature, which for paqos usually becomes linked to "membership," and an "affiliation" with a sacred mountain that is the "*apu* benefactor" of their *misa,* or medicine bundle, which will be described more in depth in the next section. For paqos, the concept of affiliation with a mountain is like the function of Christ in the Christian religion as a link to God. The collective mountain spirit serves as an intermediary between the person and the *collective.*

Remembering Atemporal, Energetic Experience and the Integration Process

Remembering and describing experiences that occur at the level of the energetic collective is challenging as it requires shifting from atemporal to temporal perception, which is limiting. Because collective energetic experience is nonsequential, without discrete boundaries, it is difficult for "the ego" to cognitively understand and integrate the knowledge into a framework because it may seem as though it lacks context since it is not defined by a *pacha,* or a specific time in space. Paqos have an easier time taking in and assimilating energetic information because the existence of the energetic collective is accepted as an integral part of the Andean cosmos and there are cultural practices and beliefs that accommodate and support it.

The re-entry process of accessing memories from these atemporal states of awareness involves an approximated process of "swallowing the energetic experience whole." For example, a bank of fog moving in over a shoreline rapidly is a nonlinear phenomenon that can't be conceptualized explicitly. It lacks definition in the way it happens. In observing such an experience taking place, the familiar boundaries that usually exist in perceiving when taking in new information are "softened" into a veil of ambiguity and mystery. Re-creating this artistically might be done using watercolor paints on a page saturated with water. Painting in this medium in this way does not allow for defined lines or edges. The paint pigments blend on the page. The phenomenon of fog is a metaphor for a guesstimate of implicit energetic experience.

The ego demands separation from experience to define itself in its temporal existence. Because the ego cannot perceive without existing in a conscious state of separation, being in a state of fluidity in connection happens in an atemporal psychic domain more expansive and multidimensional than the ego can hold. The *manos wasi* is both the receptacle that holds *energetic* experience and the sensory receiver of this experience. Paqos teach that experiencing through the belly enables one to enter a state of *fluidity*, a state of no separation. This state of fluidity corresponds to the Taoist experience of being in the flow and in balance with the energy around us.

In Peruvian shamanism, the heart is the hub of connective experience in the *manos wasi* and the vehicle through which union with others is experienced. Paqos say that the heart is where *munay*, the universal feeling state of love connecting us to the land and every living thing around us, occurs. *Minka* is a very evolved form of love based upon collective *ayni*, a state of connected reciprocity between all living things. It is *collective* state of love, different from personal love directed specifically toward another person. Collective love is associated with being in "right relationship" with the cosmos. Paqos refer to being in a state of fully developed wisdom in *munay* as *tukay munayniyoc.*

The Medicine Bundle of the *Misa*—Literal, Symbolic, Mythic, and Essential Levels of Engagement

The medicine bundle, referred to as a *misa* (or *misa*), is a grouping of up to 12 stones, or *q'uiyas*, that function as a "medicine body" for the paqo, the intermediary space between the natural spirit world and the paqo's *manos wasi*, or energy body. *Misas* are considered by paqos to be living entities that function as a paqo's alter ego, an embodiment of the universe. A paqo's *misa* enables them to "track" information outside of linear time in atemporal reality identifying possibilities of "momentum"—directions in life, through an active dialogue with the energetic patterns held in the *q'uiyas*. According to paqos, this interaction enables the *misa* carrier to remember who they are "in the eyes of creation."

There is an Andean myth that the first *misa* came into being as a stone given by a great condor sent by the creator that could heal all living things. When it was time for the condor to leave the earth and return to the creator, the condor left a stone as a gift that carried his sacred lineage and *ayni*, or heart energy, for human healers to work with. Paqos describe the *misa* as a medicine bundle of *q'uiyas* that embody the "heart fire" of the *apu* mountain spirits.

Initially, building a relationship with a *misa* begins by physically collecting stones, which over time will become symbolic of memories or feeling states. When first training to become a paqo, the student creates a beginning *misa* by finding a group of stones that they feel a natural affinity for. The individual stones become *q'uiyas* when they are assigned meaning. For paqos, meaning is not based upon a personal narrative or belief system but rather is an engagement with life and spirit.

Q'uiyas become "known" to the paqo-in-training over time as associations of what each of the stones symbolizes, emerges. The individual stones may be assigned a memory that holds a "charge," or a personality trait, which can either be a quality or feeling that the *misa* carrier is trying to cultivate or eliminate, such as courage or fear. By using intent and blowing negative patterns into the stones, the process of consciously separating from identifying with one's complexes and being "claimed" by past wounds begins. The *misa* provides a symbolic scaffolding structure to engage with areas of personal experience that remain unfulfilled, bringing them more fully into awareness. Like complexes, that may be experienced in reoccurring dreams, pressured reactions, or a sense of undifferentiated longing that have been difficult for the *misa* carrier to bring into consciousness, working with a *misa* resembles Jung's own process of connecting with the unconscious through the process of active imagination using stones.

In the early stages of working with a *misa*, the *misa* carrier's relationship with the stones is symbolic and the *misa* has a personal orientation. The *misa* provides the *misa* carrier with "a space" to work with cultural and familial imprints and wounding, and to discover characteristics of "karmic memories" being carried in their *manos wasi*.

Working with the Misa

Like the *manos wasi*, *misas* carry *kausay* energy, or life force, and need to be worked with by a paqo in an open dialogue of reciprocity, in an energetic exchange, to grow. By sitting in a quiet receptive state and "feeling into" the stones, by allowing thoughts and imagery to surface, the *misa* carrier becomes aware of disempowering belief systems that have become personal guiding mythologies. Through these realizations, the *misa* carrier can begin to release old patterns and move into a greater state of openness in relationship to the Andean cosmos.

Working with a *misa* starts by "opening" the *misa*. An "open" *misa* is a group of stones arranged in a circle together, connecting the personal and transpersonal levels of psychic engagement. First, the *mastana* cloth (a square, colorfully woven textile, with Andean symbols representing aspects of the cosmos) is carefully laid open on a flat surface, preferably somewhere in nature in a spot where an "affinity" is felt. Usually, a larger ceremonial cloth that is slightly larger is placed under the *mastana* cloth. The *misa* stones are placed in an arrangement, often circular, that intuitively "feels right" to the *misa* carrier. Next, the ceremony is opened by calling "sacred space." Calling sacred space involves asking the spirit world for assistance, calling in the three worlds and each of the four directions, following the rotational movement of the sun as it circles the earth. The *misa* carrier sits facing the *mastana* cloth with the "opened" *misa* and gradually begins to shift their focus by "dropping" their awareness into their belly and breathing and "feeling into" the earth and the *q'uiyas*.

The *misa* carrier enters a receptive, meditative state—often using the aide of the repetitive sound of a rattle or bell. Once in a quiet state of receptivity, spirit symbolically becomes matter, by imagining weaving the energy of the *q'uiyas* into the body and visualizing a figure eight motion, again using breath with focused intention. Next, an intention is set to build on and expand a connection with the cosmos by opening oneself and *misa* to receiving a stream of light energy from *Pachamama* and the *apus*. A point of connectivity between the *misa* carrier and *Pachamama* is established by imagining weaving the land into the medicine body held by the *q'uiyas*.

Initially, for a beginning *misa* carrier, the work begins with a "wounded *misa*," and like the Jungian analytic process, enters a *nigredo* phrase—a descent into the dense shadow material (*llanthu*) of personal history, using the *q'uiya* as a transitional object that "holds" the experience. As a spiritual transitional object, each *q'uiya* carries personal meaning imbued through a "heart felt" connection that grows stronger and more immediate as the relationship between the *misa* carrier and the *q'uiya* builds over time. In this stage of the work, the *misa* carrier learns to understand, or "track" their spiritual purpose by remembering and reflecting upon personal history.

The word *kuti* in Quechua means to revisit and set right what has been overturned. Using intention, the *misa* carrier engages in a process of recapitulation, consciously remembering the past with compassion. Through this process, the *misa* carrier develops a deeper understanding of the personal narratives they have created regarding the past. Like working through trauma in psychoanalysis, painful memories tied to personal history begin to become integrated. As in the analytic process, compulsions, defenses, and complexes related to shadow material rise to the surface and begin to deconstruct as they are "cooked" in the inner heat generated by bringing previously unprocessed traumatic feeling states into awareness.

Over time, usually months in the beginning, the individual *q'uiyas* change. The turnover of *q'uiyas* in a beginning *misa* is relatively rapid. *Q'uiyas* are released by the *misa* carrier and returned to nature when the *misa* carrier no longer feels an affinity to the complex wound being held by the stone. *Misa* stones that have been assigned and carry core complexes for the *misa* carrier remain in the *misa* for longer periods. Little by little, or as paqos say, "*pesay manta, pesay manta,*" the process of "dying to the old way of being" occurs, along with letting go of being identified with a limited personal narrative and persona. This process is referred to as *wañupuy*.

By engaging through an open channel of communication and self-reflection while sitting with the *misa*, the *misa* carrier prepares to release imbedded *llanthu*, or shadow patterns with a fire ceremony. The intensity of "heated" feelings decreases as energy shifts from unconscious complexes into a state of greater ego awareness, increasing deeper connection with the cosmos, or Self. The question, "What will you die to?"—meaning, "What complexes or personal issues are you ready to face?" is asked. The phrase "taking it to the fire" (*nina lauray*) refers to the purification of releasing old patterns and beliefs into the fire by creating a *despacho* or fire offering. Similar to the function of fire in alchemy, the fire ceremony is a process of purification that is the practice of clearing used in Andean medicine.

New *quiyas* that hold greater power, the spirit of *Pachamama* or the *apus*, are introduced into the *misa* and replace *quiyas* that may have symbolized past trauma. The focus of the *misa* begins to shift from a personal to a collective orientation, as is the case in individuation when a shift is made from an ego focus to the Self. Over time, through a process of *yanachakuy*, or union, an energetic imprint that reflects the *apu* mountain spirits is woven into the *misa* in filaments of light, which supports deeper connection with the Andean cosmos.[3] Relationships or "membership" to the great mountains begin to form and coagulate, as the energetic qualities of the *apu* mountain spirits are "downloaded" into the *misa* and begin to emerge in the *quiyas*.

In this phase, the *misa* is growing into becoming a collective expression of the *misa* carrier's relationship with the mountains and the land. The collective has different expressions, or ways of creating, which mirror the paqo's relationship with the land. Through developing a strong connection with the *misa*, the paqo becomes a co-creator, in service with the universe. Paqos believe that the process of creativity brings together opposites, or *yanantin*. Over time, the size of a paqo's *misa* increases as their capacity—and, as a result, the capacity of their *misa*—to hold power also increases.

Movement from the personal to the mythic collective continues as energy "sourcing" shifts from the *hucha*, or dense energy associated with past trauma and complexes into the *sami* or light collective energy of *Pachamama* and the *apus*. As the capacity to hold power grows, the connection between the land, the *misa*, and the *misa* carrier's *manos wasi* grows stronger, and the ability to become a conduit between realities, to serve as a gateway or *pacho*, becomes easier. When a *misa* carrier is no longer "claimed" by personal history, they become more focused on the collective cosmos, and through their increased *availability* (not having their perspective overshadowed by their personal complexes) they have a greater capacity to engage in a spiritual dialogue and connect with the *Pachamama* and the sacred mountains. This is when a *misa* carrier becomes a paqo.

The Paqo's Misa

In more advanced *misas* that have gone through an intensive process of purification and are now able to hold more *sami*, *q'uiyas* begin to provide an energetic link to an *apu* or a specific spiritual realm that paqos begin to use as gateways into atemporal energetic realms. The *misas* can serve as a grounding anchor between the paqo's *manos wasi* and the cosmic connection with the natural world. The paqo's capacity to hold power is a direct function of their openness and flexibility in relation to their skill in shifting between states of awareness at different levels simultaneously—in their *manos wasi*. This is determined primarily through their ability to connect using their heart energy center, or *munay*. As this capability develops, the ability to shift perception between temporal and atemporal states evolves as well. All encounters—regardless of the level of psychic engagement—involve multiple layers of information that can be experienced and understood, through the transmission of *kausay* energy. As the paqo matures and advances, the *misa* evolves and expands its capacity to hold energy in greater dimensions.

The paqo's *misa* is a vehicle for connecting with atemporal reality and has the capacity for prophecy through its "membership" with the various mountains. The more availability and conscious awareness a paqo has, the greater their capacity to hold power, or energy, and shift from ordinary reality, or *kay pacha*, into energetic experience, or *kausay pacha*. The practice of *taytanchis* is the process of talking about a profound experience after it has happened to reflect upon it.

As the *paqo* engages with the *misa* with the intent of building a reciprocal relationship of *ayni*, the paqo feeds their *misa* with energy, or *kausay kuna*, by visualizing with intention. The *q'uiyas* become imbued with meaningful associations for the paqo through active engagement and the practice of *mikhuchy*, the process of "feeding" the *misa* with psychic energy. *Misawan Kausay* refers to the practice of creating a space for bringing the different levels of psychic engagement on the physical and spiritual planes together by being in a harmonious relationship with a *misa*. Over time, a *misa* becomes a sophisticated representation of an energetic map with different levels, domains, and properties, bridging the literal level with the energetic realm.

Misas have a range of functions and their capacity to hold energy, or power, depends on the level of advancement of the paqo. *Misas* become more powerful when their capacity to hold energy increases, which is a direct reflection of the strength of the paqo's spiritual connection and *manos wasi*. A *misa de luz*, or "light *misa*," is used by paqos for their own individual spiritual work. In addition to having a *misa de luz*, more evolved paqos work with different *misas*, which each have a specific function used in service with a collective focus that is no longer personal. There are healing *misas* (*humpuy misas*) used in working with others. Celestial *misas* are made up of *q'uiyas* that hold energy specifically related to the celestial realm of *Hanaq Pacha*. *Chaska misas* are even more specialized, focusing on connection with the stars, which often symbolize the experience of returning home to a fulfilled state. A seer's *misa* has to do with creation and changing the future. Other *misas* serve as conduits to *Pachamama* and the lower world of *Uku Pacha*. Every *misa* functions as a conduit between physical reality and atemporal, other world connection that paqos source energy from.

In addition to the functions of *misas* being determined by the capacity of the paqo to hold energy and ability to move further into atemporal realms, the characteristics of a *misa* are also influenced by the energy a *q'uiya* holds. As mentioned earlier, early on a young *misa* carrier "assigns" a specific quality to each *q'uiya* that the *q'uiya* will hold that pertains to an issue the *misa* carrier is working on. As a paqo advances they find *q'uiyas* that "speak" to them energetically, and the paqo is given a sense of the specific function and purpose of *q'uiyas*. For more advanced *misa* carriers, the *misa* becomes an expression of connection at the essential level.

As an apprentice's relationship with their *misa* matures, usually one of the *q'uiyas*, called a *ñawin*, emerges that serves as the focal point, connecting all the other *q'uiyas* each with their own energetic blueprint together. The *ñawin* is the most powerful *q'uiya* in the *misa*. In addition to connecting the other *q'uiyas* together so that they can function as a whole energy body together, like a hub with spokes on a wheel, the *ñawin* also serves as the portal between the three worlds. The *ñawin* is the center *q'uiya* in a circular configuration, or in smaller *misas* with only a few *q'uiyas*, the *ñawin* is usually at the top. Sometimes a single *q'uiya* serves as a *ñawin*, as center portal. Sometime, as a *misa* grows and evolves, there are three or four stones stacked in the center of the *misa* with each representing one of the worlds. These *q'uiyas* function together to create a *chaka*, which is a bridge or ladder between the worlds. In addition, *q'uiyas* differ in terms of masculine and feminine properties, their function, their affiliation with one of the worlds, and their vibrational level. Each of these areas will be described.

Yanantin Existing with a Misa and Castaneda's Contribution

The Andean codes of *yanantin*, the relationship between masculine and feminine — or opposites, and *mansantin*, the relationship between two like energies that exist in the Andean cosmos, also can occur within *misas*. The word *llok'e* refers to the feminine principle of formless essence with potential as the composite of femininity. At more profound levels, *llok'e* is atemporal, a state of being and oneness. One aspect of this feminine energy that could be held in an individual *q'uiya* is the archetypal mother, *Pachamama*. A young *misa* that is still "wounded" could hold the energy of past trauma tied to a negative mother complex. A *q'uiya* could hold *kausay* associated with *Mama Qilla* (Grandmother Moon) or *Mama Qocha* (Mother of the Lagoon). More aggressive feminine energy, sometimes represented by the Greek goddess Artemis or the Hindu goddess Kali, might also be held in a *q'uiya*. A *q'uiya* associated with *llok'e* might also hold the feminine qualities associated with eros or intuition, and so forth. A *q'uiya* could also hold a feminine function, representing a seed or fertility. Within the *misa Llok'e* governs the left side of the body, and the left side of the *misa*.

Pana refers to the structured masculine principle governing the right side of the body, and the right side of the *misa*. An individual *q'uiya* might hold the archetypal energy of the masculine associated with a sense of agency and penetration in relation to the outer world. This *q'uiya* might hold aspects of a positive father, adding a sense of drive, or *kallpachay*, to the *misa* with the potential for breaking through atemporal spaces into the temporal dimension. The word *kallpachay* refers to the process of giving strength, which is a function of the masculine, bringing focus to making what is unconscious in a feminine state of being, conscious.

The masculine and the feminine function together. *Pana* supports *llok'e*, and jointly they bring what is essential into manifestation. The physical *q'uiyas* in the *misa* become representations holding different types of *kausay* that grow stronger over time for the paqo, the more they are worked with. The composite of *q'uiyas* in the *misa* together anchor aspects of atemporal energetic experience into a map existing in physical reality that can be reflected upon and worked with as a whole.

Integrating the masculine and feminine in this context may involve transferring personal and collective memory of numinous energetic states into conscious awareness, with the left side (having to do with the feminine) into sequential time in ordinary reality on the right side (having to do with the masculine). This occurs in a process of remembering and recapitulating while working with the *misa*, which holds both sides of the experience.

Castaneda (1981) described a process involving a transfer from the left side to the right side of the body. In *The Eagle's Gift*, Castaneda (1981, p. 167) wrote, "Don Juan had told us that human beings are divided in two. The right side of the body, which he called the tonal, encompasses everything the intellect can conceive of in normal awareness. The left side, called the nagual, is a realm of indescribable features: a realm impossible to contain in words. The left side is comprehended, if comprehension is what takes place, with the total body, thus its resistance to conceptualization." For Castaneda, the sides of the body represent the split between atemporal and temporal reality, which in a *misa* may correspond with different feminine and masculine energetic states. Later Castaneda (1984, p. 10) wrote, "No one remembers anything while in a state of heightened awareness. Remembering is an act of becoming conscious or shifting from the left side to the right side."

Castaneda is describing the shift from the left side to the right side as a shift from atemporal to temporal experience. Paqos conceptualize this energetic transfer from left to right as occurring through the interaction—and union—between *llok'e* and *pana*.

A Q'uiyas Affiliation with One of the Three Worlds

Besides linking masculine and feminine principles in *yanantin,* in some *misa* configurations of *q'uiyas*, there are *q'uiyas* linking the three worlds. A *ñawin,* or central *q'uiya*, often functions as the portal or link to this connection. The Quechua word *saywa* refers to a column of energy connecting *Uku Pacha, Kay Pacha,* and *Hanaq Pacha* that serves as a bridge between the energetic and the physical realms.

Q'uiyas placed farthest from the paqo, at the top of the *mastana* cloth, may hold the *kausay* of *Hanaq Pacha*, the upper world, the celestial realm of the *apus* and the *chaskas* (stars). A *q'uiya* placed closer to the paqo, at the bottom of the *mastana* cloth, may hold the earth energy (*hallp'a*) of *Pachamama* and the lower world of *Uku Pacha.*

A range of energetic frequency exists within each of the three worlds. *Q'uiyas* may also hold *kausay* associated with other multidimensional realms, stretching outside of upper and lower worlds. These *q'uiyas* hold *kausay* that pertains to specific qualities and frequencies, which reside in higher levels of vibration associated with celestial realms. For example, *Kama Titi* is a very high vibrational frequency that is said to exist beyond *Hanaq Pacha* that is accessed specifically for healing.

In even more advanced *misas*, a *q'uiya* might represent and take in the energy of *tiqsi muyu amaru,* which translates from Quechua to the *ouroboros* or "enlightened view of the universe" in English. The word *tiqsi* refers to a form of completeness involving the past, present, and future in time.

The Vibrational Frequencies Levels of Misas

In an active *misa*, the *q'uiyas* are linked to and correspond with the *misa* carrier's *manos wasi. Hucha* is dense energy and *layka* is dark energy. Either or both may be held in the *misa* and the *manos wasi* of the *misa* carrier, and are often experienced somatically, as pain or constriction in the belly or chest, in the physical body. *Hucha* is energy generally associated with trauma while *layka* is energy associated with evil or sorcery, with an intention for personal gain at the expense of the collective, or cosmos. *Sami* is energy at a higher vibrational level of *kausay*, often experienced in the body as expansive and open, with a felt sense of being one with the world.

The amounts of *hucha* and *sami* in a *misa* are in direct proportion to the amounts of *hucha* and *sami* found in *misa* carrier's *manos wasi.* Through the process of working with the *misa*, by clearing *hucha*, and raising the vibrational frequency, the *misa carrier* purifies their *manos wasi* and increases *kausay*. Working with the *misa* is one of the ways a *misa* carrier becomes a paqo and reflects a paqo's capacity to hold power (*kausay*). As a *misa* evolves and the vibrational level of *q'uiyas* are raised—*hucha* decreases and *sami* increases.

Payan

There are three levels of energetic frequency found in *misas, payan, kayau,* and *q'ollona,* ranging from low to higher frequencies respectively. Out of the three levels, *payan* has the densest, slowest vibrational level, with the greatest amount of *hucha. Payan* is the first level, usually found in a beginner's *misa,* often a "wounded *misa.*" At the level of *payan, hucha* from the past is carried in the *misa* and the *manos wasi. Payan* is the level where *quiyas* hold the most *hucha* (negative energy) from past trauma.

Payan involves a level of existence that occurs in a state of temporality. Temporality occurs within the boundaries of linear time—with a before and after, that can be limiting. Atemporal experience is different because it is not contextual nor constrained, within the limitations of time and space. It is instantaneous and direct, with a potential for objective clarity that transcends preconceived assumptions often influenced by *hucha,* or more specifically, ego defenses such as denial, rationalization, and repression. These ego defenses are usually activated, in reaction to memories of unpleasant experiences carrying unprocessed *hucha,* to avoid feelings often associated with *hucha,* such as anger and fear.

Q'uiyas carrying *hucha* usually have been assigned a specific traumatic memory, issue, or problematic relationship that have kept the *misa* carrier "stuck" in the past. These incomplete narratives are often held in *q'uiyas,* linked to the corresponding dense energy being carried in the *manos wasi.* The *hucha* being carried from experience creates blocks to shield against feeling the intensity of actual events happening in the present, to avoid re-experiencing a repeat of an unpleasant past event. Creating protective safeguards that screen against potentially traumatizing experiences also filter direct experience, limiting the capacity to access a fuller range of engagement in atemporal states.

The personal stories that have been created based upon a limited interpretation of life history form episodic memories that define and often restrict experiencing connection in the world and being in relationship with the cosmos. Over time, through working with a *misa* with *q'uiyas* at the *payan* level, *hucha* is cleared and *q'uiyas* affiliated with *hucha* leave the *misa.* This sometimes involves a ceremony with gratitude for the *q'uiya* that held the *hucha* to be cleared for healing. Stones with a higher vibrational frequency are found to replace the *q'uiyas* that have been released. They may hold a vibrational frequency associated with *kayau.*

Kayau

Kayau is the second level, often linked to the realm of *Hanaq Pacha,* which is the vibration of the lower celestial realm—closest to *Kay Pacha,* the middle, physical world where we live, where *hucha* is experienced. The *q'uiyas* in an intermediate level *misa* are often representative of *kayau*. *Kayau q'uiyas* are moving from a personal orientation to a more collective perspective with greater temporal fluidity, shifting more easily between past, present, and future.

K'inychi chaka translates from Quechua to English as "the rainbow circle." *K'inychi chaka* refers to the bridge connecting *Kay Pacha* and *Hanaq Pacha,* temporality to atemporality, respectively. As a *k'inychi chaka* grows stronger in a *misa,* the capacity to hold *sami* energy builds and the stones are less constrained within the context of a specific time in space; in other words they shift from holding a personal perspective to a collective orientation.

Q'ollona

Q'ollona, the third level, is the highest, with *q'uiyas* vibrating with the greatest amount of *kausay k'anchay* energy and *sami* (very pure energy*).* It is the level of the *hatunmesayoqs* and the *altomesyocs,* an extremely advanced paqos with the capacity to hold power (*kausay*) in connection with the *apus.* In the Andean cosmos, *altomesayoqs'misas* are portals between the physical reality of *Kay Pacha* and the energetic spirit world of *Kausay Pacha.*

At the level of *q'ollona,* "seeing" truth, referred to in Quechua as *chekak,* requires take in information through direct experience—through the *manos wasi*—and letting go of preconceived notions about the world and oneself. This requires moving into a receptive state of availability to engage with the living world a *Kausay Pacha,* where psychic, somatic, and energetic experience becomes integrated and experienced both temporally and atemporally, as a complex myriad of experience, separate, yet interwoven.

Through remaining open to experiencing the cosmos directly through their *manos wasi,* paqos avoid being confined by an interpretation of physical reality based on a fear of a lack of security and expand beyond the limitations of narratives that are constructs of ego-consciousness. Staying receptive enables them to access energetic experience occurring at the essential level. This involves moving into a more fluid state of consciousness through connecting with *Kausay Pacha,* a dimension much more expansive than what can be comprehended through the lens of the ego.

At the level of *q'ollona* experience is collective rather than personal, and different from experiencing separation between oneself and the cosmos, which is limited, and ego driven. This is because the ego's capacity for self-reflection can only occur through the experience of separation. In the process of assimilating direct experience, there is generally a lag between the *actual* experience and *conscious reflection* about the experience, unless one has reached the level of an *altomesayoqs* who has the capacity to hold both attention states simultaneously. This is because the *altomesayoq's* greater capacity to hold energy enables them to participate in temporal and atemporal states of awareness simultaneously.

Notes

1   See Appendix for *despacho* ingredients.
2   Jung refers to a psychic space called the mundus archetypes that in some ways resembles the paqos' mythic level of perception, an atemporal realm of "divine images" (1975 [1953], pp. 21–2).
3   Castaneda's writing corresponds accurately to aspects of shamanic experience based upon my personal experience, even though it was later discredited by some members of the Jungian community as metaphorical. This resembles String theory, which postulates that the fundamental components of the universe are one-dimensional "strings," and what is perceived is vibrational loops of string of specific frequencies rather than individual particles.
4   This resembles String theory, which postulates that the fundamental components of the universe are one-dimensional "strings," and what is perceived is vibrational loops of string of specific frequencies rather than individual particles.

References

Castaneda, C. (1981) *The Eagle's Gift*, New York, NY: Simon and Schuster.

Castaneda, C. (1984) *The Fire from Within*, New York, NY: Pocket Books.

Castaneda, C. (1998) *The Wheel of Time*, New York, NY: Simon and Schuster.

Corbett, L. (1996) *The Religious Function of the Psyche*, Milton Park, Oxfordshire: Taylor & Francis.

Eliade, M. (1964) *Shamanism: Archaic techniques of ecstasy*, Bollington Series LXXVI, Princeton, NJ: Princeton University Press.

Hoerni, Ulrich, Fischer, Thomas, and Kaufmann, Bettina, eds (2019) *The Art of C.G. Jung*, New York, NY and London: W. W. Norton & Company.

Jung, C. G. (1921) *Psychological Types* (Collected Works, vol. 6).

Jung, C. G. (1959) *The Archetypes and the Collective Unconscious* (Collected Works, vol. 9).

Jung, C. G. (1960a) *Structure & Dynamics of the Psyche* (Collected Works, vol. 8).

Jung, C.G. (1960b) 'Synchronicity: An acausal connecting principal' (Collected Works, vol. 8), in *The Structure and Dynamics of the Psyche Princeton*, Princeton, NJ: Princeton University Press.

Jung, C. G. (1963 [1955]) *Mysterium Coniunctionis* (Collected Works, vol. 14).

Jung, C.G. (1975 [1953]) *Letters, vol. 2: 1951*–1961, eds Gerhard Adler and Aniela Jaffe, trans. R. F. C. Hull, Princeton, NJ: Princeton University Press.

Knight, G. (1993) *A Practical Guide to Qabalistic Symbolism*, Maine: Samuel Weiser, York Beach.

Marian, S. (2005) *The Black Sun*, Texas: Texas A&M University Press.

Saarinen, J. A. (2012) 'The oceanic state: A conceptual elucidation in terms of modal contact', *Int J Psychoanal* 93: 939–61.

Whitmont, E. C. (1993) *The Alchemy of Healing*, Berkeley, CA: North Atlantic Books.

Winnicott, D. W. (1971) *Playing and Reality*, New York, NY: Penguin Books.

Chapter 5

The Paqos' Direct Experience— Shifting States of Awareness through Ritual

Types of Energetic Encounters

Haipay, Hamat'ay, *and* Tinkuy

In Andean spirituality, *haipay* is the meditative practice that facilitates the experiential state of *hamat'ay,* a profound connection occurring on different levels and in different dimensions, which can move between temporal and atemporal states depending on the depth of the connection. In *haipay* rituals, a state of *hamat'ay* develops by first setting an intention of connecting with *kausay k'anchay* (light energy), and then "dropping into" connection with the natural world. Entering *hamat'ay* requires shifting attention by imagining reaching deep into the center of the body and stilling the mind. In this state, the potential exists to pass into psychic spaces where thoughts do not yet exist. In psychoanalysis, these inexpressible non-verbally intermediated states resemble Ogden's (1989a) autistic-contiguous position.[1] In these psychic spaces, we sense without thinking—even if only for a moment. Maintaining a receptive state, in a practice of *hamat'ay,* brings the possibility to increase awareness of elements in the natural surrounding world, that can then be taken in and felt in the body. This is a way of connecting with *kausay.*

According to paqos, the practice of connecting with *kausay k'anchay* in *hamat'ay* occurs in silence, with humility. In Andean medicine there are three kinds of energetic encounters that build upon one another during the practice of *haipay* rituals, through experiencing *hamat'ay.* They are *tinkay, tupay,* and *taque. Tinkuy* is the initial phase, and *tupay* and *taque* encounters are more advanced.

Tinkuy

Tinkuy refers to communion and full recognition between two sentient beings, energetically touching through the *manos wasi,* which leads to an act of *tupay.*

DOI: 10.4324/9781003356448-7

Tupay

Tupay is the next phase, which paqos refer to as a "spiritual meeting." The term *tupay* is used to refer to an energetic exchange between sentient beings with full disclosure to one another of their fundamental nature—including shadow material. Because the sentient being are fully disclosing who they are to one another this involves confrontation, which if one being is of the light and the other dark—may involve conflict.

All ceremonies are *tupays*. Paying attention to direct experience through a *tupay* is an atemporal energetic encounter with *Wira Cocha*, the living essence of the natural world. Paqos teach that truth is discovered through a *tupay* relationship with *Wira Cocha*, the living cosmos, through being attuned to experiencing *kausay pacha* in the present rather than being distracted by an imagined personal narrative tied to the past that is projected onto the future.

Through initiating a *tupay*, one of the ways paqos move into psychic states of connectivity with *Wira Cocha* is through joining energetically with the *collective* of "the land," by dropping into receptive psychic through their *manos wasi* in the "sacred space" of ceremony. Focusing on opening one's *manos wasi* to linking energetically with *Pachamama*, the land becomes the paqos' conduit into the experience of *collectivity*, from an individual to the universal state of the *energetic collective*. In Quechua the phrase *kallpa wan tupay* translates literally as "a sacred meeting with energy." Paqos use the phrase *pachawan tupay* to refer to the sacred ritual of forming physical and spiritual connection with the atemporal "cosmic dimension" through the *manos wasi*.

In *tupay* ceremonies, such as "calling" *Pachamama* and the *apus* with intention, often through prayer and song, creates a "sacred space," that functions as a doorway into the energetic spirit world that facilitates shifts in consciousness from temporal into atemporal experience. Paqos call these invocations *kallpachayway-chis*. Calling sacred space through *kallpachaywaychis* is always the first step in any ceremony and are a means of engaging with the atemporal spirit world and to enter deeper connection with the spirits in *Uku Pacha* (lower world), *Kay Pacha* (middle world), and *Hanaq Pacha* (upper world). The purposes of ceremonies include but are not limited to introducing oneself and connecting with the spirits of the land, healing, entering vision states, initiations, and strengthening the *misa* (medicine bundle).

Taque

Taque is the most advanced phase of connecting with another being and describes bringing harmony through the joining of energy fields, and "remembering one's place in creation." The act of joining together similar energy body bubbles of light is called *musichayuy*. In addition to connecting with the spiritual presences in the cosmos such as *Pachamama* and the *apus*, it also involves connecting with one's *misa*. Ceremonies performed individually and, in the community, based upon symbolic practices and rituals may also provide a framework that serve as a *k'inychi chaka* (bridge) to enter states of atemporal spiritual connection.

There are different types of ceremonies based upon the ritual of *haipay* described earlier. *Supan haipay* is an individual ceremony, practiced alone. *Yanantin haipay* is a ceremony involving a male and a female, while *masantin haipay* is a ceremony between two people of the same sex. *Ayllu haipay* is performed as a group.

Supan Haipay

In Andean medicine, there are many individual ceremonies or forms of *supan haipay*, performed with the intention of opening a channel and connecting with the living Andean cosmos, *Wira Cocha*, that follow specific rules of engagement. A process of connecting, involving creating an observing ego or shifting into an impersonal perspective, takes place, which enables the paqo to move into a stance of "not knowing." The paqo adopts an attitude of innocence, or receptivity without judgment, enabling them to embrace the mystery of the cosmos through direct experience. From this nonattached position, the paqo develops the capacity for "sacred play," where everything becomes synchronistic, and they are open to the possibility of experience unknown, invisible realities.

In Quechua, there are specific words or phrases that refer to the steps or stages of entering into deeper connection with the cosmos. Most practices of *supan haipay* begin with *mast'ay,* the practice of formally introducing oneself in ceremony to the spirits of the land. *Mast'ay* also includes stating the intention of becoming available to forming a connection with the spirit world, which may include *Wira Cocha, Pachamama,* the *apus,* the celestial realm of *Inti Tayta* (Father Sun), *Mama Quilla* (Grandmother Moon), and the *chaskas* or *qollurs* (stars). The Quechua word *mast'ay* literally means "making oneself available"—in other words, opening to dimensions beyond consensual reality. This is experienced as connection through dropping into a state of surrendering.

According to the paqos, while in a state of consciousness that extends beyond ego-consciousness and into the celestial realm, a *saywa,* or column of energy may be experienced as descending from the upper world of *Hanaq Pacha*, the celestial realm of light beings into the *misa* and middle world of *Kay Pacha.*

After introducing oneself in prayer to the spirit world and stating intention for connection, next the paqo concentrates on quieting their mind and entering into a state of *sucana,* "being not doing." The analogy of scuba diving corresponds with this process. Beginning scuba diving one often has the experience of being underwater, slightly above the ocean floor, and watching and waiting for dirt that has been "kicked up" by rapid thrashing movement to slowly settle down again to the bottom before visibility is regained. One learns quickly in these circumstances that other than softly breathing one must remain quiet and motionlessly suspended. Any attempt to rush or "move through" the process will inevitably prolong it. This process of slowing down and waiting for things to settle in diving is like the process the shaman uses in shifting states of awareness.

Mañaquiy is another meditative practice involving invocation with the intention of moving into deeper energetic connection with *Pachamama* and the *apus*. *Mañaquiy* takes place after a greeting of *mast'ay* occurs. While *mast'ay* is a formal introduction often made to the spirits of the land in places one has not visited before, *mañaquiy* is performed when a relationship between the paqo and the spirits of the land has been established.

The words of invocation used in *mañaquiy* are an expression of manifestation because the words themselves have an essence that connects the three worlds of *Uku Pacha*, *Kay Pacha*, and *Hanaq Pacha*. *Mañaquiy* is also used in opening ceremony by paqos. Intention is set with words in prayer, spoken silently or out loud as to call sacred space, introduce the purpose of the request for connection to the *apus* and *Pachamama*. It involves dropping into a receptive state that allows implicit feelings to enter one's awareness.

In *mañaquiy*, after clearly setting intention with words, by then transferring one's attention to the feelings associated with the words in the heart and the belly, the paqo becomes more fully present—and available to connecting with the Andean cosmos through the body. The somatic event of receiving an energetic connection may be sensed as a tingling, a sense of expansiveness, seeing color or light, or feeling a heartfelt connection of being part of something greater.

After connection is made through *mañaquiy*, paqos drop into a silent state of *chinq-ay* that may be felt through their *y'ankay* or belly. *Chinq-ay* literally translates as "be silent." When the word *chinq-ay* is pronounced, there is a pause between the two syllables that indicates that the silence is the focus of the meaning of the word. When the paqo can still their mind and *manos wasi* and move deeply into the quietness, *chinq-ay* becomes the gateway for entering atemporal otherworld dimensions, where there are no words—only a felt sense of the greater cosmos. Although there are no words, there are deeply felt sensations through connecting with *kausay k'anchay* (light energy), and then from that point of connection psychically surrendering to a sense of being one with the natural world that often involves a profound sense of being held. For some paqos, these sensations are accompanied. with color and smell. The experience of *chinq-ay* often includes feelings of gratitude, compassion, and love, in being in relation to the natural world.

Yanantin and Masantin Haipay

In addition to being an individual practice of invocation, moving into a receptive state of *mañaquiy* also occurs between two people coming together to build connection between them, the *apus*, and *Pachamama*. These relationships between different types of *kausay* energy are not only found in *misas* and the relationship between an individual and the cosmos, but they also apply to relationships between people. *Yanantin* and *masantin haipays* are encounters involving two people, opposite sex, or same sex, respectively. *Ayni karpays* are sacred rites of energy transmissions involving an exchange of the totality of knowledge and linage between the *poq'pos* or energy bodies of two paqos. *Yanantin* and *masantin haipays* can also be a "transmission" of energy from a teacher to an apprentice during an initiation ceremony, called *rantin*.

*Rantin i*s an energetic transmission of *kausay k'anchay* (light energy) that is a replacement or exchange of energy in the *manos wasi*. During shamanic initiations, through *karpay* rites, a paqo's ancestral lineage as a medicine person and body of knowledge is transmitted energetically from their *misa* into the initiate's *misa* through physical contact and convocation, while calling on the spirit of the land. Through a heart connection of *munay*, a *rantin* may formalize alliances between a paqo and an initiate in *karpay* ceremonies as well as harmonizing and feeding energy in the initiate's *misa* and *manos wasi*. During the altered states that take place during initiations, paqos experience a sense of well-being or being energized along with a sensation of expansion. Sometimes a vibration or tingling, accompanied by a buzzing sound, is experienced, with everything appearing more vivid. Some paqos have described this experience as a process involving "rewiring of the energy body."

A *karpay* is a process not a single event because the energy "download" goes through a period of gestation in the transmission receiver's *manos wasi* and *misa* after the initial transmission as it is being integrated. During the initial phase that takes place after receiving *karpay* rites, the initiate is more vulnerable to outside influences because the energy field of the *manos wasi* has been opened and is more permeable.

In some ways like distressing events causing overwhelming trauma states to be held in the body as implicit memory that are too difficult for the ego to assimilate initially, integrating an intense transmission of *kausay* energy after an overpowering connection with the *apus* in ceremony or an initiation also takes time to become integrated in the *manos wasi*. In a re-entry process, after undergoing a forceful *rantin* during a *karpay* initiation, the unintegrated energetic experience held in the body gradually becomes incorporated both somatically and psychologically as it moves into ego awareness. Assimilating energetic experience to make meaning of the intense experience that has occurred is a blending and layering process, which begins as a nonverbal feeling state. In this context, for paqos, making meaning refers to the development of the capacity for embodiment, to live life to the fullest.

The incubation process of integrating the *kausay k'anchay* into the *manos wasi* and *misa* received during the *karpay* rites that follows takes about three months. The transmission receiver or initiate's dedication to *supan haipay* practices such as *chinq'ay* and *mañaquiy* will help to expand the capacity to move beyond a personal orientation into open-ended fluid states. Spending time in "flow states" in *supan haipay* will increase their receptivity and availability to connect with the *apu* mountain spirits. As the initiate incorporates the *kausay k'anchay* received in the *karpay* rites in to their *manos wasi*, they grow in their capability to mirror the collective cosmos and can create relationships and form connections at higher vibrational frequencies, with higher value.

The shamanic lineage being transferred from a paqo to an apprentice is referred to as *paqo wachu*. *Machu kuna* is the ancestral energy that a *misa* carries. Paqos say that blood, culture, and karma are the three ingredients that make up lineage. Lineage begins with collective archetypal ancestry that then becomes conscious through cultural expression and made personal through karmic embodiment and ego identification.

In *yanantin* and *masantin karpay* ceremonies, the paqo invokes connection with *Pachamama* and the *apus.* Once sacred space is called and intention is set, the paqo touches the initiate's three energy centers *y'ankay, munay,* and *y'anchay* (Belly, Heart, and Mind, respectively) and *misa* with their *misa* and through this process the *paqo wachu* is transferred. During the initiation process, the student's capacity to hold power (energy) in their *misa* and *manos wasi* increases.

Sometimes, the master paqo will also give the initiate a sacred *q'uiya* (stone) imbued with energy, to add to their *misa.* A *khuya rumi* is the gifting of a stone from a *paqo* to a student. In this initiation process, receiving the master paqo's embodiment of knowledge in connection with the land strengthens the apprentice's capacity to hold energy in their *misa,* and their availability to connect through their *manos wasi* also grows stronger.

There are many types of initiation ceremonies, or *karpays,* with different purposes and functions. For beginning students, the ceremony of *jununakuy* helps to facilitate moving into a receptive state of union and connection with the *apus.* *K'anchaq karpay*, which literally means "bright light of energy initiation ceremony," is a ceremony between paqos and their students to promote growth on the Andean spiritual path. *Kallpa hap'inachiy* is another powerful ceremony that helps initiates drop into more profound states of connection with the *Wira Cocha.* Paqos also perform the sacred Incan rites of *Kallpa t'aqwinakuy,* for personal healing and transformation.

Mosaq karpay rites, an advanced initiation into a "new rites of passage," have to do with a new identity aligned with a paqo's soul's purpose for healing, transformation, and embodiment for a new vision of times to come. *Mosaq karpay* rites have to do with the collective on the mythic level and, because of this, are considered a "nonpersonal" way of being. Paqos have described *mosaq karpay* rites as "a return of light and a return of the Inkas." The purpose of *mosaq karpay* rites are to "connect back to lineage and walk hand in hand with creation."

Ayllu Haipay

Ayllu haipay is a *karpay* ritual performed in a group. *Ayllu haipay* is carried out as a group practice for deeper connection in the community and is a way of aligning with the collective in the cosmos. Paqos begin all *haipay* ceremonies calling sacred space. In *supan haipay* rituals, the focus is on introducing oneself, calling upon and connecting with the spirit world of the Andean cosmos. When calling sacred space as an *ayllu,* the ritual is often more involved and frequently starts with calling sacred space from the four directions. The elements associated with the different directions may vary, depending on the paqo. In my experience, paqos practicing from the Q'ero tradition often consider aspects of the mythic beings of *Amaru,*

Chocochinchi, and *Apucheen,* while paqos who focus on Incan traditions place greater emphasis on *Inti Tayta,* Father Sun. The following descriptions are a combination of elements from the spirit world invoked by different paqos that I have observed in ceremonies.

Energy from the east is awakening and regenerative, the powerful energy of *Inti Tayta,* or Father Sun. Facing the west is sometimes associated with purification and clearing *hucha,* because the light of the sun disappears in the west. The energy from the west is used by *brujas,* or sorcerers, who work with the dark. The west is also the realm of timeless dreamtime. The directions of north may refer to a place of spirit and mystery and the meta language of spirit, with the south being associated with the healing feminine, power, and/or the wind. The north and south support and balance each other.

In addition to calling sacred space from the four directions, spirits from the three worlds of *Uku Pacha, Kay Pacha,* and *Hanaq Pacha* are called by following the movement of the sun, the pivotal element. This starts with beginning the ritual facing east, the direction of the rising sun, and finishing with facing west. *Apucheen,* the mythic condor, is called in association with the celestial realm of *Hanaq Pacha*—with the ascended masters, *Inti Tayta* or Father Sun, *Mama Qilla,* or Grandmother Moon and the stars, calling for visions and dreams. *Chocochinchi* is called, with all the plant and animal beings in relationship as a source of growth and power in *Kay Pacha. Amaru* is called in relationship to *Pachamama,* as a symbol of rebirth.

In the process of calling sacred space, other cosmic beings are called by name, including *Pachamama* (Mother Earth), the *Santa Tierras* (earth spirits), *Mama Cocha* (Mother Water), the four elements of *Wyra* (wind), *Nina* (fire), *Unu* (water), *Tierra* (earth), and *chaskas* (stars).

Spirits from a specific location are also included. The *apus* are each called individually by name and collectively as a group. The term *apu kuna* is used to call the *apus* collectively. The phrase *yupana kuna* means "all of the holy mountains." In ceremonies, the names of the *apus* of the sacred mountains called include *Salkantay, Ausangate, Mama Simona, Picol, Manuel Pinta, Wanaquari, PachaTuscon, Pijchu, Sacsayhuaman, Wiraqochan, Pukin,* and *Senq'a.* Other powerful Andean *apus* such as *Alangoma, Quelque Punqo, Sawasiray* and *Pitasiway,* and *Umantay,* to name a few, are also called upon during ceremony. These *apus* often become *apu* benefactors of a paqos' *misa.* The *apu* benefactors serve as conduits between the paqo's *misa* and the spirit world and are always named when a paqo is calling sacred space.

In *ayllu haipays,* sometimes the members of the *ayllu* perform the ritual of calling the spirits together, naming each of them individually in song often using rattles. The meditative rhythm of the song and sound of the rattle helps still the mind from distraction and the "chatter" of thinking.

This practice usually occurs during fire ceremonies when individual *despacho* offerings are given to the fire. Before a *despacho* offering is given to the fire, a cleansing ritual usually takes place that includes the participation of everyone present. This ritual is done for the purpose of purification. In the fire cleansing ritual, four individuals approach the fire at a time from each of the four directions, holding their *misas* to their torso. The *misa* is next laid on the ground next to each person facing the fire. *Hucha* is released from the *manos wasi* with intentional focus using sweeping arm and hand gestures in three stages, first pulling *hucha* away from the body toward the fire in a counterclockwise direction, next pulling energy into each of the three energy centers from the fire directly, and then pulling energy from the fire and sealing it in each of the three energy centers making circular clockwise motions. Finally, the *misa* is picked up by the *misa* carrier and moved in a circular clockwise direction over the fire three times, to purify the *misa*. Once this ritual is completed by everyone present, as an *ayllu* the individual *despachos* are carried by each person to the fire and carefully placed on top of the flames. Once the *despachos* have been placed on the fire it is important not to look at them to avoid undoing the intentions that have been "downloaded" into the *q'intus* in the *despachos*. The ceremony is complete, and the participants turn away and leave the fire.

In some *ayllu haipay* ceremonies, after sacred space is called, a shift is made into a silent state as a group. While *chinq-ay* is practice of profound silence in *supan haipay, thaiqay* describes a trance state often occurring in a person during a group ceremony who is in a state of deep tranquility. According to the paqos, spirits look for people in a state of *thaiqay*, who, because of their state of silence, are more open and available to receiving messages. Like other meditative states, *thaiqay* is achieved through intentional receptivity.

Intentional Receptivity

As a paqo's connection with the cosmos develops, they build the practice of acquiring power using "intentional receptivity." In Andean medicine, intentional receptivity refers to the process of becoming open, attending, and bearing witness to the immediacy of what is happening in the surrounding world—without any preconceived notion of what is taking place.

States of "intentional receptivity" are an aspect of psychic healing and mystical experience in Andean medicine that provides agency toward manifestation. In addition to being an act of focusing with the mind as a practice toward spiritual connection, "intentional receptivity" is a function of the *manos wasi* because it is an energetic, intuitively "felt" state that may include but is not limited to operations that are ego-directed.

Over time, shifting perception from the physical to the imaginal, to the energetic realms becomes easier by developing the ability to "feel" into the experience through the *manos wasi*.

In addition to shifting into deeper connection through the *manos wasi*, by staying present in an open state of "beginner's mind" paqos use their intent to increase their capacity to hold power. This is accomplished by moving from a personal position into an energetic state of collectivity and shifting their state of attention.

This attention transfer to an energetic state of collectivity becomes a somatic state of embodiment, experienced in the totality of one's being more powerful than the limitations of a mental exercise (Mindell, 1993). It is a fluid, organic process, of sensing a connection with the cosmos that arises spontaneously, in a state of seeing not doing.

Like the practice of meditation, entering the energetic realm is a process of "holding space," allowing experience to emerge by "letting go," and learning how to shift the focus away from cognitive operations using the mind to body awareness. Through intentional receptivity, a paqo's ability to shift their focus and drop into profound psychic spaces of profound silence through *chinq'ay* grows stronger, and their *manos wasi* becomes more attuned to *kausay pacha*. Their capacity to perceive different aspects of *Wira Cocha* deepens as well, and they begin to experience nuances that continue to become more intricate and multifaceted as the paqo evolves. An understanding of *Wira Cocha,* as the living cosmos, expands into a more differentiated awareness of the light essence of everything, containing the totality of all the worlds, including but not limited to *Uku Pacha* (the lower world of *Pachamama)*, *Kay Pacha* (the middle world), and *Hanaq Pacha* (the upper world). In this process, *qepe* (the past), *kunan* (present), and *nawpi* (future*)* comes together in atemporal reality as one.

Paqos refer to the focusing of intent as *muñana*. The intent gives the structure and the direction of the energetic experience in the *manos wasi*. It creates the temenos through which conscious intersection with the collective leading to transformation can occur. Paqos believe that the universe mirrors the intention created by a paqo and when a paqo's intent is clear and focused, this will be reflected to the paqo by the universe in a relationship of reciprocity, that is nonnegotiable. Castaneda (1998, p. 54) has written, "Intent is what sends a shaman through a wall, through space to infinity."

Intentional receptivity often involves "softening" one's vision into a relaxed semi out-of-focus state and *seeing* the energy in the spaces around objects, or— in the epic film *Star Wars,* the way Jedi warriors learn to work with "the force." Transferring between states of awareness starts by entering a receptive state using intent, and seeing things "as they are," in the present moment, without preconceived notions. Vision is a function of availability or receptivity, which includes intention, focus, and perception. Intentional receptivity usually involves shifting one's mode of perception from seeing and hearing to bodily responsiveness.

Intentional receptivity is an attitude of awareness toward the outside world, as well as inward practice. While participating in an *ayahuasca* ceremony a couple of decades ago, I had an experience that illustrates this phenomenon. During the first stages of an *ayahuasca* journey, there is often a great deal of mental stimulation and activity. Being someone that does not particularly enjoy the experience of hallucinogenic drugs, I was finding the intensity of the increasing neural activity in my brain annoying, wishing for it to end. Like diving under a large wave to avoid being pummeled while body surfing, I discovered that by setting intention with my mind to shift my attention state or awareness into my belly, I could drop underneath the mental stimulation and "feel" my way deeper into the energetic experience. Even though I was consciously aware that my brain was still engaging "full speed," I was able to drop into a calm centeredness, enabling me to experience energetically merging with the jungle around me through the perceptual shift.

Phases of Orientation: Physical, Collective, and Energetic

There are three phases of orientation—personal, collective, and energetic that take place through the process of intentional receptivity in connecting with the cosmos through the *manos wasi*. In Quechua they are called *pachayki, pachaqaway,* and *qaway kusaq,* respectively.

Pachayki is temporal. It involves a personal orientation specific to one's own state in life using the *y'anchay,* or Mind. The meditative practice of self-observation in the act of *reqsequiy* and decision made to keep or eradicate behavior based upon its effect on one's spiritual path in the process of *qaway kusaq* are examples of *pachayki.*

Pachaqaway is more advanced than *pachayki* because it moves beyond reflecting upon one's personal life to reflecting upon one's relationship and standing in the greater universe, from a position of collectivity. As paqos experience the universe as both temporal and atemporal, *pachaqaway* is a state that bridges both realms of temporality.

Qaway kusaq, is an atemporal energetic state of oneness with *Wira Cocha,* often experienced as a state of ecstasy in connection with the Andean cosmos.

Using a description of an *ayahuasca* experience again may help to illustrate differences between these levels. The vision experienced in an ayahuasca ceremony usually entails three stages that correspond to *pachayki, pachaqaway,* and *qaway kusaq.* During ayahuasca vision ceremonies in the Amazon, it is common to experience being eaten by the giant anaconda spirit of the jungle. This first stage of dismemberment involves coming face to face with the shadow, that takes apart the physical body and identity as it is personally experienced in *pachayki.*

If a psychic shift is made from an attachment to the physical body, by surrendering to the dismemberment process in the first phase of this *ayahuasca* journey, it is possible to move beyond persona and physical form and join with *Amaru,* the great serpent that facilitates transformation in the sacred initiation process. This phase is *pachaqaway,* the transition from moving beyond the limitation of identifying with a physical form, and toward experiencing an expanded state of collective identity.

Transcending beyond a physical identity and entering the experience of being a part of the celestial realm of the stars is exhilarating and liberating, taking place in the realm of *qaway kusaq.* The experience of becoming one with the cosmos happens through the *energetic* field of the *manos wasi,* when personal identity tied to a physical body falls away, and having form no longer matters. It is possible in this state to psychically merge with the elements in states of light, air, and water. This is an example of *qaway kusaq* at the essential universal level.

Sourcing from the Collective of the Land

In states of intentional receptivity paqos also move beyond a personal perspective into *qaway kusaq,* through sourcing from *Pachamama,* the expression of the collective subtle body of all living things. In Quechua, *allpa kamasqa* means the "life giving earth energy" of *Pachamama.* The process of sourcing from *Pachamama* is called *kaipai.* For Andean paqos, the "collective of the land" is the *energetic* manifestation of *Pachamama* that exists both inside and outside of time and space that they derive power from through connection. The power that is acquired through sourcing *allpa kamasqa* is called *kallpa.* For paqos, connecting with the land is a means of linking to the "source" of the *collective,* which is the definition of empowerment.

This energetic attunement with *Pachamama* creates a link that becomes the conduit to experiencing the collective of the land as existing beyond the structure of linear time and space. The land provides the medium to shift from experiencing an individual psychic state, into the universal expression of the energetic collective. What paqos refer to as "the land" contains both physical reality and the energetic realm, aspects of *Wira Cocha.* Through energetically anchoring into the land in meditative states using intention, paqos experience "crossing over" between psychic levels of engagement, linking the *energetic, symbolic,* and *literal* states of existence.

Connecting with the collective of the land takes place in a state of *ayni,* a "right relationship" of reciprocity with *Pachamama* and the *apus* through *karpays.* A *karpay* is an energy transfer ritual usually made with blowing *kausay* energy with intention into *k'intus,* which is *moraya* or a kind of "energetic food." Paqos believe that a *karpay* transmission of *kausay* awakens vision, enabling one to become more open and observant of what is happening in the Andean cosmos.

For paqos, working on their connection with the land helps them to ground the experience into a perspective framework that can be assimilated into conscious awareness. Paqos often develop a deeper connection with the land through making a spiritual pilgrimage, or *paq'o wachu.* They often create *despacho* and *q'intu* offerings for *Pachamama* and the *apus* in acts involving *karpays* before a journey, or along the way.

On pilgrimages and during ceremonies, an intentional shift is often "sensed" by the paqo as being in a fluid, expanded energetic state with no separation between oneself and the cosmos. In Quechua the phrase *kallpa wan tupay* translates literally as "a sacred meeting with energy." In these states, paqos frequently experience seeing energy particles of light surrounding the mountains or in the atmosphere and feel a vibration pulsing in their bodies. They may also have a universal feeling of love, *munay,* in the heart.

Power Spots: Altars in the Land

Within the collective of the land there are different kinds of altars, or power spots, that paqos source from called *pucharas,* that have different functions and physical characteristics. *Paqarinas* are *pucharas*, often residing in caves, springs, and other bodies of water that are mythic places of origin where creation is reenacted. They are feminine manifestations in nature that are portals connecting the lower world of *Uku Pacha* with the middle world of *Kay Pacha,* and the *Mama Cochas,* the sacred water spirits of glacier lagoons.

Wakas are holy places where the veil between realities is thin, that are *pucharas* used for communicating with other worlds. *Wankas* are *pucharas* usually found in the forms of large rocks called *hatun rumis* that hold the lineage of the ancestors and serve as a protector of crops, health, and well-being. *Wankas* are also sometimes found in the shape of a cross.

Saywas and *sacanas* can be types of *pucharas* connected with *Hanaq Pacha* that are specifically tied to the land. *Saywas* that are *pucharas* are energetic luminous markers that are mysterious pillars or columns of energy connecting *Pachamama* to the celestial bodies. *Sacanas* are solar markers, like *Machu Pichu* used to measure time through relationship with a trail of light that creates a halo of a fundamental map of navigation.

Like the land carrying different types of energy and forms of energy configuration this also occurs in the physical and subtle bodies—and the *manos wasi.* Paqos work with the arrangement of energy both collectively and individually to promote healing. The next chapter will focus on healing practices pertaining to the *manos wasi.*

Like the land carrying different types of energy and forms of energy configuration this also occurs in the physical and subtle bodies—and the *manos wasi.* Paqos work with the arrangement of energy both collectively and individually to promote healing. Chapter 6 will focus on healing practices pertaining to the subtle body and the *manos wasi.*

Note

1   The autistic contiguous position refers to the process of attributing meaning to experience in which raw sensory data is organized through forming pre-symbolic connections derived from bodily sensations, primarily through the surface of the body.

References

Castaneda, C. (1998) *The Wheel of Time*, New York, NY: Simon and Schuster.

Mindell, A. (1993) *The Shaman's Body: A new shamanism for transforming health, relationships, and the community,* New York, NY: HarperCollins Publishing.

Ogden, T. H. (1989a) 'On the concept of an autistic-contiguous position', *International Journal of Psychoanalysis* 70: 127–40.

Ogden, T. H. (1989b) *The Primitive Edge of Experience*, Abingdon, Oxfordshire: Routledge.

Chapter 6

Experiencing the Energetic Realm through the Body— Temporality and Atemporality

Atemporality and the Energy Body

The paqos' explanation of the energy body called the *manos wasi* and Jung's depiction of a collective subtle energy body are each described as carrying memories of ancestral lineage, as templates of wholeness. This kind of information is not available in the physical body that exists in a state of temporality (which is subject to gravitational pull due to existing in a state of matter). This amount of information is only available in an atemporal, energetic state where the phenomenon of gravity does not exist.

Rovelli (2019, p. 67) has written, "Spacetime is the gravitational field—and vice versa." Rovelli's statement indicates that matter creates the experience of temporality. Because we have physical bodies—comprised of matter—we are generally only able to conceptualize time as temporal.

Jung has written:

> *The absolute knowledge, which is characteristic of synchronistic phenomena, a knowledge not mediated by sense organs ... such forms of existence can only be transcendental, since, as the knowledge of the future or spatially distant events shows, it is contained in a psychically relative space and time, that is to say an irrepresentable space-time continuum.* (Jung, 1960b, p. 90)

Somatic Awareness in Healing

According to both Jungians and paqos, deep primordial states are held somatically in the subtle body, or *manos wasi*. They both agree that the body functions as a cumulative warehouse of nonverbal unconscious experience that can be brought into awareness through accessing liminal spaces existing between unconscious memory and ego-consciousness.

Jungian analyst Mara Sidoli (2000) has stressed the importance of attending to nonverbal body communication by attending to every subtle detail taking place within a session. She approaches her analytic work with clients by listening to the

DOI: 10.4324/9781003356448-8

client's verbal communication and silence and observing changes occurring in her own and her clients' bodies concerning breathing patterns, tension levels, and skin tone, as well as any other noticeable indicators presented by the autonomic nervous system. In working with psychotherapy clients, Mindell (1985) has developed a process in which the client "amplifies" or expresses urges he or she is experiencing through the body through movement to gain greater sentient awareness.

Jung entertained the idea of working symbolically through the body. He has written, "And to be in an abdomen would mean most probably that we were in the mother, in a condition of development or beginning. That point of view would throw a particular light on our symbolism" (Jung, 1996, p. 24).

According to paqos, *y'ankay*, the energy center in the belly, functions as the vessel that holds the memory of implicit, energetic experience, while *munay*, the energy center located in the heart, is where connection with the natural world and others is felt and experienced (that is, love and gratitude). *Y'anchay* is the energy center of the mind located in the forehead and top of the head pertaining to mental clarity and vision. The body is both the vessel that holds energetic experience and the receptor of the experience. Paqos believe that the body knows how to heal itself, and that the role of a healer is to move energy to activate the memory of a healed state in the *manos wasi*.

In my own process, I have learned to move into a state of heightened states of awareness, by "dropping" into my body, sensing through the "belly," and "connecting" energetically with the earth by "feeling into it," kinesthetically. I have found that by entering a receptive state and attending to body sensation, it is possible to shift the experience of the "assemblage point," a phenomenon described by Castaneda (1984, p. 168), into a state of awareness centered in the somatic body. When the assemblage point shifts, perception moves into the realm of nonordinary reality, the "focus" of experience transfers from discrete thoughts and images to somatic *energetic* experience.

Energy Blockage in the Body

Wilhelm Reich (1990), a colleague of Freud and Jung, described how painful experiences that are suppressed that can be recollected but are shut off from awareness in the present moment, along with repressed memories that are too traumatic to remain conscious, become stored as "character armor" in the body. Both agree that assimilating and integrating traumatic experiences held in the body as *hucha*, or blockage, requires removing the energetic obstacle, frequently held in the belly by rearranging the energy in the body, or *manos wasi*.

According to paqos, there are two ways of rearranging energy in the *manos wasi*. The first is through the extraction process of removing negative energy and the second is through soul retrieval when lost parts that have become split off are reintegrated in the *manos wasi*.

Both processes have counterparts in psychoanalysis and psychotherapy.

Dismantling Blockage and the Extraction Process in the *Manos Wasi*

Current body-oriented therapies, largely derived from Wilhelm Reich's (1990) early work in Orgone Therapy, have focused on using breath and movement techniques that enhance sensation in the body, enabling defensive body armor to be made conscious and released through the physical body. Like the paqos' description of the energetic experience of being in connection with the collective of the land—seeing energy particles of light accompanied by the sensation of energy running through the body—during Reichian breathwork sessions these sensations are also frequently experienced. In Reichian therapy the experience of energy moving through the body is referred to as streaming.

While Reich breathwork focuses on releasing energetic blockage in the body with an emphasis on breath, for paqos the release of *hucha* occurs through an extraction process.

In Andean medicine and other forms of shamanism, the process of extraction refers to the removal of dense energy or *hucha,* corresponding to what Reich was referring to in his description of character armor, which creates a deadening of *kausay* and produces blockage. The dark energy of *layca* is another more active form of negative energy associated with intrusive thought forms or obsessions. On a larger scale, *layca* is sometimes the result of disincarnate sentient beings, considered to be evil spirits, that attach to, feed off, and overshadow a person's *manos wasi.*

According to paqos, the difference between evil and benign sentient beings is that benign beings do not draw energy, while evil beings associated with *layca* are parasitic—likewise, *brujas* or sorcerers, who work with *layca* for personal gain at the expense of the collective, while paqos work with *sami* in *ayni,* a relationship of reciprocity to eradicate *layca* in service of the collective. In Andean medicine and other forms of shamanism—as well as psychoanalysis and other forms of psychotherapy—souls are believed to be autonomous, and no one has ownership or the right to impose or take something that is not freely given in a relationship of *ayni.* Regardless of theoretical orientation, this is the definition of abuse. Like working with adults caught in cycles of abuse in psychoanalysis and psychotherapy, in Andean medicine, healing is consensual and will only occur at the level and to the degree the person undergoing the healing is willing to accept. Healing is a translevel process often involving the four levels of psychic engagement.

In addition to releasing *hucha* being carried in the body, through the process of *reqsequiy,* like most forms of psychotherapy, healing also involves identifying and releasing limiting guiding myths and core belief patterns that have become imprinted on the *manos wasi.* Like depth psychology, healing in Andean medicine involves a prospective perspective of envisioning a healed state of wholeness. The universe mirrors back intent, and intent is the function of vision, which is a function of openness or availability.

Both *layca* and *hucha* are often the result of patterns associated with addiction, dark familial lineage, and family trauma, as well as shock to the *manos wasi* due to a sudden accident or negative event. The understanding of the causes of trauma to the *manos wasi* are similar in Andean medicine, although the actual events are often different due to cultural dissimilarities. In modern culture, familial trauma is more often caused by abuse or neglect, while in the Andes trauma is often the result of hardship living in the elements under harsh environmental conditions.

In the extraction process, attachments, or energetic cords binding *layca* to the *manos wasi* are cut in a ceremonial process that always begins with an invocation. Sacred space is called, inviting the luminous light beings of the Andean cosmos, the *apus* and *Pachamama*, asking for support and protection during the process. Next, using intention, the paqo shifts into a receptive dream-like state to receive information regarding the location and nature of the energetic attachments to be removed from the *manos wasi*. Frequently, incense is used in the clearing process. Quartz crystals that have previously been cleansed and infused with *sami* are sometimes held by the paqo during the extraction process.

In some ceremonies, ones that tend to occur in more remote villages, a whip is used to drive the negative spirits away from the person's *manos wasi*, Sometimes negative energy being removed from the *manos wasi* is transferred into a quartz crystal (which is cleaned through ritual with intention after the ceremony), or a dried llama fetus, which is then given back to *Pachamama* through a burial ritual or fire ceremony.

Soul Loss

Paqos refer to psychic fragmentation due to traumatic experience as "soul loss," like the concept of dissociation in psychoanalysis. Patrick Harpur (2000) has described soul loss as something that takes place within the subtle body, which he has explained as a daimonic, imaginative body, which is a soul that can be lost and retrieved by a shaman who journeys to other worlds in a process some refer to as "soul retrieval" (Ingerman, 1991).

In his writing on nonordinary reality, oriented from the perspective of Western culture, Harpur (2003) has proposed that lost soul parts are aspects of conscious awareness that exist outside of the experience of the rational ego and leave the body in the "out of body" experiences and "near-death" experiences. This is when we can perceive our actual physical form from outside of ourselves. Both psychoanalysis (Bromberg, 1996, 1995; Ogden, 1989; Winnicott, 1958 [1945]) and shamanism view the psychic fragmentation that occurs as a defensive response to a traumatic event to be a separation from consciousness. Soul loss is a form of illness associated with a lack of power, which may manifest as localized pain, fear, and phobias, and a lack of creativity. In soul loss, elements of the psyche that are memories, or parts of oneself that experienced trauma, split off psychically and become frozen atemporally as implicit trauma in the unconscious.

Soul loss is a construct that not only applies to Andean medicine, but to most forms of shamanism. Both Andean medicine and psychoanalysis view psychic fragmentation—or soul loss—to be an atemporal state. Mircea Elaide (1992, p. 215) has stated, "Disease is attributed to the soul's having strayed away or been stolen, and treatment is reduced in principle, finding it, capturing it, and obliging it to resume its place in the patient's body." Soul loss can occur as the result of birth trauma, accidents, surgery, depression, addiction, and other unresolved traumas. Some shamans also believe that parts of the soul may be given away in grief or loss.

In Jungian psychology the intrapsychic phenomenon of *abaissement du niveau mental* (Jung, 1979, par. 213), a lowering of the level of consciousness and psychic energy due to fatigue, illness, violent emotions, and shock, corresponds to the concept of soul loss. A difference between psychoanalysis and Andean medicine is that paqos believe that soul fragments leave the psyche and the *manos wasi* rather than becoming repressed.

In *Demons of the Inner World: Understanding our hidden complexes*, Alfred Ribi has written:

The modern analyst deals with soul loss in essentially the same way as the shaman. He helps the patient elevate into consciousness fragments of his psyche that have been withdrawn into the unconscious or have come to life there. Dream work and the active imagination technique play an important role in this process... Soul loss can occur other than by spontaneous wandering away or withdrawal of the soul. More often the soul is stolen by a sorcerer, a hostile shaman, or a vengeful spirit. Sorcerers and sorceresses are not personal figures but archetypes in the sense that, as we have seen in the case of projectiles, the effect emanates from the archetype. (Ribi, 1989, p. 84)

Soul Retrieval

Andean paqos perform the practice of soul retrieval or bringing split-off soul parts back to the *manos wasi*, starting in the current *pacha* (an allocation of energy in a specific point in time and space). In both shamanic practice and psychoanalysis, past trauma cannot be processed and worked through unless the trauma victim is in a psychologically safe environment. In soul retrieval ceremonies, after calling sacred space, the paqo journeys to locate the lost parts or soul fragments of the person's psyche, that became spilt off due to a traumatic event while the person remains in a quiet, receptive state. In both analysis and soul retrieval ceremonies, by moving from explicit memories of personal experiences (that is, *pachas*) into implicit unfelt feeling states, experiential layers become more consciously delineated.

Paqos, like other shamans, travel in the middle world of *Kay Pacha* (which some shamans refer to as the astral plane) to coax the lost soul fragments to return to the psyche, in the *manos wasi* after creating a "safe space," in the present, in some ways like the analytic container. When movement is made from implicit feeling states associated with fragmented memories into the current *pacha,* the intricate nuanced experiential layers become more consciously delineated.

Unlike trauma work where the intent is to help the analysand remember and process memories of the actual traumatic events that led to aspects of the psyche (or soul) splitting off and become fragmented because feelings in reaction to the events were too overwhelming to hold consciously, in shamanism the intention is to remove memories of the events from the mind and *manos wasi.* Paqos and other shamans do not share explicit information about what they uncover regarding the past trauma, to avoid reactivating the trauma in the psyche. However, like psychoanalysis, when the split-off psychic parts begin to become reintegrated, repressed feelings related to the split-off memory of the traumatic event may be re-experienced as the lost psychic fragments are recollected and become conscious. In both soul retrieval and trauma work, a greater capacity for more complex perception develops by weaving together an understanding of the implicit and explicit of the experience of the past, present, and future.

References

Bromberg, P. M. (1995) 'Psychoanalysis, dissociation, and personality organization', *Psychoanal. Dial.* 5: 511–28.

Bromberg, P. M. (1996) 'Standing in the spaces: The multiplicity of self and the psychoanalytic relationship', *Contemporary Psychoanalysis* 32: 509–35.

Castaneda, C. (1984) *The Fire from Within,* New York, NY: Pocket Books.

Elaide, M. (1992) *Shamanism: Archaic techniques of ecstasy,* Princeton, NJ: Princeton University Press.

Harpur, P. (2000) *Daimonic Reality: A field guide to the otherworld,* Enumclaw, WA: Pine Winds Press.

Ingerman, S. (1991) *Soul Retrieval,* New York, NY: Harper San Francisco, a division of HarperCollins.

Jung, C. G. (1960a) *Structure & Dynamics of the Psyche* (Collected Works, vol. 8).

Jung, C.G. (1960b) 'Synchronicity: An acausal connecting principal' (Collected Works, vol. 8), in *The Structure and Dynamics of the Psyche Princeton,* Princeton, NJ: Princeton University Press.

Jung, C. G. (1979) *Collected Works of C.G. Jung, Volume 9 (Part 2),* eds Gerhard Adler and R. F. C. Hull, Princeton, NJ: Princeton University Press.

Jung, C. G. (1996) *The Psychology of Kundalini Yoga,* Princeton, NJ: Princeton University Press.

Mindell, A. (1985) *Working with the Dream Body,* Boston, MA: Routledge.

Ogden, T. H. (1989a) 'On the concept of an autistic-contiguous position', *International Journal of Psychoanalysis* 70: 127–40.

Ogden, T. H. (1989b) *The Primitive Edge of Experience,* Abingdon, Oxfordshire: Routledge.

Reich, W. (1990) *Character Analysis,* New York, NY: Farrar, Straus and Giroux.

Ribi, A. (1989) *Demons of the Inner World: Understanding our hidden complexes,* Boston, MA: Shambhala Publications.

Rovelli, C. (2019) *The Order of the Universe*, London: Penguin Books.

Sidoli, M. (2000) *When the Body Speaks: The archetypes in the body*, ed. P. Blakemore, Hove: Brunner-Routledge.

Winnicott, D. W. (1958 [1945]) 'Primitive emotional development', in *Collected Papers: Through paediatrics to psycho-analysis*, London: Tavistock, pp. 145–56.

Part II

Atemporal Experience and Re-Entry

Chapter 7

A Personal Account of Mystical and Re-Entry Experience

Most of the writing in the following chapter, except the last entry, was written 14 years ago, following a series of life-changing events that happened after receiving my first series of initiation rites from the paqos, with the *apus*[1] in the Andean mountains in Peru (Bryon, 2012). It is a personal account of what I experienced as atemporal encounters with the energetic realm of the *apus* and the re-entry process that followed. While I have returned to Peru many times since these initial mystical experiences, perhaps because shifting between atemporal and temporal states was unfamiliar to me at the time, this first transition back was extremely challenging for me.

Most of the dated passages in italics are an account of the mystical process that took place over the course of several days, followed by entries describing my re-entry process after returning home. The content in this chapter was written when I was still very close to the experience and illustrates my struggle in trying to integrate and draw meaning from what had happened to me. As is usually the case, working with the atemporal numinous material felt almost impossible to put into words, and expressing what transpired became a process of approximation. At best, these verbal descriptions are only vague recollections of *direct experience*. None of the following personal experiences that I describe were drug induced.

The entries begin during a pilgrimage I had made with the paqos to the sacred mountains of *Waki Wilka* and *Alangoma* in 2009. The text included between the entries was written primarily during the first several months after my return. At the time of the writing, I was still using the terms "shaman" and "shamanism" interchangeably with the words "*paqo*" and "Andean medicine," the terms used by the Andean medicine people. In my later writing, I use the words paqo and Andean medicine as they are closer to "the source."

June 5, 2009

While sitting on the top of the mountain with my eyes closed, I felt myself entering a trance state. I saw a series of doorways or openings of light with five points each that opened up on to each other so that one doorway opened into another doorway, and on to another. I began to experience a succession of

DOI: 10.4324/9781003356448-10

waves of convulsions, or intense shaking that echoed through my entire body. I heard a voice keep telling me to "hold it," and I understood that holding the energy meant containing it physically by maintaining a focus of intent through the process. Intuitively I knew that my ability to "hold" the energy in my body would determine the degree to which I would be able to integrate the power or energy being downloaded that I was receiving from the mountain. (Bryon, 2012)

In the process of shamanic initiation, power (energy) is "layered" into the physical body as light. While sitting on the mountaintop in a visionary experience, feeling myself being infused with energy, I realized that my personal narrative was there—and would always be there. I have heard Peruvian shamans say that we do not get rid of our egos; instead we move beyond the ego into a "flow" state of fluidity by entering a dialogue with the land, through our hearts and bodies. This "flow" is beyond words, personal narratives, and stories.

June 7, 2009

Over the course of the next several days, in ceremony, I felt intense waves of energy continually running through my physical body. At certain times, when I experienced contractions in my solar plexus and belly, the process became painful. At one point, I felt I was in labor and giving birth in the process. Afterward the waves subsided, I felt incredibly energized and in a state of euphoria. Throughout this entire process, although in trance, a part of me remained conscious. On some level, I was aware that this was necessary; otherwise, I would not have the intentionality needed to "hold" the power. (Bryon, 2012)

June 8, 2009

At times, I had the sense of going through the doorways and looking into a mirror reflection. It was not an actual mirror but seemed more like an energetic aspect of myself that I needed to face. I heard myself telling the reflection that I would meet it. We were equals. I knew, through the state of connectivity, that I was an equal with everything I was experiencing, as we were all the same. We were all energy. I sensed that to claim my power and hold the energy that I would be required to face, as equal, whatever I saw or experienced. It was necessary to honor the experience, and myself. Sometimes the reflection I was looking at became dark. I told the reflection that I was willing to face what it had to show me. I realized this as an aspect of my own shadow that I was seeing and needed to come to terms with. (Bryon, 2012)

June 10, 2009

During these couple of days, I had faint memories of what felt intuitively, to be a past life. In Peru, perhaps with these same Apus, a time I had misused power. I had the sense in that moment that this was in the past and would no longer claim me. I had returned, committed to serving the light of the collective.

I tracked the dark memory to a thread I still experience in myself linked to my competitive nature. I noticed it. In making the shift from the personal to the collective, I remembered that we do not get rid of our personal shadow; rather we need to become aware of it, and then place it on the shelf. I was aware that, consciously, a shift in awareness is made by attending to, and focusing on the light. Through this, it became clear to me that I could witness my own personal narrative, complexes, and inter dynamics, acknowledging that these elements of my psyche exist and then shift the focus to the energetic level where the personal becomes "ground," in the background, and the collective becomes "figure," or the primary focus. (Bryon, 2012)

In Throughout these experiences in Peru, I felt the presence of an inner figure that existed in the imaginal realm. At times, it felt like energy, while at other times it assumed the appearance of a giant bird, or "birdman." In service of this connection, I spent time in active imagination, engaging with it in dialogue. I also did a series of paintings trying to capture the essence of the "birdman" energy, Figure 7.1 being an example. Before these encounters, I remembered initially meeting this being several years ago in a dream, in the form of a snake. Then, before going to the Amazon, I experienced its presence again as a black jaguar that surrounded and protected me during an *ayahuasca* ceremony. Later, I learned that the jaguar was the spirit of the Amazon jungle.

Figure 7.1 Apu Spirit - Painting by the Author.

Eventually it occurred to me that these animal forms—the snake, the jaguar, and the bird—were the same mythological beings found in the cosmology of Peruvian shamanism—as *Amaru* the snake, *Chocachinchi* the jaguar, and *Apucheen* the great condor. At the time (see Chapter 4 on mythic beings) I was somewhat perplexed and wondered if perhaps I had "plugged" into a collective shamanic experience that was influencing my dreams and visions.

June 12, 2009

Over the course of the several days of "energetic layering," I was in constant dialogue with an inner figure who assumed the form of a bird/man. At times during the process of "energetic layering" I would see with my eyes closed an intense golden yellow light that completely surrounded me. Within the light, I saw doorways consisting of five points, and the energetic outline of a bird with extended wings—all composed of a radiant light. A couple of times these visions would shift, and I experienced myself shifting into the form of a bird. I felt what it was like to grow wings, and to stretch them. I felt myself flying and soaring—flapping my wings aggressively—then gliding with the momentum. I could feel myself circling higher in the air, and then diving through the air closer to the earth. I do not remember ever before experiencing such a great sense of freedom. I loved the experience of stretching my wings as far out as they would go and gliding with the breeze. I looked down at the earth and noticed how small everything looked. At times, I was reluctant to look down when I realized how far above the earth I was. I remember hearing the voice of my ally, the birdman, saying to me, "If you are asking for visions, you must be willing to see." I promised that I would try to hold the intention to look at what I was shown. (Bryon, 2012)

In Jeffrey Raff (1997, 2000, 2008)[2] has described what he refers to as psychoidal figures and has written that our inner figures and egos need each other to grow in these other realms. He has described "the ally" as the intermediary, or necessary conduit between the ego and psychoidal experience. As I reflect on my initiatory experience in the *collective energetic,* I remember that the emanations of light came through the energetic shape of a bird, *Apucheen.* For me, this bird became the ally—the bodhisattva to the energetic realm. *In The Wheel of Time* Castaneda (1998) has written:[3]

The Eagle, that power that governs the destinies of all living things, reflects equally and at once all those living things. There is no way, therefore, for man to pray to the Eagle, to ask for favors, to hope for grace. The human part of the Eagle is too insignificant to move the whole. (Castaneda, 1998, p. 202)

In I have heard the comment that Castaneda was writing in metaphor and that Don Juan was fictitious. Although his writing can easily be understood and worked

Figure 7.2 Ecstasy - Painting by the Author.

with symbolically in the realm of ordinary reality, as one moves deeper into the veil, from the symbolic into the energetic realm, what Castaneda is describing, for me, was an actual experience.[4]

For me, the bird/man was a being and energy at the same time. I felt a connection being in "his" overwhelming presence and at the same time being "awe struck" by the tremendous energy I was surrounded in. Figures 7.1 and 7.2 show paintings that were made shortly after I returned home.

In *The Fire from Within*, Castaneda (1984) stated,

> *The old seers actually saw the indescribable force which is the source of all sentient beings. They call it the eagle, because in the few glimpses they could sustain, they saw it as something that resembled a black and white eagle of infinite size … They saw that it is the eagle that bestows awareness. The eagle creates sentient beings so that they will live and enrich the awareness it gives them with life. They also saw that it is the eagle who devours that same enriched awareness after making sentient beings relinquish it at the moment of death.*
> (Castaneda, 1984, p. 38)

The next set of entries in italics were written a couple of months after I had returned home and was actively in the re-entry process.

August 26, 2009 (A reflection a couple of months later)

As I began receiving karpay *rites (initiation ceremony) from the paqos, when "lineage" from their* misa *(medicine bundle) was transmitted into mine, I found myself dropping into an atemporal experiential state which felt to me to be in a realm beyond words, where everything is connected. Although I could not put words to it, in a deeply calm state, I often had the sense of being outside of time, and that the past, present, and future were accessible simultaneously because everything was one. When I attempted to put words to the experience and describe it, I was immediately back in a temporal state and outside of the experience.*

   This is when I discovered that language exists in a state of temporality. I came to understand that temporal reality requires context, anchored in experiencing the outer world of physical reality, sequentially, while atemporal or extra-temporal reality is not necessarily a linear experience. In addition, to atemporal and temporal experiences not conforming with each other, in deep atemporal meditative states, a sense of separation between oneself, others, and the world drops away and everything is experienced as being connected. This is frequently described as a state of ecstasy and a felt sense of "coming home." I learned through the initiations I was experiencing that the deeper one "drops into" a state of connected experience of oneness, the less differentiated the experience becomes and it can feel as though multiple points in time are accessible at the same time and can be experienced simultaneously.

   In states closer to the surface of ego-consciousness, such as the imaginal realm of dreams and reverie, and implicit trauma states that are being re-experienced, "everything" is not necessarily happening at once, but the sequential timelines that exist in and help organize experience in consensual, physical reality can bend and are inescapably bound to an order of past, present, and future. Jumps are often made back and forth between a "then and now," and an imagined future. (Bryon, 2012)

August 14, 2009

Two months after returning home, I have spent time working in the inner realm trying to recapture and comprehend the essence of the experience. As my journey into the inner world of energetic experience deepened, I began to sense that the energetic realm lay beyond what I have understood to be the archetypal regions, into a place where separation and form no longer exists. Some alchemists refer to this as the prima materia. The Cabalists call this the "veils of negative existence." Part of my motivation was a need to articulate in writing what I experienced in initiation in Peru, the other motivator being a strong longing to return to the state of conjunctio.

   As I spent more time in this energetic state, symbols, images, and even archetypes themselves began to feel superficial, and I sensed there was more. The concept of a continuum of the energetic collective emerged from this state, and I sensed that this might be a link to understanding what I had experienced. The conceptual construct of a continuum of an energetic collective includes the psychoidal realm and ranges from the subtle body into the land. The continuum I imagined exists at the essential energetic level where there is no form or separation. Intrapsychically, it intersects Jung's proposed continuum that ranges from instinct to archetype. The point of contact where the continuums intersect is experienced within the subtle body. The point where the continuums touch pierces the veil between the energetic collective and ordinary reality. My hunch is that what I am proposing is only a superficial description of something that is vast and beyond all human senses, and the energetic collective would not exist on a continuum at all—because it is not linear and exists beyond time and space.

As I continued to explore the realm of the energetic collective, trying to go deeper, this state of vision of light began to change, or rather, I began to change, and it began to feel like fire. As I attempted to write or describe what I was experiencing, I began to lose the sense of where I ended and where the energy began, and my words stopped making sense. I sensed that my ego was beginning to decompensate. I began to feel I was losing myself—becoming consumed in the fire. It was very frightening and disorienting. I stopped writing and struggled to find my footing in this world again. I sat with the medicine bundle of my misa *and went to see my acupuncturist who put needles in my feet. I tried to feel my body and to remember mundane things like what I had for dinner the night before. I began to wonder if I would go crazy and not find my way back.*

As I tried to talk to people close to me, I realized that my speech was becoming too tangential. I could see the concern in their eyes, and I knew that intuitive leaps I was making in my thinking were creating gaps that were becoming too great for anyone to follow closely. The fire of the light became increasingly uncomfortable, and I found it becoming harder to disengage. So, I stopped. When I visited my analyst, Jeffrey Raff, he told me that I needed to "will" myself back from the other world and close the door to the veil of the other world for the time being—to shield my ego and sense of identity. He said that I was in the chaos of the prima materia and that I needed protection.

Although I had spent pages writing about the function of the land in Peruvian shamanism, what I had been writing about, trying to explain finally began to made sense to me experientially, and I began to embody the understanding. Edinger (1985) has written about coagulating spirit into matter in, "The Anatomy of the Psyche." I felt that the land and the shaman's misa *serve as the ego's shelter, a way of anchoring the energetic experience. In connection with the energetic collective, the shaman is the doorway that the electrical current runs through, and without a way of grounding the experience, they would be burned up, in the fire of the divine. For the shaman who is working with the energetic collective, the land is essential and the Great Mother, the temenos holds the energy. It is the protection against chaos and madness.*

It was then that the purpose of archetypes and symbols began to make sense, and I began to understand their necessity. Among other things, the images and symbols function as the ego's protection against the chaos of the prima materia. In re-entry, the symbolic image becomes the philosopher's stone, the way to come back with meaning. It is the buffer and the insulator—the psyche's way of coagulating energetic experience. In supervision conversations, Nathan Schwartz Salant told me that coming back from the other realms was literally a birthing process. In "The Imaginary Twin," *Bion (1950) has described the process of splitting as the mechanism that allows the formation of symbols to occur.*

I started looking for ways to ground myself using my thinking function as a means of separation from the actual energetic experience. I began looking for answers by revisiting psychoanalytic theory, reading material that previously had not seemed to me to be of relevant interest. I started to notice a tie between the development process in early object relation and my own re-entry experience. I began to wonder if the shaman's connection of the land through the subtle body, provided a temenos, or container, that helped to facilitate the ego's process of separating from the energetic collective—similar to what happens during infancy when the ego separates from the symbiotic relationship with the mother and forms as a separate identity.

Sadly, I realize that I do not live in a culture that supports these kinds of experiences and know that I must find a way to return to and connect with the land. If I were living in Peru, I would have the support of my village, my allyu. *Other shamans would understand and help me create* despachos *or fire offerings for* Pachamama, *the Great Mother. I am thankful for the mentors I have had that have helped me in this writing project, but I realize, that I feel very, very alone. In our extraverted culture, those of us who have these kinds of experiences often become introverted—spending time in solitude. I realize I must turn to my inner figures or* allyus *to digest and metabolize what has happened.* (Bryon, 2012)

The intense separation experience that happens during re-assimilating into one's life and collective culture after a mystical encounter is painful. There can be an unexpected grief reaction of feeling like an outsider—alone, disoriented, and a little "crazy." While all of this is uncomfortable, the worst part of the experience—by far—is feeling cut off from the incredible connection of being in oneness, longing to return, and living with the fear of never being able to find a way back.

Personal Narrative of Re-Entry Experience at Three Months

Three months after returning I found myself continuing to process my inner experience of where I had been, and noticed changes in my relationships with my children, partner and peers. I became increasingly aware of a greater focus toward the inner world and intensity in the need to connect with the energetic collective. At one point my son said, "Mom, you have been crazy since you came back from Peru." I realized that I was different. Similar to what I frequently hear people in the midst of a depression say when they think they are still functioning well, I was surprised. I had thought I had been containing the inner turmoil I was experiencing in my attempt to return to "civilian" life. A couple of months after my return, a couple clients commented that I seemed different since I "came off the mountain." I heard my analytic training supervisors comment that I seem more grounded. In professional settings with colleagues, I find that I tend to censor my thoughts less and say what is on my mind. Some people seemed drawn to this while others seemed put off by it.

Personal relationships during this phase of re-entry became difficult. During this period, I noticed that I was receiving more attention from peers—to a point. I sensed an attraction on their part to the energy that I brought back with me after my encounter with the energetic collective that perhaps they couldn't quite identify. Yet I found that these same colleagues had difficulty tolerating a sustained connection. As I looked into the eyes of my peers, I could clearly see that they were not relating at all to what I was saying even though they were trying. I wondered about what felt like a desperate need to be understood and to experience a sense of connection at a "soulful" level. I saw that I frightened them, or perhaps facing their own potential dismemberment became threatening. I mused to myself that this was because it was easier to talk about shamanic experience rather than to be in the experience.

At the time, I questioned what it was in me that felt compelled to share my experience. I wondered if I had a narcissistic need to be seen as a mystic or as one who "speaks with" the spirits. I thought back on the sequence of events that had occurred in my life after returning from Peru. In an attempt to reintegrate myself back into my life, I "downloaded" the experience into writing. I wrote solidly for six weeks and completed my required thesis project for analytic training, that (according to the training manual) was supposed to take a couple of years. At the time, I felt I had no choice but I needed some place to put the energy of the experience. Because I neglected to follow proper training protocol, a couple of my peers commented that my behavior had appeared entitled. What right did I have to finish something when everyone else had been required to dedicate more time? Why did I think I was different? I wondered if this might be true—yet I also understood that my creative endeavor was an attempt to separate from the experience by describing it. I heard myself saying, "This isn't about me." I tried to explain that I did not think I was different and that this was not about me—it was about the experience. As I reflected upon it later, I realized that I was inflated with the archetypal energy. It felt as though I had been "along for the ride," being dragged along by a momentum of energy that was bigger than I was. (Bryon, 2012)

July 30, 2009

A part of me wanted to communicate what I had experienced and was experiencing in an attempt to re-ground myself. I struggled to find language to describe what had happened to me, yet I felt self-conscious. I felt "crazy" and was sure colleagues would say I was delusional if they knew what was going on in my mind. Perhaps I was paranoid. I know I was scared. Saying that I had experienced spirits flying through the walls and coming up through the floor—and speaking seemed over the top. I remained silent and tried to "pass."

I spent days reading what others had written about their experiences in nonordinary reality, and wrote pages and pages myself, trying desperately to understand what had happened. I diagnosed myself as schizoid and read object relations theory written by analysts such as Fairbairn (1952) and Guntrip (1970). The early primitive states they were describing—accompanied with the need to be encapsulated in a bubble—fit my experience. Even if it was a "severe diagnosis," being able to label myself was comforting—because the part of me that was doing the diagnosing was outside of the experience. At least part of me was acting like a psychologist—even if the rest of me felt crazy.

I read Thomas Ogden's (1989) work on the "autistic contiguous position." Ogden has described psychological states that occur in infancy, during which everything is processed as sensory experience—before an actual awareness of discreet physical form exists. The analytical part of me understood that a part of me had "regressed" in reaction to the intense energetic experience. It felt as though part of me had "tapped" into a time in my psychological development before I had words. I kept reading. (Bryon, 2012, p. 191)

The Re-Entry Adjustment Over Time

A year later, I returned to the Andes to work with the paqos and underwent another initiation ceremony and another encounter with nonordinary reality. This experience and re-entry process was less difficult, which I attribute to two factors. After going through the initial re-entry process, I discovered that I would be able to return to being in a state of connection with the *apus* and the energetic collective, which was incredibly comforting, and I no longer was feeling the loss of abandonment. In addition, I had survived the initial re-entry process and was more familiar with the process. The influx of energy was less overwhelming, perhaps because my capacity to hold the energy in my *manos wasi* had increased.

The last entries (Bryon, 2012) were made the following year, in 2010, when I had returned to the Andes and was with the paqos on the holy mountain of Ausangate.

June 16, 2010

Sitting cross-legged in the moonlight at the base of the great mountain of Ausangate in my state of vision, I saw a wormhole of light, and sensed the presence of the Birdman, who instructed me to stay focused on the light. As had

Figure 7.3 Wings - Painting by the Author. Merging with the *apu* "winged beings" symbolized by gestural white brush strokes creating the feathers of an outline of a bird, with a bright golden egg shape interior, against a dark background.

occurred in my dream a year before, indiscernible dark objects were flying past me at rapid speeds. I focused my intent toward staying connected with the light. Staying focused on the light required concentrated intention, to avoid becoming distracted by what was quickly moving by me. I sensed that I was being given some kind of test.

As this vision process continued, I felt myself merging with the Birdman. Then I became a bird. As I soared effortlessly high in the sky, I became aware of extending talons where hands had been. I felt an incredible freedom of movement in stretching them. Almost automatically, I experienced swooping down and grabbing a small animal that I carried off with me. With my prey in my grasp, I aggressively flapped my wings, rising higher and higher into the moonlit sky.

Being someone who shies away from eating meat, the small part of me that was still human felt a bit horror-struck at what I sensed was to become the fate of this small, innocent creature. Suddenly I found myself swiftly pulling the animal close to me, ripping into its flesh with my beak. I began to eat and devour it. I was surprised to discover that what I had previously considered an aggressive instinctual act had an element of tenderness that felt extremely intimate.

Figure 7.4 Ausangate - Painting by the Author. An abstract painting of shades of white and blue created through gestural brush strokes, conveying a sense of energetic movement.

I felt deep affection toward the prey I was eating—sensing we were one in the same—an integral part of nature.

Then out of nowhere from the dark sky above, a great Condor appeared abruptly. It dipped down, swiftly snatched me up, and began devouring me. The great bird consumed my heart, and then my intestines. Strangely, this act also felt very loving to me. I experienced being held and cared for. A moment before I was being eaten, I had been eating—and loving my prey, holding it close to what had been my heart. I heard the soothing voice of the Birdman telling me that I had entered his realm and that my heart and stomach as they had existed were gone. The Condor started packing these areas of my body with light. I felt the presence of the light living inside of me.

Then the vision shifted. I heard Ausangate's commanding voice calling me "mejo" as I had heard in the past. I looked down and saw that I had the arms of a young adult or adolescent male. My upper torso was bare except for decorated armbands, a neck ornament, and a headdress I was wearing that was made up with feathers. My skin was dark. I looked up and saw a great, intimidating, and magnificent figure standing in front of me, who was also wearing an ornamental headdress made of brightly colored feathers and gold, on a scale much grander than the one I was wearing. I was humbled and awed in his presence. He was so tall that I could barely see his face, which was both the face of a bird and the face of a man. The figure instructed me to continue to reach and direct my gaze higher. I attempted to reach my vision to meet his eyes, which was at a height far beyond what I could see.

In that moment, I realized that I was in the midst of a ceremony—and in the process of being sacrificed. I was not afraid. Somehow, I knew that this was a great honor and act of divine love. I fell into a state of ecstasy, surrendering into a sacred communion. At some point, I became aware that I was standing on a raised platform, in midday sunlight, in front of a mass of hundreds of people. My hands were extended out to them, and I was speaking. I knew intuitively that these were my people, and that I was in some leadership role of knowing and trying to convey a message. I did not understand the words I was speaking.

The vision shifted and my body became altered again, to what felt like to me to be the image of a wise old woman. I was experiencing myself as her, within her body. Then the vision changed again, and I was walking upstairs of light, made of light. I knew that I needed to trust that somehow, I would be held—even though I appeared to be literally walking on air. I agreed that I would sacrifice everything to the light. Then I was walking through fire. I kept looking up—higher and higher and I felt my personal self dropping away. Staying in open relationship with the light required concentrated intent on my part. I felt myself continually stretching, constantly reaching for, and moving toward the light. As I moved higher, I was aware that I was losing my identity and sense of self, yet somehow, I maintained my focus—I became the focus. (Bryon, 2012)

August 2, 2009

While sitting on top of the mountain. I experienced the intense white light of the energetic collective running through my body as an intense electrical current. I saw the energy emanating from the mountain range in front of me as I felt it pulsing through me. Over time, the vibrant light shifted into an energetic outline of a bird.

Later, as I reflected on the experience, the bird became the anchor in my mind of what I had experienced. After I returned home, I painted the bird that I then saw in my mind's eye. In my dreams, I accessed the energetic state through the bird image. The bird images appeared to me in a state of receptivity.

I found myself painting images of "worm holes" into a vibrant white light. Sometimes the faint outline or gesture of a bird would enter the imagery on the canvas. I painted the picture I held in my mind of what I had experienced on the mountain over and over again, attempting to find a way of conveying the profound experience representationally. I also wrote about the experience—the original draft was the beginning of what I am writing now.

Figure 7.5 Wormhole - Painting by the Author. An abstract painting with white gestural brush strokes extending outward against a black background, creating a sense of movement, with semi-symmetrical interior detail indicating two small, circular openings.

… Each night in my dreams I returned to the mountain, and once again became immersed in the vibrant light that now felt like home to me—and to my soul. I felt the momentum of the energy as a forceful drive that needed to be expressed and given form in this world.

The length of time we carry the charge of the afterglow of numinous experience in our luminous body depends on our willingness to engage with our vision of the experience and to keep it alive in our Mind—and Heart. At deep levels of profound energetic collective experience, a faint thread of conscious awareness is held by being with the feeling. Following the feeling of energetic experience is the only means of connecting with the experience at a pre-conscious level. This is because these states exist at a preverbal and pre-image level—and feeling states are the only channel available to us at deeper levels. Once an energetic experience can be felt, it can be recapitulated—and processed. (Bryon, 2012)

I am aware that I would have still been able to access the energy of the experience even if had not "morphed" into a bird, but the bird image added dimensionality to the memory of my vision experience.

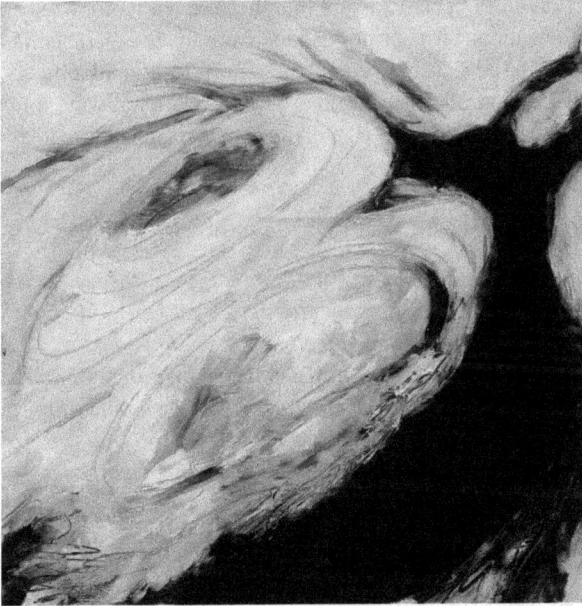

Figure 7.6 Flight - Painting by the Author. A black and white abstract painting of the winged body of a bird in flight.

August 21, 2009

After returning home, I repeatedly dreamt of snakes. I had dreams of snakes lying by my feet at my computer as I wrote and of carrying them around in my pockets. Snakes became my companions in the inner world. In one of my dreams, a powerful snake split the floor open beneath me. In another dream, I was taking energy from a large snake in the other world and giving it to baby snakes in this world that lived in caves. The snake dreams I experienced provided my psyche with a metaphor for working with and assimilating the powerful energy of Amaru *associated with the numinous experience.*

I had the following dream: I was standing up somewhat precariously on a platform where there were multiple caves forming a dirt wall that were housing for snakes. To the left, in a realm that I can feel but not see, I sense the presence of a giant snake. I was asking the snake to help provide the energy that would bring the snakes back so that they could live in their houses. I know it is my job to help it by bringing its energy into "ordinary reality" to feed the baby snakes. There are small caves/cubbies of dirt stacked against a wall and I am on a table reaching to put the energy in the caves for the snakes. I saw a small snake peering out of one of the caves. I knew it was being timid in approaching me because it knew I was still afraid of snakes, and it did not want to scare me.
(Bryon, 2012)

As I worked with the dream, I became aware that these caves symbolized transitional spaces to house the energy I was bringing back from the *energetic collective*. Snakes, being creatures of the earth, became the transformational objects that would coagulate the expression of spirit into matter in a relational way, implying connection. The caves helped provide the organizing schemata necessary to assimilate the energy.

November 8, 2009

I dreamt the shaman saw me and knew I was coming back to work with him and I saw him acknowledging that he saw me and I saw him. The night after I dreamt I saw the shaman again, I started feeling a burning and a lot of energy. I could taste the energy. Although at times it felt empowering, I can't say it was comfortable ... it was somewhat disorienting. In my own analytic process, I had worked with the energy as movement toward a deeper relationship with the snake. I went to a weekend training class, still feeling like I was on fire. I spoke in the class and realized people were having difficulty tracking my "intuitive leap," so I decided to be quiet and started drawing snakes on my notepad to contain the energy. While I was doing that, I looked over to the left on the page—an inch from where my pen was—and noticed a worm that was moving. I was stunned. I was in Denver, in freezing weather, and had not bought fruit ... so I wasn't sure where the worm came from ... especially since it hadn't been on the page before. It had a small greenish, white body and a black head ... The fire continued, and I felt pretty disoriented. (Bryon, 2012)

The following excerpt was written six years later, after a serious, life-threatening car accident. The paqos and I were on our way (in separate cars) to Utah to meet a group for a workshop on Andean medicine. That day, prior to leaving Denver, Adolfo had warned that in our car ride we were entering into a potentially dangerous situation that we needed to be mindful of and call upon the *apus* for protection.

October 26, 2015

Next week will be one year since I survived a near fatal accident when the car I was a passenger in, slammed into the back of a semi on an interstate freeway. In addition to other bodily injuries as the result of the impact, a five-gallon bottle of apple juice flew from the back seat into the front window and shattered, before hitting me in my head slightly above my left eye. I must have had my eyes closed because I didn't see anything. I remembered thinking upon impact about past descriptions I had read on traumatic brain injuries that occurred when the frontal lobe of the brain hit the inside of the skull and then bounced back to the posterior area of the skull. I assumed that was happening—I wasn't aware of the flying apple juice bottle at the time.

Figure 7.7 Self Portrait - Painting by the Author. An abstract painting of a woman with a black eye.

I retained consciousness and climbed out of the car despite a cracked sternum, a broken ankle and a sprained ankle and a large gash over my eye. I remember not feeling any pain but experiencing a black cloak of fog descending over my head that dropped down to my nose, and I was trying to see underneath. My husband helped me out of the car and told me that the iris of my right eye (that is normally hazel green) had turned light blue (I moved into a full-blown trauma response).

Soon after I remember "helping" the paramedic that had arrived, perform a mental status exam on myself and informing him, I had no loss of consciousness. I also remember asking everyone within hearing distance to help me find a rental car so that we could continue to Utah to facilitate the workshop with the Andean medicine people that had been planned for over a year. Then the ambulance came.

After arriving at the hospital, the ER doctor convinced me to spend the night in the hospital after sternly explaining that leaving with a cracked sternum could be fatal. After getting a wheelchair and a cast I forged ahead to Utah the next day. I was going come hell or high water (still actively in my trauma reaction). Close friends expressed concern about my refusal to rest in bed. After completing the workshop, I ended up with bronchitis. Coughing with a cracked sternum was incredibly painful and I finally agreed to spend a couple of days resting.

This accident occurred six weeks before a painting show that I had not started preparing for. A series of self-portraits became the overarching theme. Prior to the accident I had decided to paint on a larger scale, which proved to be a little awkward. These paintings (Figures 7.7, 7.8 and 7.9) are from this body of work.

Figure 7.8 Dissociation - Painting by the Author. An abstract painting of two separate heads of a woman with black eyes, one at the bottom of the canvas and the other upside down at the top, with colorful, gestural brushstrokes in between.

Figure 7.9 Transcendence – Painting by the Author. A gestural painting of a large elephant against a colorful abstract background of red, green, and blue indicating water or land, at dusk.

People that I respect continued to suggest that I really hadn't processed the trauma—I hadn't. I recognized the fight verses flight trauma response behavior in my insistence to attempt to facilitate the ten-day workshop for 40 people. I found myself wading through layers of psychological grief until I became conscious of the somatic experience in my body. I re-experienced the pain in my nose that felt like it had been broken and remembered the pain of chipping all my front teeth, that had since been repaired. Moving into the core of the somatic memory felt grounding and brought a sense of relief. (Bryon, 2012)

Six months later, during a Reiki session, I remembered being outside of my body (up to the left) and seeing a circle of light beings, perhaps angels, surrounding me. Now looking back, I found it curious that I did not remember this aspect of the event until I remembered the experience in my body. I'd been struggling with writing about nontemporal reality for a couple of years now, and now having two sets of memories of the same event has added fuel to the fire. Is it possible to split and have two sets of memories for the same event? (Bryon, 2012)

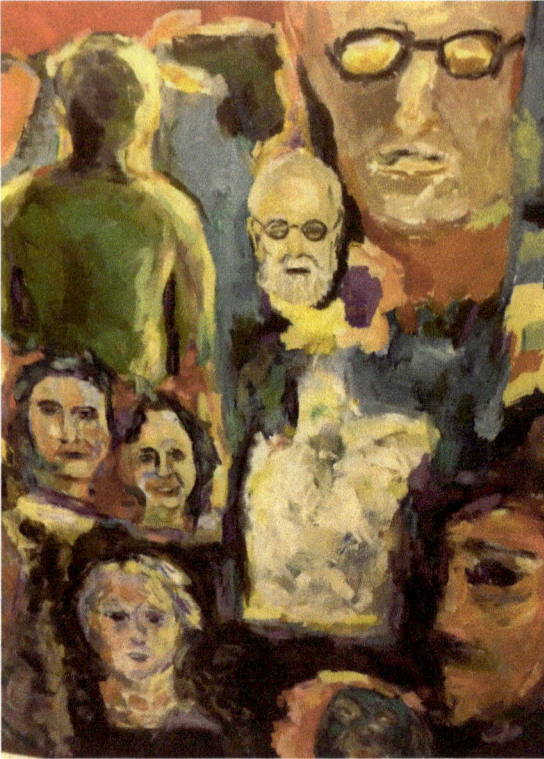

Figure 7.10 Ancestors - Painting by the Author. A colorful grouping of the heads of different people in different sizes combined with the outline a larger greenish figure.

While reviewing the experience, now 14 years later, I learned about supersymmetry theory in physics, which is discussed in Chapter 9. Supersymmetry theory states that all particles have undiscovered pairs, and that as energy increases the distinction between matter and force disappears.[5] At the University of Queensland, Dr. Stefan Forstner has described the phenomenon of quantum superposition as, "the quantum effect where particles exist concurrently in multiple places."[6] In addition, while writing this book (April 2023), I came across *The Big Book of Near-Death Experiences* by P. M. H. Atwater (2007) who has conducted research since the 1950s, investigating the accounts of more than 3,000 adults. I realize that what I experienced after my car accident coincides with her description of near-death experience (NDE). At the time, in my trauma state, I didn't realize how serious my condition was. I remember after arriving in Utah, Adolfo performed a soul retrieval ceremony on me and instructed me to rest.

Atwater (2007) has written:

In those scenarios in which the near death or near death-like experiencer had an out-of- body episode, those I spoke with said they first viewed their body from a point directly above or from a top corner of the room. Many claimed that after vacating their body, they "floated" elsewhere in a bodiless state. Initially, though, the main "staging area" was the left side of the room, especially the upper left corner... (p. 46) .... I found myself in a different place ... it was a different dimension than what we know in the physical. Things were not concrete and fixed, but somehow "fluid" yet not liquid. I conversed with a group of people there. They did not have physical bodies but were more of an energy that was iridescent. I had no fear. There was a sense of peace, almost as if I was dreaming, but I wasn't dreaming ... The experience was not of this world, so to explain it in regard to this world cannot be done. (Atwater, 2007, pp. 74–5)

Quoting Melvin Morse, MD (1990), from his book *Closer to the Light: Learning from children's near-death experiences*, Atwater (2007) continues:

The near-death component cannot be explained by research ... The light is the key aspect of the experience—the transforming element that originates outside of our bodies. It is, claims Dr. Morse, identical to the light experienced, spoken of, and written about by mystics. (Atwater, 2007, pp. 74–5)

Atwater (2007) and Morse and Perry's (1990) descriptions resonated with my own experiences. Atwater (2007, p. 104) also wrote, "The experience is then usually, but not always forgotten, to be remembered later when some signal triggers its memory," which for me was the Reiki session.

String theory emphasizes the behavioral properties of the particles of the strings and can be applied to higher dimensions with the implication that all known particles have undiscovered pairs. The idea that there are undiscovered pairs for the particles is something called supersymmetry, and it applies to superstring theory only: it says that matter and force are in a sense the same. As energies are increased, or distances reduced, the distinction between matter and force disappears.[7]

Notes

1   Collective Mountain spirits in the Andes, sometimes referred to as "the winged beings."
2   J. Raff, personal communication (2008).
3   Don Juan's description of the Eagle has been interpreted as being a symbol for the Self, a representation of the numinous. Within the context of ordinary reality, it is easier to understand Castaneda's description of the spirit of the eagle in his writing as a symbolic metaphor for mystical experience.
4   Over the last 14 years during my return visits to Peru, sitting in ceremonies with *altomesayoqs* I have heard flapping wings and the voices of the *apus*, the winged beings, or

collective mountain spirits, and have heard the paqos on multiple occasions enter into dialogues with them. The conversations have often involved being given direction about an upcoming mountain pilgrimage or answering questions regarding one's spiritual path. I have also experienced being touched on my head, shoulders, and back by what felt to be massive wings flapping against me during a healing ceremony. Since I can find no other explanation than this is a physical manifestation of the *apus* from an atemporal dimension, I have placed trying to understand how these experiences are happening on the shelf since they do not fit with consensual reality.

5   Conversation with Dean Rickles, April 14, 2023.
6   https://www.uq.edu.au/news/article/2020/10/need-be-two-places-once-it-may-be-possi ble#:~:text=Quantum%20physics%20has%20demonstrated%20that,also%20exist%20 in%20multiple%20places.
7   Conversation with Dean Rickles, April 14, 2023.

References

Atwater, P. M. H. (2007) *The Big Book of Near-Death Experiences*, Virginia Beach, VA: Rainbow Ridge Books LLC.

Bion, W. R. (1950) 'The imaginary twin'. In *Second Thoughts*, London: Maresfield Library.

Bryon, D. (2012) *Lessons of the Inca Shamans, Part I: Piercing the veil*, Enumclaw, WA: Pine Winds Press.

Castaneda, C. (1984) *The Fire from Within*, New York, NY: Pocket Books.

Castaneda, C. (1998) *The Wheel of Time*, New York, NY: Simon and Schuster.

Fairbairn, W.R.D. (1952) *An object relations theory of psychoanalysis,* New York: Basic Books.

Guntrip, H. (1970) In M. Brierley, 'Schizoid Phenomena, Object Relations and the Self' London: Hogarth Press and Institute of Psycho-Analysis. 1968. Pp. 437. International Journal of Psychoanalysis 51:540-546.

Morse, M. (with Paul Perry) (1990) *Closer to the Light: Learning from children's near-death experiences*, New York, NY: Villard Books.

Ogden, T. H. (1989) *The Primitive Edge of Experience*, Abingdon, Oxfordshire: Routledge.

Raff, J. (1997) 'The felt vision', in D. F. Sander and S. H. Wong (eds) *The Sacred Heritage: The influence of shamanism on analytical psychology*, New York, NY: Routledge, pp. 79–90.

Raff, J. (2000) *Alchemical Imagination*, Berwick, ME: Nicolas-Hays.

Raff, J. (2008) personal communication.

Rickles, D. (2023) personal communication, April 14.

Chapter 8

Making Sense of the Re-Entry Experience

The Aftermath

Initially, this writing was an effort to try to find a way of explaining the experience, and hopefully to convey to others what this was like. In addition to feeling disoriented by the atemporal experience I could not explain, emotionally I felt an incredible sense of loss coupled with a longing to return to the state of oneness (Bryon, 2012). Ulanov, (2017, p. 23) has written, "Touching the psychoid realm can feel like losing your mind as well as being ushered into bounty, amplitude, full measure, solidity, that no matter how great the damage through trauma these unconscious processes go on, there to be accessed, and people do access them and know joy and gratitude."

Now, years later after re-integrating back into my life, and shifting between atemporal and temporal states multiple times over the years in my work with the paqos and in my own meditation practices, my purpose of including the material on my conceptualization during the initial re-entry process is to add another layer of understanding from a personal perspective. Most of this chapter was written while still close to the "afterglow" of the energetic experience. Since this initial encounter, I have wrestled with understanding atemporality, the primary motivator in writing this book.

After my return, besides reading the writings of Carlos Castaneda, I read about alchemy, the Qabalah, and what Jungians with an archetypal orientation had to say, to try to find some sort of road map that would help me to navigate the re-entry experience.

Ulanov has written:

We may abhor the psychoid as undoing of inner structures we rely on, fraying boundaries we need for definition of self and the world, mixing up time senses, space senses, and other senses we have carefully differentiated to discover a self-sense. Instead, touching the psychoid can make us feel we enter not a unified reality but boundlessness itself ... In addition, the psychoid dimension moves us out of cultural assumptions, motifs we have relied on ... We succumb to the dread of cultural disintegration. (Ulanov, 2017, p. 55)

DOI: 10.4324/9781003356448-11

Initially, the re-entry process after returning from states of ecstasy was disorienting. The following chapter will present alchemical and psychoanalytic theory, as well as different psychoanalytic perspectives that I explored that seemed to relate to mystical and re-entry experience. My conceptualization of re-entry while I was actively in the process went in three different directions—diagnosis, metaphors in contemporary culture, and alchemy and depth psychology.

Because the experiences did not fit with my understanding of consensual reality, as a psychologist, and psychoanalyst in training who had spent a couple of years working in psychiatric hospitals, I often resorted to seeing myself through a diagnostic lens. Most likely, this was a defensive reaction I was using to try to separate myself from the experience using an orientation based in psychoanalytic theory—an attempt to make sense of what was happening to me, using a "skill set" I was familiar with. Diagnosing myself from the perspective of a clinician was my way of distancing myself from what felt delusional. By acknowledging that these experiences did not comply with consensual reality—and that others were not seeing the world the way I was—provided me with a way of orienting with "the real world," and offered a sense of sanity.

I eventually shifted away from a diagnostic lens. I found metaphors in contemporary culture that helped to "humanize" my reaction to the experiences, adding some levity and compassion. It was comforting to find examples and stories from others who had a similar emotional response. It helped me to normalize the experience and feel less alienated.

I also drew from my Jungian orientation and explored concepts in mysticism and alchemy searching for explanations. Alchemy is primarily process oriented, as a method that focuses on explaining how material shifts from one state to another. It was useful discovering parallel processes moving from spirit to matter that seemed applicable. I am very grateful for the support and guidance I received from my Jungian analysts, Nathan Schwartz-Salant and Jeffrey Raff, who had some understanding of what I was going through and helped me to feel not so alone.

Now, years later, I have discovered that the atemporal phenomenon I experienced seems to align with the "blurring experiences" described in quantum physics outlined in Chapter 9, moving from atemporal to temporal states. Describing blurring, the physicist Carlo Rovelli has written:

> Time determined by macroscopic states having to do with the quantum indeterminacy[1] (i.e., lack of specificity) of things produces a blurring … which insures—contrary to what classic physics seems to indicate—that the unpredictability of the world is maintained even if it were possible to measure everything that is measurable … Temporality is profoundly linked to blurring. The blurring is due to the fact that we are ignorant of the microscopic details of the world. The time of physics is, ultimately, the expression of our ignorance of the world.
> (Rovelli, 2019, p. 123)

During my initial re-entry process, I was unaware of the theories of quantum physics, which would have been useful in explaining the experiences from a scientific perspective. Having a viewpoint grounded in sciences would have offered credibility. Perhaps I would not have relied so heavily on my diagnostic lens as a psychologist. I have heard people say that we use the tools available in our toolbox—meaning we use the concepts we are familiar with in formulating our understanding. While most of the text in this chapter was written while I was immersed in the re-entry experience, I have added reflections from my current perspective, as I now have a different vantage point that feels more integrated.

Loss of Connection and the Longing to Return

In *Hero with a Thousand Faces*, Joseph Campbell (2008) has explored the problem of re-entry and cites numerous stories and myths to illustrate the point. He has also raised the issue of not wanting to come back. In extreme cases, the intensity of the desire to return to a state of connection can become so overpowering that it develops into a compulsion, like Richard Dreyfus's character's reaction in the film *Encounters of the Third Kind*, directed by Steven Spielberg in 1977, after a numinous experience with aliens.

Atwater (2007, p. 105) has written that after one has experienced being one with the universe, that becomes the primary focus. After a numinous encounter, the experience of one's "personal" life in temporal reality may seem bland compared to the intensity of numinous connection with the *energetic collective*. What is often missing after such an experience is a channel that allows an active exchange or dialogue with the *energetic collective* to continue. This potentially helps to alleviate extreme feelings of loss of connection. Establishing an "energetic link" takes time, and often doesn't happen during the first re-entry experience. My experience is that it takes multiple times of going through re-entry to maintain an ongoing sense of connection when there is familiarity with the process and an understanding that one can return to that state of connection. Ultimately this comes from knowing that one can find their way back.

Alain Connes,[2] the physicist who studies noncommutativity, wrote a science-fiction story about a woman who had the experience of seeing the world without blurring. He has written in her words: "(I) have had the unheard of good fortune of experiencing a global vision of my being—not of a particular moment, but of my existence 'as a whole'. And then open returning to time, I had the impression of losing all the infinite information generated by the quantum scene, and this loss was sufficient to drag me irresistibly into the river of time …This re-emergence of time seemed to me like an intrusion, a source of mental confusion, anguish, fear, and alienation."

Atwater (2007, p. 113) has written that "it takes the average person at least seven years to adjust to the aftereffects—some much longer." Frustration is frequently felt after experiencing a deeply moving event that one does not have words for.

According to Castaneda (1984), "No one remembers anything while in a state of heightened awareness" (p. 10). The inability to put something into words often happens after having a profound religious experience, in a state of ecstasy. During the re-entry process, one often has the awareness of forgetting something important and experiences loss as a result. There is often the feeling of loss of connection— and awareness. This is due to intuitively remembering having the embodied experience of being a part of all things, followed by the experience of only being connected to what exists in the isolated bubble of what is accessible in temporality. The configurations of the "bubble" in temporality create limitations that form the contextual patterns of how we can access the world.

Carlos Castaneda's (1984) description of his own atemporal experience coincides with Rovelli's (2019) explanation of blurring, when a shift is made from atemporality into temporality and information is lost. The concept of blurring in physics occurs when a shift is made from atemporal to temporal states as described in Chapter 9 and re-entry after profound shamanic experience.

The richness of our perception on the left side was a post-facto realization. Our interaction appeared to be rich in the light of our capacity to remember it. We became cognizant then that in these states of heightened awareness we had perceived everything in one big clump, one bulky mass of inextricable detail. We called this ability to perceive everything at once intensity. For years, we had found it impossible to examine the separate constituent parts of these chunks of experience; we had been unable to synthesize those parts into a sequence that would make sense to the intellect. Since we were incapable of those syntheses, we could not remember. Our capacity to remember was in reality, incapacity to put the memory of our perception on a linear basis. We could not lay our experiences flat, so to speak and arrange them in a sequential order. The experiences were available to us, but at the same time, they were impossible to retrieve, for they were blocked by a wall of intensity. The task of remembering, then, was properly the task of joining our left and right sides, of reconciling these two distinct forms of perception into a unified whole. It was the task of consolidating the totality of oneself by rearranging intensity into a linear sequence. (Castaneda, 1981, p. 170)

The information cannot be retrieved cognitively because thinking about something requires being separate from it. Ulanov (2017, p. 56) has written, "What we relied on to guide us—our ethical standard, our confidence in our own perception, our spiritual maxim connected to truth, what Jung called … our ruling principle is here completely useless."

The experience can only be accessed through what paqos refer to as the *manos wasi,* which initially occurs somatically. The linear sequence, or narrative happens after the energetic experience is assimilated somatically.

The Loss of a Familiar Orientation during Re-Entry

Re-acclimating to daily life and routine is challenging after having a mystical experience because one feels fundamentally changed and sees the world differently in ways that seem unexplainable. After an influx of energy, sensations are more intense and acute, so it is hard to step out of the experience to find a vantage point.

In *Letters to a Young Poet*, Rilke has written:

Because we are alone; because we stand in the middle of a transition where we cannot remain standing with the new thing that has entered our self, because everything intimate and accustomed has for an instant been taken away. (Rilke, 2002, p. 64)

Von Franz has said that when material crosses the threshold into the unconscious it "becomes altered in its quality and when it comes back into consciousness it becomes altered again" (1992, p. 58). In science-fiction films there are many examples of this phenomenon. In *The Fly*[3] a scientist who enters a different realm upon returning begins to metamorphose into a fly, after transporting a fly back with him in a fused state. Rip Van Winkle, a short story written by Washington Irving (1819-1820)[4] struggled after being asleep for twenty years, coming back to find a world that he no longer recognized. It can feel disorienting when what felt true is no longer true. Returning and trying to adjust to daily living after intense atemporal energetic connection demands flexibility and a willingness to drop assumptions and preconceived notions that may not seem congruent with how we understand nonordinary reality.

Castaneda said, "When a man learns to see not a single thing he knows prevails. Not a single one ... Once we see nothing is known; nothing remains as we used to know it when we didn't see" (1971, p. 235).

There are many stories of time travelers who re-enter into the atmosphere and land in a different time and place. After having a numinous experience with the other realm, the longing for reconnection can become a raison d'être or driving force. Stepping outside of the limits of our personal narrative regarding consensual reality changes the ways in which we interact with the world, and it can be quite unsettling. In experiencing a longing to return to an alchemical state of *conjunctio* after a numinous experience, there is often a sense of frustration associated with the re-entry process of "coming back."

The stories that emerge after energetic encounters may be a way of confirming the experience with the unknown. Trying to put these experiences into words is an attempt to extract the real value from the experience by putting it into a framework that we can understand. Paqos believe that true essence of experiences cannot be described in words. I was forced to learn that trying to focus on "working through" the personal narrative simply did not work. Like Hercules attempting to clean out the stables on Mount Olympus, it felt impossible because there was too much to try to assimilate. Instead, I learned to "shift," or change channels of perception so that I could experience the *energetic* realm, by shifting out of my personal narrative (Bryon, 2012).

It is impossible to describe what the experience was like to others because there are no words for it in the English language. The experience of re-entry may feel like trying to communicate with a language barrier in a foreign county or shifting from *seeing* in color to seeing in black and white, while retaining the memory of what it was like to see in color. For the person returning, trying to communicate to others can be incredibly lonely because the tools needed to describe the experience are lacking. Trying to explain to others what seeing in color was like can seem impossible—especially if there is no context or common representation for the experience. The Quechua language has words that reference these states that I have included in Chapter 5. Even so, they are descriptors that are useful in communicating among people who have shared a similar experience—they aren't the experience itself.

Intense encounters with the energetic collective can be both jarring and transformative. Often people are left with the feeling that they have no way to integrate the experience into their existing frame of reference. Some people do not return to their "day jobs." For other people who have become overly identified with their personas and the way they present to the world, they may swing the opposite

Figure 8.1 Re-Entry - Painting by the Author. An abstract painting of colorful brush strokes emanating from a yellowish white circular center.

way and experience a regressive restoration of the persona (Jung, 1953a), trying to revert to how they were before. This results in shutting out the experience to return to what had seemed to be normal, choosing to negate and dismiss the numinous experience. These reactions are often coupled with a disconnection from feelings and rigid thinking.

An Understanding of Re-Entry from an Alchemical and Depth Psychology Perspective

In his later years, Jung wondered whether he was dreaming the dream or if the dream was dreaming him. The question becomes, are we assimilating the numinous experience back into a context of ordinary reality—or are we transforming the experience of ourselves, while the experience remains constant? My hunch is that we are doing both. The *opus* or work of the alchemist was to transform *prima materia* into gold—and in the process of doing work the alchemist was also transformed. An alternate view would be that the experience of the *energetic collective* remains in the realm it occurs in and instead we shift between states. Could it be that the shift has nothing to do with "working through" or circumambulation? The experience is not linear and therefore not reductive. It feels more ephemeral in nature, unattainable, with a texture like fog that moves in and out of awareness. Although mystical experience is not transferred back into cognizance explicitly, the essential meaning is carried as memory in the form of an energetic imprint that becomes a defining filter in the way we see the world.

In *Myth and Reality*, Mircea Elaide has written about the ideal of the Taoists as a state of "primordial unity" (1963, p. 84). He wrote:

> *The aim is no longer to reiterate the cosmic creation; it is to recover the state that preceded the cosmology, the state of chaos. But the line of thought is the same: health and youth are obtained by a return to the origin, be it "a return to the womb" or a return to the cosmic Great-One. So, we may note the important fact that, in China too, sickness and old age are believed to be cured by "return to the origin."* (Eliade, 1963, p. 84)

Qabalists have referred to a state that resembles the shadow side of re-entry as the *qliploth*. In *A Practical Guide to Qabalistic Symbolism*, Gareth Knight has written that mystics view separation as an illusion and "evil," and the *qlipoth* is the denial of unity. Knight (1993) has said, "The only unity is in the Unmanifest" (p. 28). This happens in the atemporal, energetic realm. Moving into a *qlipoth* state occurs each time there is a leap to a higher level of consciousness, or vibrational frequency (a higher *sephiroth* or node), on the tree of life (the symbol for the soul of man and the universe), which Knight (1978, p. 25) has described as "emanations of the spirit of God or man in its progress from a noumenal existence (things we can never know) to its building a physical vehicle in the phenomenal world (the world we are aware of)."[5] These kinds of "energetic jumps" into a state of a higher vibrational frequency create a state of disequilibrium until they can be incorporated.

Knight (1978) has explained that if we could see the whole picture, we would understand that being born is like dying because we are leaving a state of connection and being thrust into a state of separation in assuming a physical body. He has written, "There are many people who look upon anything destructive as evil, but this may be because they take the short instead of the long view and consider any change as a threat to their security" (Knight, 1978, p. 131).

Edward Edinger (1972) has described a state of separation, of the ego's identification with the Self. He said that all experiences of alienation are ultimately alienation between the ego and the Self (p. 39). Whether one falls into the popular metaphysical trap of believing that the ego can manifest anything it desires or becomes inflated and over-identified with the energy of numinous experience, ultimately one eventually enters a death phase of *mortificatio*, an awareness of being separate. Edinger says that this is because it is impossible for the ego to recognize having a religious experience unless it ceases to be identified with it. After a blissful state of fusion, there is a sense of feeling the "death" of the loss of connection.

The Orphan's Journey and Separation from the Participation Mystique

Jung refers to the wounding that occurs in this transformation. "Look not upon me because I am black because the sun has scorched me" (Schwartz-Salant, 1989, p. 31). Jung writes that the "orphan" or lapis inherits the wealth of the rich widow and the "serpent's poison" (Schwartz-Salant, 1989, p. 31). Here, Jung is talking about receiving the "riches" of the inner world, while at the same time facing the inner demons of the shadow as one loses the protection of their persona, or social identity that has worked in the past. The Qabalists (Knight, 1978) would equate this to being burned by what lies beyond the veils of negative existence.

Jeffrey Raff Watanbe,[6] refers to the "orphan phase," as one of the necessary stages in the individuation process. Being an orphan usually brings about a sense of separation and isolation. This can be a painful process, which may initiate the beginning of a dismemberment cycle, or deconstruction of life as it has been.

In alchemy, re-entry can seem to correspond with being in a state of the *prima materia*, associated with chaos and undifferentiation. Nathan Schwartz-Salant (1998)[7] has written about the experience of separation after a *coniunctio*, or state of union in *The Mystery of the Human Relationship*. He has described it as the alchemical shadow experience of *nigredo* and has asserted that a *nigredo* state always occurs after a *coniunctio* experience, which must be faced each time transformational movement is made. A contributing factor to the experience of a *nigredo* state is that the ego has no point of reference for the nonverbal *energetic* experience, and it is experienced as being beyond its control. Nathan Swartz-Salant has also described re-entry as a re-enactment of the birth trauma involving separation from the symbiotic relationship with the sacred. In personal conversations with Nathan, whom I had reached out to during my own struggle with re-entry after reading his books *The Mystery of the Human Relationship* (1998) and *The Black Nightgown* (2007), he explained that the process of re-entry often requires re-experiencing early personal history. In the re-entry process, the spirit re-enters the body in a new configuration that can be hard to consciously assimilate—which is why a "sturdy" ego is essential in this type of work. He reassured me that through the process of struggling to find equilibrium, integration can occur with a sense of homeostasis.

Discovering theories and finding descriptions that corresponded with the re-entry process felt somewhat comforting because I realized that others had shared a similar experience. Yet the theories were descriptions, outside of the felt experience. The new ways of understanding were not a substitute for the profound heart connection I had experienced and the deep sense of longing, wanting to be back on the mountain. I also turned to psychoanalytic theory and continued trying to identify the overwhelming emotional state I was finding myself in.

Sulfuric Energy and Mania

In addition to experiencing a state of confusion—and entropy, re-entry after a numinous encounter often includes feeling an abundance of energy, as if one is on fire. Jung termed being inflated by archetypal energy as a *mana* personality (Jung, 1953). This condition can resemble the paranoid state of grandiosity associated with a mania of feeling highly "energized," like you can do anything. Even though the aftereffects of a numinous experience may appear subtle, they can become disruptive as well.

According to Von Franz (1980), this phenomenon occurs when an archetype that has been activated in the unconscious emerges into ego-consciousness. Synchronistic events originate in the mythic realm of psychic engagement, existing in atemporal and temporal states as described in Chapter 10.

The intense download of energy that often happens during a mystical experience frequently possesses a sulfuric quality. In alchemy, sulfur is the substance that ignites and causes explosions. It can be beneficial in the early stages of a creative or transformative cycle, but it will eventually need to ground, or one may begin to feel consumed by it. Von Franz has described sulfur as the "the natural light hidden in matter—and the destructive fire" (2002, p. 184).

Direct and sustained exposure to the *energetic collective* can have a sulfuric effect. This energy can feel archetypal and manic because it can overwhelm the ego. Uncontained, the experience of sulfur feels like an unrelentless drive or compulsion that can be addictive and exhausting.

The alchemists understood the need for the vessel to hold the *prima materia* in its process of transformation. If the vessel is strong enough to hold the sulfuric energy, working with this energy can create amazing things. It can feel like it is the substance that blasts rocket ships into warp speed and back. If harnessed, using sulfuric energy can be effective in transitions, because of the driving thrust and force of momentum it can provide.

Extroverted Re-Entry: The Risk of Becoming Inflated

Emotionally, returning from a numinous experience may create an urge to share and connect with others, accompanied by a sense of urgency, with a need to "blurt out" and express the overpowering feeling associated with the experience. Perhaps it is the actual numinous energy of the *conjunctio* itself that is brought back from the experience that creates the urge to express oneself and to be understood. The "urge to merge" can become somewhat of a trickster, wreaking havoc in the psychic field.

The intensity of energy one "picks up and brings back" after a numinous encounter can be difficult to tolerate for those around them. The *manos wasi* (energy body) of a person returning from a state of oneness after a numinous experience is expansive and open. They are often carrying an "afterglow" and feel a "burning desire" to share their experience, while those around them may feel bombarded by the intensity and intruded upon. In conversations, Schwartz-Salant[8] has said that this is because this kind of "expanded state" tends to constellate projections in others because energetically it sets up the experience of "bumping up against" the unconscious in the psychic field.

Although she is writing about people who have had a near death experience (NDE), there are similarities between NDE and re-entry. Atwater has written:

> *All near-death experiencers want to talk about it. They want to tell everyone in the whole wide world what happened to them and what they think it means. Adults, however, learn to clam up—how fast depends on the response from significant others.* (Atwater, 2007, p. 122)

Talking about an experience in a debriefing situation after a traumatic event can mitigate the long-term effects associated with the experience, and the support of a group is a curative factor, as is the case with Alcoholics Anonymous (AA) in the treatment of addiction. However, in the context of re-entry, sharing the experience with others who have not had the experience is generally not helpful—and can even become detrimental. Because others have no way of relating to it, unless they have been through a similar experience themselves, this often is disruptive and annoying, as it usually is a "one-sided down-load" rather than a relational exchange and as a result tends to interrupt whatever is going on. .

The cartoon character *Casper the Friendly Ghost* comes to mind. The underlying theme in the cartoons involves Casper continually trying to establish a friendship with everyone he encounters but because he is a ghost without a body, he is not fully in the world and scares people. His affable overtures toward other people startle them and they become extremely uncomfortable and run away because Casper is threatening consensual reality. Casper repeatedly is left feeling lonely and disappointed.

The question arises, is the sulfuric experience inherent property of the energy due to inflation, or is it a manic defense, a compensation for the loss of omnipotence as the result of the separation in the re-entry process? According to McWilliams (1994), acting out and denial are the core defenses associated with manic personalities. The energetic experience of "spinning" may serve as a buffer from emotional suffering, usually related to traumatic separation and loss.[9]

Trauma and the Return

As described, initially re-entry can be terrifying when it does not fit into what is understood to be consensual reality. If the experience of disequilibrium becomes too threatening or overwhelming for the ego to process, integration does not occur, and the experience may become split-off and encapsulated in a disassociated state. The feelings that come up during this process can be particularly challenging if unresolved early childhood wounds are reopened. Perhaps this is due to the intense symbiotic experience of connection that often happens during mystical experience followed by a devastating sense of abandonment if there is no sense of knowing how to return to the blissful state. Jungians have spoken of becoming engulfed by the "terrible mother" (that is the mother complex).

Schwartz-Salant (1998) has described the Northwest Coast image of sisiutl, the two-headed serpent, which can be applied to understanding the process of re-entry. He has stated that faith and a quest for truth, which happen to be primary principles of most religions, bring about the healing transformation, and that holding the tension opposites between the sense of one's own identity and the longing for a fused state is challenging.

As Schwartz-Salant (1998) has described, during the process of re-entry, traveling through and reliving the intensity of early states of infancy and childhood development can often feel on the inside like —and resemble on the outside—psychopathology. In my work with trauma clients, who have often become disassociated or disconnected from affect that had become too overwhelming to feel, as they have approached "opening up" to the experience, they often describe a fear of being "swallowed up in a black hole." Although this is not something they have experienced physically in their outer world, in the inner world they are acutely aware of the feeling.

Christopher Bollas (1987) has suggested that ego structure is a form of deep memory, derived from the symbiotic relationship with the mother. If we were able to trace this back even further, it is possible that we would find a memory of the experience of being within the *energetic collective* that is the original template for the infant state of maternal union. If, according to Bollas (1987), ego structure "is the trace of a relationship" (p. 50), then returning from an encounter with the *energetic collective* would require us to retrace our memory pathways through our early infant experiences back into our adult schemata and perception of ordinary reality. Potentially, every early childhood experience and stage of psychic development may be relived and re-experienced during the process of returning from a shamanic encounter.

Moving from a state of blissful union experienced in energetic atemporality back into what Schwartz-Salant (1998) has described as the *nigredo* after a *conjunctio* can bring about states of deep anguish and emptiness due to the sense of alienation that often comes from separation.

James Grotstein has written:

> *The black hole is an experiential term which has recently become frequently mentioned by patients suffering from primitive mental disturbances, especially during attachment disruptions ... The patients' usage of the term seems to convey a sense of a catastrophic discontinuity of self, of falling over the abyss into the void. It frequently designates a phantasy of their inner mental geography, connoting a picture of a disrupted landscape with a sudden, unexpected confrontation with a cliff, abyss, or hole which seems to be pulling one over its edge. One of the most frequent statements made by these patients is that they "have no floor," by which they mean they have no inner source of security. The "black hole" conveys the experience of meaninglessness and nothingness ... and represents the ultimate traumatic state of disorganization, terror, chaos, randomness, and entropy ... clients have described the fear as getting lost in the void of outer space, in something that is infinite and alien—where there is no connection and no meaning.*
>
> (Grotstein, 1990, p. 377)

The fear of being mentally ill is common among people who have had a NDE (Atwater, 2007). The *Diagnostic Statistical Manual IV* introduced the religious or spiritual problem V-Code (V62.89). Although the initial proposed descriptions were more inclusive, including NDE and "problems in relationship with a transcendent being," before they were shortened to "questioning of spiritual values," this was a shift away from pathologizing spiritual experience to allowing for diversity (Turner et al., 1995, pp. 435-444).

Now, fourteen years later, reflecting back, I recognize that trying to understand the re-entry experience through a diagnostic lens not only provided an attempt to find footing in consensual reality through my training as a psychologist, but it was also a means of describing the severity of the mental distress I was experiencing and an acknowledgment of how discombobulated I felt.

Introverted Re-Entry: A Schizoid Experience

In 2009 I wrote:

> *While I believe the intensity of the re-entry experience is acute, it can feel and appear like a schizoid personality organization or mania and for this reason I am also using a diagnostic lens to create a framework using analytic language as a starting point, not to pathologized the experience. Re-entry is an adjustment reaction rather than ego syntonic. My hope is to create a foundation to*

conceptualize the stark reality of shadow side of the experience from the inside out that can be built upon. (Bryon, 2012)

In addition to experiencing a sense of mania at times, there are other introverted reactions to re-entry. Some people have a sense of being dissociated and may turn inward and become reclusive. Many medicine people—or shamans—have gone through early traumatic events or physical illnesses and as a result have an easier time shifting into dissociate states associated with otherworld experience (Eliade, 1964). While having the ability to shift into altered states is necessary in "otherworld" experience, the transition back may lead to feelings of alienation, and—in extreme moments—a fear of psychosis if one is living in a culture that does not support these kinds of experiences.

Because the influx of energy can be so overwhelming, coupled with a deep longing for connection while at the same time feeling a strong sense of alienation, the re-entry experience can feel schizoid. After returning from my experience in Peru, I found myself diagnosing myself, my clients, and my analyst as schizoid for a period. Most likely the experience I was living during re-entry was so engulfing that it was spilling into my more emotionally intimate connections. (Luckily my analyst had a sense of humor and had also had mystical experiences. Fortunately, I was also in a period of my analytic training when I was receiving a lot of case supervision.)

Millon (1969) has described individuals with schizoid character organization as threatened with the experience of "non-being." The overwhelming feeling of separation that can occur during re-entry resembles his description of the schizoid experience. He stated, "Detachment from others and alienation from self are the principal features"… with a tendency toward "over-sensitivity." He has written:

Denied the power or desire to experience the joy, love and vibrancy of a "personal" life, schizoids become devitalized and numb, wander in a dim and hazy fog and engage in activities and thoughts which have minimal purpose of meaning. Why should they desire, aspire, or seek to achieve when nothing can spark their flat and spiritless existence or provide them with the feeling of personal pleasure or joy? Thus, they move through life with impenetrable barriers to shared meanings and affections and estranged from the purposes of society, or the spontaneity, delight and triumph of selfhood. (Millon, 1969, p. 308)

Millon's (1969) description of characteristics of the experience of individuals with a schizoid personality disorder corresponds with the introverted shadow experience of the re-entry process. The key difference between the re-entry process and Millon's description of the schizoid character is that re-entry is a transitional phase often accompanied by feelings associated with an overpowering sense of loss of separation. While, metaphorically, in re-entry there can be a sense of going from seeing in color to tones of grey, different from the schizoid condition, it is an acute grief reaction rather than a chronic way of being. The feeling of living in a heightened state of sensitivity and at times feeling overwhelmed and alienated in our Western culture—and alone—also contributes to feeling detached from the outer world.

Grotstein has written:

> *This state of abjectness has been studied by Spitz, Sartre, Harlow, Winnicott, Balint, Bion, Tustin, and others. It was described by Winnicott (1960) as the "failure to go-on- being" and later as infantile depression (Winnicott, 1963). Bion (1962), in his conception of the "container and the contained," described the failure of mothers of schizophrenic patients to be able to absorb and defuse their infants' "fear of dying." Balint (1968) referred to this phenomenon as the "basic fault." Other authors refer to it as fragmentation, annihilation anxiety, organismic distress, and dissolution. Laing (1960) lists implosion, engulfment, and petrification as the extreme experiences of ontological insecurity result-ing in derealization (of the object world) and depersonalization of the self.* (Grotstein, 1990, p. 378)

Guntrip's (Brierly, 1970) writing on the "in and out programme," touches on this experience as well. Guntrip (Brierly, 1970) has described the schizoid experi-ence as a regressive longing to return to an uroboric, "womb-like" state, a longing for love and complete connection—a *conjunctio*. Yet as soon as this connection is experienced, it is often followed by annihilation anxiety, and the fear that loving something or someone (that is, object) will destroy it. The anxiety leads to with-drawal, to defend against destroying what is loved or losing one's own identity in the experience of the connection. A difference in the re-entry experience is that there is not a sense of ambivalence in wanting to return to the state of *conjunctio*.

In *Primitive Mental States*, Peter Giovacchini (1996) has explained that the chief defensive behavior of a person with schizoid personality organization is with-drawal. This is because of the internal turmoil they experience through engaging with external objects, or relationships. Giovacchini attributes this tendency toward "flight" after becoming overwhelmed is because they primarily experience the world somatically and lack the ability to integrate symbolic experience. Similarly, in re-entry, initially the focus is on somatic integration of the energetic "download" that has occurred in the *manos wasi* before symbolic representation has developed.

In her writing McWilliams (1994) has demonstrated a sensitivity to the schizoid condition, which is relevant to the re-entry process. She has written, "The most adaptive and exciting capacity of the schizoid person is creativity. Most truly ori-ginal artists have a strong schizoid streak—almost by definition since one must stand apart from convention to influence it in a new way" (McWilliams, 1994, p. 192).

Many writers and artists have created works that describe the experience of alienation and intense feelings of loneliness after an experience with the numinous.

Rilke has written, "Because we are alone; because we stand in the middle of a transition where we cannot remain standing with the new thing that has entered our self; because everything intimate and accustomed has for an instant been taken away" (2002, p. 64). As Rilke suggested, what is familiar is gone, but perhaps even more importantly, when one returns to their outer awareness one is forced to separate from the experience of union.

McWilliams (1994) has said that the primary goal of therapy with schizoid patients is creative activity, which can occur through the process of making works of art, scientific inventions, and discovery, and/or working with innovative theories and concepts. This approach is also beneficial during the imaginative engagement phase of the re-entry process.

More psychological research is needed that describes the process of re-entry. Because mystical experience is primarily nonverbal, developing an understanding is somewhat of an exercise in "toggling" back and forth between intellectual descriptors and the actual emotional experience—like moving between thoughts and affect in working through a trauma experience. My hope is that this topic will become a field of analytic study to help other members of modern culture in transitioning back from intense mystical experience.

The re-entry process occurs in stages. Initially, the internal psychic structure for symbolic representation does not exist, and the experience is incongruent with an orientation in consensual reality, which is why it is so confusing. It is coupled with an overwhelming sense of loss while at the same time trying to exist in a state of "energetic overload" without context. When returning to this culture, it requires a period of transition to reacclimate. The next chapter will describe the phases that occur in the re-entry process.

Notes

1   Quantum indeterminacy is the assertion that the state of a system does not determine a unique collection of values for all its measurable properties.
2   Connes, A., Chereau, D., and Dixmier, H. (2013) cited in Rovelli (2019 p. 123).
3   The film *The Fly* (1986).
4   "Rip Van Winkle" is a short story written by Washington Irving (1819–20), published in *"The Sketch Book,"* based on a German folktale about a farmer who encounters a group of dwarfs and then falls asleep for twenty years and then returns to his life and discovers everything has changed.
5   This corresponds with the state of entropy in "blurring" described in Chapter 9.
6   J. Raff (personal communication, 2008).
7   During these initial mystical experiences in Peru, I was carrying a copy of Edward Edinger's (1985) book, *Anatomy of the Psyche*, with me, and conceptualizing some of what I was experiencing from a Jungian alchemical perspective was helpful. In addition to reading Carlos Castaneda' and Edinger's books, the writings (and later conversations) with Nathan Schwartz-Salant were also extremely beneficial.
8   N. Schwartz-Salant (personal communication, 2009).

9   A means of separation is essential for the ego to survive the intensity of the experience. The question becomes, what is strong enough to serve as a container that will not be burned up when touched by the process? What does not contaminate the process, and what is flexible and adaptive enough to contain it? Jung understood this to be a function of the symbol, which provides a psychological means for coagulating and focusing the energy in a way that enables a separation to occur between the ego and the archetypal energy of the Self—in Jungian vernacular. In shamanic terms, the symbol can offer a bridge between conscious awareness in ordinary reality and the *energetic collective*.

References

Atwater, P. M. H. (2007) *The Big Book of Near-Death Experiences*, Virginia Beach, VA: Rainbow Ridge Books LLC.

Bollas, C. (1987) *The Shadow of the Object*, New York, NY: Columbia University Press.

Brierly, M. (1970) Schizoid Phenomena, Object Relations, and the Self: By Harry Guntrip, London: Hogarth Press and Institute of Psychoanalysis. 1968. Pp. 437 *International Journal of Psychoanalysis* 51:540-546.

Bryon, D. (2012) *Lessons of the Inca Shamans, Part I: Piercing the veil*, Enumclaw, WA: Pine Winds Press.

Campbell, J. (2008) *Hero with a Thousand Faces*, Princeton, NJ: Princeton University Press.

Castaneda, C. (1981) *The Eagle's Gift*, New York, NY: Simon and Schuster.

Castaneda, C. (1984) *The Fire from Within*, New York, NY: Pocket Books.

Edinger, E. F. (1972) *Ego and Archetype*, New York, NY: Penguin Books.

Edinger, E. F. (1985) *Anatomy of the Psyche: Alchemical symbolism in psychotherapy*, Peru, IL: Open Court Publishing.

Elaide, M. (1963) *Myth and Reality*, New York, NY: Harper & Row.

Eliade, M. (1964) *Shamanism: Archaic techniques of ecstasy*, Bollington Series LXXVI, Princeton, NJ: Princeton University Press.

Giovacchini, P. (1996) *Primitive Mental States*, Northvale, NJ: Jason Aronson, Inc.

Grotstein, J. S. (1990) 'Nothingness, meaninglessness, chaos, and the "Black Hole" II—The Black Hole', *Contemporary Psychoanalysis* 26: 377–407.

Jung, C. G. (1953a) *The Relations between the Ego and the Unconscious* (Collected Works, vol. 7).

Knight, G. (1993) *A Practical Guide to Qabalistic Symbolism*, Maine: Samuel Weiser, York Beach.

McWilliams, N. (1994) *Psychoanalytic Diagnosis: Understanding personality structure in the clinical process*, New York, NY: Guilford Press.

Millon, T. (1969) *Modern Psychopathology: A biosocial approach to maladaptive learning and functioning*, Long Grove, IL: Waveland Press Inc.

Raff, J. (2008) personal communication.

Rilke, R. M. (2002) *Letters to a Young Poet*, London: Dover.

Rovelli, C. (2019) *The Order of the Universe*, London: Penguin Books.

Schwartz-Salant, N. (1998) *The Mystery of Human Relationship*, New York, NY: Routledge.

Schwartz-Salant, N. (2007) *The Black Nightgown: The fusional complex and the unlived life*, Wilmette, IL: Chiron Publications.

Turner, R. P., Lukoff, D., Barnhouse, R. T., and Lu, F.G. (1995) 'Religious or spiritual problem: A culturally sensitive diagnostic category in the DSM-IV', *Journal of Nervous and Mental Disease* 183: 435–44.

Ulanov, A.B. (2017) *The Psychoid, Soul and Psyche: Piercing Space/Time Barriers*, Einsiedeln, Switzerland: Daimon.

von Franz, M-L. (1980) *Projection and Re-collection*, La Salle, IL: Open Court.

von Franz, M-L. (1992) *Psyche and Matter,* Boston, MA: Shambhala.

von Franz, M-L. (2002) *Aurora Consurgens*, Toronto: Inner City Books.

von Franz, M-L. (2002) personal communication.

Chapter 9

Phases in the Re-Entry Experience

The Initial Phase of Re-Entry: Somatic Perception

Using an alchemical framework, the ego's process of reorienting to the outer world, or becoming "re-embodied" after a numinous experience, is a process of coagulatio. In *Anatomy of the Psyche*, Edinger has written:

> *In essence,* coagulatio *is a process that turns something into earth. Earth is one of the synonyms for the* coagulatio. *It is heavy and permanent, of fixed position and shape … Thus, for psychic content to become earth means that it has been concretized in a particular localized form; that is, it has become attached to an ego.* (Edinger, 1985, p. 83)

According to Edinger (1985), coagulatio is a process of creation that is a function of the ego, and the means for grounding and embodying the numinous experience. Paqos believe that for an energetic experience to be meaningful, one must be able to "grow corn with it." In other words, for an experience to be valuable it must be anchored in practical application in everyday life, and assimilated in a way that the information is useful and relevant from the ego perspective.

After being "touched" by numinous experience, the ego goes by shifting from a nonverbal energetic experience to conceptualization, first through imagery and symbols, and then in words. Through the process of embodying energetic experience in the *manos wasi*, the ego enters a state of disequilibrium, because it moves into realms of experiencing that cannot be accessed and described through words. The experience is first understood through symbols, metaphors, and images before words can be used to describe the experience.

The three phases of re-entry after mystical experience are somatic perception, imaginative engagement, and narrative integration. The first phase, somatic perception, refers to the nonverbal body experience of holding and integrating the intense influx of energy somatically. The second phase, imaginative engagement, describes the transitional state of working with emerging symbols and imagery through creative acts and dream material, to begin to assimilate the experience

DOI: 10.4324/9781003356448-12

cognitively. The third phase, narrative integration, refers to the personal story that grows out of reflecting upon the events, feelings, and imagery associated with the experience. Each of these states will be examined and the process of movement from somatic experience to ego-conscious will be explored, with the commonalities between them (Bryon, 2012).

This begins in the phase of imaginative engagement when the ego develops a symbolic means of referencing the experience. Next, during narrative integration, the ego assimilates this experience into its cognitive schemata by expanding and updating the understanding and perception of reality to accommodate the atemporal experience. Previously held beliefs and assumptions about reality must be adjusted to adapt to and incorporate the experience.

The first phase involves integrating the influx of energy into the *manos wasi*. When shifting back to temporal reality after being in a state of connection with the atemporal energetic realm, in the somatic perception phase, the *energetic* experience is sensory, experienced as a non-ego state. Being touched by a numinous experience often leaves one with a sense of having undergone a life-changing event that has left them psychically "carrying" the archetypal force. It is a time of turning inward. The memory of being in the state of connection with *Wira Cocha*, the cosmos is often experienced emotionally in the heart as a sense of universal love, or as a sense of well-being.

Re-entry can also be accompanied with a great sense of loss. Initially, a young shaman's process of re-entry into the outer world after an initiatory experience can be painful because of an intense sense of separation and alienation after being "held" in security of a felt sense of connectivity with the natural world.

Physically it can be experienced as a vibration, sense of expansion, tingling, expansion, depending on the strength and depth of the connection. In *The Eagle's Gift*, Castaneda wrote,

> *My body began to shake, out of control. I had a sense of duality. Perhaps what I call my rational self, incapable of controlling the rest of me, took the seat of a spectator, some part of me was watching as another part of me shook.* (Castaneda, 1981, p. 70)

This initial phase of re-entry, at the level of the *energetic collective,* is a state of consciousness during which a mental framework involving differentiated imagery does not exist, which is why it is a non-ego state. The imagery associated with the energetic experience is often of a continual state of light energy with no form or perceivable structure. Everything is experienced simultaneously in an energetic state of no-separation. There is less of a sense of "being in" and more of sense of "fusion." "Being in" implies a relationship of being imbedded in something, with a point of reference while "fusion" is experienced as a state of nondifferentiation between interior and exterior.

Figure 9.1 Numinosity - Painting by the Author. A gestural painting with a golden-white interior of brushstrokes extending outward into a blackish-blue background.

Bollas (1987) has stated, "The experience of the object precedes the 'knowing' of the object" (p. 39). In other words, we experience our world before we know our world, through sensing somatically. It is impossible to stay close to the actual experience using cognition because the rules describing processes involved in ego-functioning do not apply. Thinking is a sequential operation and energetic states of oneness are experienced as undifferentiated and atemporal. Like trying to explain the acausal phenomenon of synchronicity as a causal event, attempting to "bend" energetic experience to "fit" immediately back into temporal spatial reality distorts the experience. Thinking involves discernment—which requires being outside of the experience to describe it, and this is a function of the ego.

The realm of the energetic collective can only be consciously accessed through the irrational intuitive and sensate functions—which are not processes involving the ego. Like a fog bank that moves in rapidly along a coast, it is nonlinear. Painting such an event realistically would involve a layering process of circular gestural paint strokes, made with a large brush. The mood could not be captured by precise mark making. The fog metaphor corresponds with the integrative layering that happens when assimilating mystical energetic experience.

Neither experience can be accurately described using words, which are at best an approximation. Because these experiences occur at the fringe of consciousness they are only remembered implicitly without details, undefined by discrete boundaries.

Preverbal Experience, Somatic Experience, and States of Ecstasy

The first phase of re-entry into the external world after a profound sense of one-ness with the universe, which paqos experience in states of ecstasy, is a profound awareness of being part of something greater, rather than being outside of it and understanding oneself in contrast with another. The infant's early symbiotic rela-tionship with the mother and the "oceanic" psychic state (Ackerman, 2017; Freud, 1930) at birth corresponds with the profound spiritual experience of being one with the world in deep meditative states experienced in many indigenous cultures such as the Andean medicine people.

In *Playing and Reality*, Winnicott (1971) has described, how at birth, an infant is in a state of union through a symbiotic relationship with the mother and expe-riences through feeling at a pre-symbolic level where there is no differentiation between itself and the world. This uroboric state corresponds to being in a state of energetic connection where no reference to time and space exists and there is no separation between internal states and the external world. Preverbal states in infancy and the transition from an atemporal existence into an understanding of duration and temporal experience parallels the re-entry experience back to the "day world" after experiencing a state of ecstatic oneness after a primary shamanic ini-tiation. Because the experience is pre-symbolic, and therefore nonverbal, it is not bound by linear time (Valkonen-Korhonen, 2019). The phenomenon of time does not occur because there is no language construct that can be used as means of delin-eating between the past, present, and future. This is the realm associated with the primordial unconscious. In these kinds of atemporal states, separation between self and "other" doesn't exist. Often a sense of "where one ends, and the world begins" is lacking.

Sander (2008) has written, "What would it mean for caregivers to think in terms of systems instead of individuals; in terms of process instead of structure; in terms of a flow of sequence, recurrence, and expectancy within the recurring exchanges between themselves and their charges instead of thinking in terms of isolated events?" (p. 168) … "We begin life 'connected,' as part of each other" (p. 170).

The paqos' states of ecstasy correspond with memories of implicit experience in early infancy based upon secure attachment. Bowlby (1958) has written that there is an innate need for attachment in infancy for healthy adult relationships to occur later in life. Secure infant attachment develops into a capacity for connection in relationship with reciprocity, or *ayni*. Siegal and Sieff (2015) have described a shared relational state as resonance, which—using their words— "occurs when we allow ourselves to be influenced by an internal state of another person" (p. 156). Object relations analysts have described the need of both infants and adult psych-otic patients to find a "safe holding environment" and "space inside the mother" (Summers, 1994, p. 128). In adulthood, these "holding spaces" are internalized, selfstates that exist within our psyches.

The Intensity of Ecstasy

Bromberg (1979, 2008) has described how traumatic experiences too overwhelming to become integrated consciously become stored as implicit memory. This often occurs somatically and applies to preverbal experience and states of ecstasy as well. Paqos believe states of ecstasy associated with intense "downloads" of *kausay* energy are held in our luminous energy bodies, which are the templates that encode this energetic material in the substance of our physical bodies. The paqos refer to the luminous body as *runa kurku k'anchay*, which translates as "luminous light body." Assimilating and integrating implicit experiences, whether energetic states of ecstasy or traumatic experience too intense to be held consciously, requires moving it from a somatic state, into ego-consciousness.

The Quechua word *mast'ay* means "making oneself available"—in other words, opening to dimensions beyond consensual reality. During the somatic perception phase of re-entry, the energy received assimilated somatically in the *runa kurku k'anchay*. This occurs before the next phase, imaginative engagement, begins, when making meaning and the process of psychic integration begins.

The Second Phase of Re-Entry: Imaginative Engagement

The second phase of re-entry, imaginative engagement, is when symbolic imagery begins to enter ego-consciousness through dreams and actively playing with the material that emerges imaginatively in states of reverie and in acts of creative expression. In this phase, psychic movement is made from the energetic collective into the mythic and symbolic levels of engagement.

In *The Eagle's Gift,* Castaneda (1981, p.170) explains that by creating memory markers, the "vivid, moment to moment recollections" can be reassembled from the actual experience. Having a point of reference as a memory anchor while in an altered state, using symbols that can provide cognitive scaffolding, aids the process of memory retrieval.

In depth psychology the points of reference are conceptualized as symbols that surface from the archetypal realm of the unconscious. Jung (1950) and Von Franz (1999) believed that the process of working with and integrating a numinous mystical experience occurs through circumambulation, "moving around" the symbolic archetypal material in contemplative states of receptivity, allowing associations to spontaneously emerge and amplifying the imagery using collective myths and motifs that relate to the psychic material. The richness of numinous experience requires a symbolic form or image to anchor it, originating in the collective unconscious. This practice of integration eventually becomes grounded in the body when one has an "a-ha" moment.

Jung (1934, par. 320) and Hillman (1983, p. 2) are proponents of "sticking to the image" by staying close to the actual imagery and not focusing on the interpretation of the image. They have advocated for tracking the course of images and allowing

Figure 9.2 Kausay - Painting by the Author. An abstract painting with a circular shaped center, surrounded in an orange ring, on a dark blue-black background.

them to stand on their own rather than reducing them down to a single construct to find inherent meaning. This approach adheres to the intelligent natural order of the imaginal realm without trying to "fit" it prematurely into a conceptualization. This approach is not applicable during the somatic perception phase of re-entry because it is impossible to anchor to an image in the formless *energetic* realm. However, it can be helpful in the imaginative engagement phase, when symbols begin to emerge, because it enables the experience to become grounded temporally through form.

The power of numinous energy can be overwhelming if it is not directed or channeled in a meaningful, creative way. Finding ways of directing psychic energy through creative expression enables inner unformulated experience to be assimilated and communicated in the external world. This creates a bridge between implicit and somatic experience in the inner world and explicit representation so that a sense of connection in the day world can begin to become established. Having a link between numinous experience and everyday living can help to facilitate reintegration in the re-entry process and potentially mitigate the intense feelings of loneliness and alienation that often occur after a profound mystical experience.

Dreams and Active Imagination as Vehicles for Integration

In addition to creative acts of expression, in the imaginative engagement phase working with a dream or active imagination in states of reverie is another way of beginning to integrate energetic experience. This may include revisiting the memory of the experience and reengaging with it in the imaginal realm through the process of active imagination. The depth of the connection to these experiences can vary depending on state of mind, intention, and receptivity. It has been my experience that there is a cumulative layering effect of meaning as the image is worked with over time.

Experiences in nonordinary reality and the imaginal realm that are not expressed creatively or recorded in writing immediately are often lost—the way dreams are often forgotten as the dreamworld fades away and the day progresses. Deeper, nonverbal experiences become even more difficult to access because they do not rely on practices associated with ordinary memory retrieval. Cues that facilitate recognition are often not available because of the intrinsically unique nature of the experience.

The Transitional Space between Fantasy and Reality and Artistic Expression

Ogden (1985) has stressed the necessity of the existence of a sequence of time in organizing thoughts, feelings, and emotions through symbols. Symbols help us create ourselves as subjects to reflect on. .

Winnicott (1971) has written extensively about the psychological realm of transitional space existing between fantasy and reality where creative, symbolic play occurs, which he has stated is necessary in the development of a well-functioning, autonomous ego. Like an infant learning to discriminate between inner and outer objects, or internal and external reality, forming relationships with "transitional objects" becomes the means for learning how to move between subjective and objective states. Transitional objects serve as a bridge between atemporal and temporal experience because they are not completely under the jurisdiction of the ego. They do not become reified, reduced to something that is concrete existing in the external world. Winnicott (1971) has described this kind of psychic engagement as the intermediate area that creates a space in infancy between primary creativity and objective perception.

Winnicott disagrees with Melanie Klein's (1930) premise that transitional objects cannot be a mental internal representation. According to Winnicott (1971), transitional objects—or symbols—can be anything imbued with psychic energy. An object or symbol may become a substitute and a temporal reminder of an unformulated *feeling* experience in an act of creative play that can provide a means of transitioning between unconscious and conscious states, and atemporal and temporal reality. Winnicott's (1971) description of a multi-dimensional transitional space is useful because it allows for simultaneous arboreal movement in different directions to be brought together, outside of the time–space paradigm of consensual reality, between the past and the present, and conscious and energetic experience.

The importance of the process of creative play that Winnicott (1971) has described may also be applied to understanding the process of imaginal engagement during the re-entry process that also occurs in the transitional space between the *energetic* realm and conscious reality, which can be bridged through working with images symbolically and through creative acts.

For an artistic act to have meaning, it must involve the imagination and become an automatic experience through the creation of a symbol. Creative acts and the formation of symbols are ways of constructing a foundation from which to build meaning that can become vehicles for integrating numinous experience. The creative act becomes the means from which to engage in an open dialogue with atemporal energetic experience.

The creative act itself occurs within a transitional space, emerging as an expression within the temporal time and space paradigm. In this way, the creative act carries the atemporal energetic experience being held somatically and manifests it in a form that is witnessed and processed by the ego. Ceremony and ritual are two forms of creative acts that can become ways of engaging with the *energetic collective*. The *temenos* created in ceremony functions as a bridge intersecting soma and psyche, and atemporal and temporal states of reality.

Creativity as an Agent of Change

Creative expression becomes the organizing agent of the numinous experience and becomes the catalyst and channel for self-reflection. The act of creating enables energy to be transformed into matter, and what has been unconscious to become consciously differentiated and assimilated by the ego in a meaningful way.

Unlike the numinous experience itself, the physical creation of the memory as art form does not dissipate over time but remains constant. In the spirit of the action painters of the abstract expressionist art movement, it becomes a record of the experience. Art critic Clement Greenberg (1971, p. 118) has stated that the artist should be less focused on *representing* a subject and more focused on recording the artist's *experience* of relating to the subject. The work of action paintings such as those of Lee Krasner and Jackson Pollock are an example of a process that illustrates creating a record of the movements and gestures made by layering paint on the canvas.

The creative act is an illustration that documents the nonverbal experience and may serve as an explicit method of communication that can then be referenced and described because it exists in a temporal dimension. The actual act of creating when the artist is in the "flow" of the experience is the expression of spirit and becomes a means of organizing the *energetic* experience. Nonverbal, automatic creative acts fall close to subtle body experience, while creative expressions involving images and words are activities of the psyche closer to ego-consciousness.

The creative expression may take on many forms—from the mounds of mashed potatoes Richard Dreyfus builds after his interaction with aliens in the film *Close Encounters of the Third Kind*[1] to an artist's painting after a numinous dream. Creative expression provides a venue to enter dialogue with energetic experience because it introduces temporality through linear time (creating art is a process), and separation in space (the artist is separate from the art being created). This phase of integration involves a process of recapitulation as a means of weaving imagery together that can "hold" the experience, to create a method to communicate numinous experience, essential in reintegration. This occurs symbolically, in a transitional space.

Winnicott wrote, "It is creative apperception more than anything else that makes the individual feel that life is worth living" (1971, p. 71). Apperception is the means through which new experience is woven into and transformed into a narrative tapestry of past experience by the individual to form a new whole. In other words, it is the perception of new experience within the context of past experience.

The Third Phase: Narrative Integration

The third phase of re-entry, narrative integration, involves integrating the imagery and symbols that have emerged through processing the energetic experience into conscious awareness as the ego "codes" and assimilates the memory of the experience into the cognitive schemata, or general body of working knowledge based upon consensual reality through verbal language.

Constructing a personal narrative facilitates the development of a personal narrative that then makes implicit feeling states more consciously accessible. The act of verbally recollecting an experience enables paqos to assimilate the memory into meaningful personal narratives. In *The Power of Silence*, Castaneda described a process of recollecting that refers to this process of engagement in his statement:

> Sorcerers start their recapitulation by thinking, by remembering the most important acts of their lives. From merely thinking about them, they can then move on to actually being at the site of the event. When they can do that—be at the site of the event—they have successfully shifted their assemblage point to the precise point where the event took place. (Castaneda, 1998, p. 145).

Piaget and Constructing a Narrative

Shifting between ordinary and nonordinary reality states requires constructing a permeable personal narrative that can adjust to the ongoing changes of the living experience. Shamans are aware that recapitulating experience into our personal narratives determines who we are at any given moment in consensual reality.

Piaget's (1937) model of early cognitive development is useful in understanding how the mental maps we create to understand our world are formed. The cognitive mechanisms involved in early sensory motor processing correspond to the way energetic experience is incorporated in the *manos wasi* during the process of integrating numinous experience. In both situations, the ego moves into a state of disequilibrium as it encounters novel, unmapped experience, previously inaccessible using verbal or visual language. Prior to this, no functional structural method of sequencing or internal scaffolding exists. Integrating implicit energetic experiences into conscious awareness requires a means of coding and assimilating the experience. If no cognitive schemata or body of working knowledge exists, then one must be created. As described in Chapter 8, the first re-entry experience after an intense energetic encounter is often extremely uncomfortable and alienating because there is no existing mental map that can be used to organize and make sense of what has happened.

After reliving the implicit feelings associated with the experience in the present, a cognitive schema becomes constructed through forming a personal narrative. This enables the implicit memory from the past to be consciously differentiated from the present, placing it into a sequential format that can then be described, named, and communicated to others. This is how the numinous experience, which may have initially felt disorganized or chaotic, becomes differentiated and contextualized.

The narratives we create determine our character based upon our perception of our own past (Bollas, 1987). The personal story we form about ourselves, based upon our subjective recollection of our experience can keep us confined to limiting assumptions we have made about the world or construct new ways for us to see and perceive reality.

Being able to work with an event within the context of it happening in the past, provides a vantage point to step outside of the experience and reflect upon it. Wallin (2007) has described a mindful or meta self, that is the part of us that can think about thinking, and the part that allows us to step outside the limitations of prior experience to perceive it as it is. Wallin has written that this stance of mindfulness is a function of secure attachment and healthy ego functioning. It is what enables the process of remembering to occur after the ego has been stretched by a dismemberment experience or a state of disequilibrium. This leads to the formation of a *metacognitive* framework. Metacognition refers to the objective capacity to think about thinking, or in other words to obtain a conscious position beyond personal narrative.

More psychological research is needed that describes the process of re-entry. Because mystical experience is primarily nonverbal, developing an understanding is somewhat of an exercise in switching back and forth between intellectual descriptors and the actual emotional experience—like moving between thoughts and affect in working through a trauma experience. My hope is that this topic will become a field of analytic study to help other members of modern culture in transitioning back from intense mystical experience.

Note

1 Film, 1977.

References

Ackerman, S. (2017) 'Exploring Freud's resistance to the oceanic feeling', *Journal of the American Psychoanalytic Association* 65: 9–31.

Bollas, C. (1987) *The Shadow of the Object*, New York, NY: Columbia University Press.

Bowlby, J. (1958) 'The Nature of the Child's Tie to his Mother', *International Journal of Psychoanalysis* 39:350-373.

Bromberg, P. M. (1979) 'Interpersonal psychoanalysis and regression', *Contemporary Psychoanalysis* 15: 647–55.

Bromberg, P. (2008) '"Grown-up" words: An interpersonal/relational perspective on unconscious fantasy', *Psychoanal. Inq.* 28: 131–50.

Bryon, D. (2012) *Lessons of the Inca Shamans, Part I: Piercing the veil*, Enumclaw, WA: Pine Winds Press.

Castaneda, C. (1981) *The Eagle's Gift*, New York, NY: Simon and Schuster.

Castaneda, C. (1987) The Power of Silence, New York, NY: Simon and Schuster.

Castaneda, C. (1998) *The Wheel of Time*, New York, NY: Pocket Books.

Edinger, E. F. (1985) *Anatomy of the Psyche: Alchemical symbolism in psychotherapy*, Peru, IL: Open Court Publishing.

Freud, S. (1930) *Civilization and Its Discontents* (Standard Edition, vol. 21).

Greenberg, C. (1971) *Art and Culture: Critical essays*, Boston, MA: Beacon Press.

Hillman, J. (1983) *Interviews: Conversations with Laura Pozzo on psychotherapy, biography, love, soul, dreams, work, imagination, and the state of the culture*, New York, NY: Harper & Row.

Jung, C. G. (1934) *The Practical Use of Dream-Analysis* (Collected Works, vol. 16).

Jung, C. G. (1950) *A Study in the Process of Individuation* (Collected Works, vol. 9i).

Klein, M. (1930) 'The Importance of Symbol-Formation in the Development of the Ego', *International Journal of Psychoanalysis* 11:24-39.

Ogden, T. H. (1985) 'On potential space', *Int J Psycho-Anal* 66: 129–41.

Piaget, J. (1937) *The Construction of Reality in the Child*, New York: Basic Books, 1954.

Sander, L. (2008) *Living Systems, Evolving Consciousness, and the Emerging Person*, New York, NY: Analytic Press.

Siegal, D. J. and Sieff, D. F. (2015) 'Beyond the prison of implicit memory', in *Understanding and Healing Emotional Trauma*, London and New York, NY: Routledge.

Summers, F. (1994) *Relational Perspectives in Psychoanalysis*, eds Neil J. Skolnick and Susan C. Warshaw, Hillsdale, NJ: The Analytic Press.

Valkonen-Korhonen, M. (2019) 'On experiencing time and timelessness', *IJP Open—Open Peer Review and Debate* 6: 1–23.

von Franz, M-L. (1999) *Archetypal Dimensions of the Psyche*, Boston, MA: Shambala.

Wallin, D. J. (2007) *Attachment in Psychotherapy*, New York, NY: The Guilford Press.

Winnicott, D. W. (1971) *Playing and Reality*, New York, NY: Penguin Books.

Part III

Integrating Psychoanalysis, Andean Medicine, and Quantum Theory

Weaving Together Theories of Psychoanalysis, Andean Medicine, and Quantum Theory

It has been exciting to discover, now years later, the shared commonality between psychics, different schools of psychoanalytic thought, and Jung's theories with my own mystical experience. Explanations of atemporal experiences found in physics and psychoanalysis can be applied to re-entry, which provide another perspective that may deepen understanding and provide an objective perspective that may be more quantifiable. The interpsychic correlation between oceanic states, the relationship between conscious and unconscious, and the energetic field in relation to time and space will be explored in the context of Jung, complexity theory and intersubjectivity in psychoanalysis,[1] and current theoretical physics, referred to in this paper as quantum theory. There are significant commonalities in ways of conceptualizing temporality and atemporality in the experience of time, as well as in understanding the links between physical and energetic realms that create reality. The purpose of this chapter is to demonstrate the considerable overlap that exists among these fields.

Quantum physics aligns with Jung's ideas regarding the archetypal realm of the psychoid, and the paqos' experience in the practice of Andean medicine. As a psychologist and Jungian psychoanalyst who has spent years with the Andean paqos, I have worked to integrate these different modalities as a clinician, while undergoing mystical experiences with the aftermath of re-entry. It has been validating to discover compatible explanations for these experiences in the theories of modern physics, which have also spilled over into complexity theory in psychoanalysis.

The Roots of Complexity Theory and Loop Quantum Gravity Theory

The psychoanalyst Robert Galatzer-Levy is a proponent of applying scientific theory to psychoanalysis as a way of understanding subjective experience. He has written:

> *The psychoanalyst may have some difficulty in accustoming himself to the idea of spaces of events and psychological forces. However, the power of mathematical thinking lies in the variety of different phenomena subsumed under one*

DOI: 10.4324/9781003356448-14

theory, provided certain conditions apply ... (The methods) provide a system-
atic method for describing the qualitative changes that arise from quantitative
change. (Galatzer-Levy, 1978, p. 929)

While trying to subsume atemporal and mystical experience under one theory is problematic, as such an approach is too reductive, not allowing for the unique-ness of the experience itself (a weakness in relying solely on mathematics), it may be useful to view these phenomena—as paqos would—as a *pacha* (an allocation of energy at a point in time and space).[2] In Andean medicine the universe of *Wira Cocha* consists of many *pachas* that together create an infinite whole. This aligns with string theory, that waves and particles cannot exist at the same time but are descriptions of electrons that can exist in different states. It is also consistent with the psychoanalytic thinking that the psyche consists of different selfstates with dif-ferent emotional, cognitive, and perceptual characteristics (Bromberg, 2009; Kohut and Wolf, 1978) that emerge depending on contextual demands and circumstances. In each of these theories different aspects of energetic experience, including states of consciousness, are woven together as a comprehensive whole in which there are laws, codes, and patterns existing under certain conditions that create an orderly universe.

Jerome Sasin and James Callahan (1990) have studied the structure of behavior, particularly regarding change and agree with Galatzer-Levy's (1978) sentiments of finding a theory with universal application that can be applied to psychoanalysis, while withstanding the rigor of physics. Louis Sander (2002) also advocates for an inclusive approach that synthesizes scientific and psychoanalytic theory. She has written:

We began with the challenge of integrating emerging knowledge at the bio-
logical, developmental, and psychotherapeutic levels and chose to see if a way
to do this might be to find basic principles of process in living systems that
would apply at each of these levels. In turning now to the psychotherapeutic
level, especially "within the psychoanalytic framework," we can think of the
therapeutic process essentially as a process bringing change to the organiza-
tion of consciousness, that is changing the way we are aware of ourselves in the
context of what is going on around us, which allows us to put together a new and
more inclusive coherence of ourselves within our own particular environment of
life support. (Sander, 2002, p. 37)

In these statements, these psychoanalysts are proposing an orientation bring-ing together psychoanalysis and physics, which was the precursor to complexity theory in the psychoanalytic school of intersubjectivity. Complexity theory grew out of the hard sciences, especially physics that was first applied to complex bio-logical systems (von Bertalanffy, 1968; Waddington, 1977). Many of the theories presented in quantum physics that correspond with complexity theory[3] drew from psychoanalysis (Galatzer-Levy, 1978; Sashin and Callahan, 1990; Spruiell, 1993;

Thelen and Smith, 1994; Stolorow, 1997; Ghent, 2002; Coburn, 2002; Sander, 2002; Seligman, 2005).[4]

The view that there are certain inherent properties in the universe that effect conscious experience is also consistent with Andean medicine, with roots grounded in ancient "Incan codes" or "Incan technology." The term "technology" is used by Andean medicine people to describe the ancient rituals of the Incans because of the exact specificity of the practices. While the Incan civilization is known for their advanced engineering and architectural abilities, all activities were based upon the precise movement of the sun (*Inti Titi*) and the stars (*chaskas*). As described in Chapter 2, the paqos practice being in the right relationship (*ayni*) with the cosmos through their capacity to hold and work with energy (*kausay*) based upon Incan these principles. All living beings are an aspect of *Wira Cocha*, which in complexity theory corresponds to the premise that our understanding and relationship to the life space we live in is rooted in the circumstances in our backgrounds and surroundings. In both Andean medicine and complexity theory the dynamics of our engagement are constantly evolving and changing in response to our ever-changing world.

Complexity theory or dynamic systems thinking in psychoanalysis has been explained in the following statement by Emmanuel Ghent:

> *A great many developmental features that appear to be driven by a built-in genetic program or design, are, in fact, the spontaneously emergent, and therefore the never completely predictable, resultant of the interplay of embedded, embodied, and environmental elements.* (Ghent, 2002, p. 762)

Rather than attempting to reduce psychic experience into a more rigid model that corresponds with mathematics, it allows for unique, intersubjective experience that is an interplay between quantitative and qualitative design. Phenomena described in quantum theory is based upon probabilities rather than absolutes. The approach of complexity theory in psychoanalysis came out of the principles that define quantum theory and corresponds with codes in Incan technology that define the properties of energy.

Quantum Physics, Oceanic Experience, and Space as an Energy Field

The theoretical physicist Carlo Rovelli has written, "Time and space are real phenomena. But they are in no way absolute" (2019, p. 66). Based upon Einstein's work, he (Rovelli, 2014a) has explained that space curves where there is matter and that space cannot stand still. Everything in the universe vibrates and is always expanding (Rovelli, 2017).

The effect of gravity on time causes it to move more slowly. According to loop gravity quantum (LGQ) theory, movement in space occurs as gravitational waves that cause time to slow down near planets because time is slowed down by mass. The curve of space is related to matter due to the phenomenon of gravity.

Time also passes more slowly as rate of change of movement, or speed, increases[5] or, in other words, for a moving object, time dilates from the viewpoint of another observer (Rovelli, 2017). These factors combined cause space to move "like the surface of the sea," indicating that space is not empty (Rovelli, 2014a, p. 9).

Paqos would agree with Rovelli's statement:

> *There is no such thing as a real void ... one that is completely empty. Just as the calmest sea looked at closely sways and trembles, however slightly, so the fields that form the world are subject to minute fluctuations, and it is possible to imagine its basic particles having brief and ephemeral existences, continually created and destroyed by these movements.* (Rovelli, 2017, p. 31)

Einstein's (1954) description of space moving like the sea and Rovelli's (2014) explanation of quantum theory fit with descriptions given by both early psychoanalysts (Saarinen, 2012) and paqos regarding the state of oneness in oceanic experience, described in Chapter 2. Paqos say that it is possible to experience oceanic states consciously,[6] while psychoanalysts such as Freud and Jung have disagreed as to whether it is possible for consciousness to exist in this state (Ackerman, 2017). Quantum theory in modern physics has developed an explanation as to how both are possible, if using observation as an indicator of consciousness.[7]

After Einstein's (1954) theory of relativity was accepted, a complementary wave–particle duality theory was proposed in quantum physics (Heisenberg, 1962) that included the actuality of both waves and particles in explaining the behavior of electrons in relation to atomic structures, which are mutually exclusive but both necessary in developing a broader and deeper understanding of the properties of electrons (Rovelli, 2014a;2014b). Seligman (2005) has applied Heisenberg's work to conceptualizing complexity theory in psychoanalysis, that elements interacting together alter one another and the system they exist in. He has noted:

> *[I]ntervening in a system may change the nature of the system. This is perhaps most famously articulated in Heisenberg's uncertainty principle, which posited that measurements of atomic particles change the properties of the particles themselves, heralding the revolutionary scientific attitude that was further articulated in complexity theory. Even as this approach emerges from atomic science, it also is apparent in everyday life. When my daughter was eight, while looking at the swirls on her frozen yogurt cone, she said, "Isn't it cool how each time you take a bite, it's a new pattern?" This all parallels the contemporary analytic assumption that our attitudes and interventions change the entire analysis.* (Seligman, 2005, p. 295)

Invisible and Visible Realms of Existence

Recognizing electrons as particles explains their physical existence at a specific place in time that is observable[8] (that is, temporal, and three-dimensional), while predicting the behavior of elections conceptualized as waves in string theory describes the existence of electrons atemporally, as one-dimensional objects. In atemporal conditions, they exist in an unseen range (that is, a wave as an estimate of probable positions) that cannot be pinned down exactly. The physicist Dean Rickles has described this as:

> *Quantum theory itself has wave-particle duality for the electron: increasing knowledge of the particle-like aspect decreases knowledge of the wave/field-like aspects, and vice versa. String theory treats all particles, electrons included, as vibrations of strings [one- dimensional objects]. These strings are then quantum mechanical, with the quantized modes corresponding to specific particles. The strings wrap around hidden, compact space dimensions to generate the kinds of stuff we can observe at our human scales (and down to particle accelerator scales).*[9]

Perceiving particles that can be physically observed is explicit, consciously taking place in temporal reality. A three-dimensional space is a mathematical space in which three values (coordinates) are necessary to locate the position of a point. However, when electrons are conceptualized as waves, they cannot be observed in a physical reality and as a result—according to quantum theory (Rovelli, 2014), do not exist as such, so are in an atemporal state. For example, according to Rickles, in a personal conversation:

> *The wave aspects of an electron exist in a 3N-dimensional space [configuration space], which when there are many electrons becomes very large (e.g., for three electrons, you have a 3x3 dimensional space in which the system exists). When measurements are made, the particle-aspect is manifested, and this reduces to ordinary 3-D space.* (Rickles, 2023)

With the introduction of string theory that followed,[10] the particle–wave "duality" became understood to be a function of context, based on a one-dimensional paradigm between two points involving position and momentum. String theory proposed understanding electrons as both particles and hypothetically as waves, to predict the range in which a particle could potentially emerge in time and space. In addition, in string theory, different particles are thought to have dissimilar vibrational patterns suggesting that they can potentially exist in distinct realms. This is congruent with practices in Andean medicine. Many paqos have the capacity to consciously exist energetically in different dimensions, with different energetic frequencies or levels.

In quantum theory, the focus has shifted from studying the substance of the strings in time and space and moved toward exploring the qualities of space and time itself as a network (Rovelli, 2008).[11] Rovelli (2017) has stated that observable reality exists within a moving energetic field (space) where elements of energy can only exist in relationship to other elements, through interacting (that is, colliding) with one another. According to Rovelli (2014a), in quantum theory, this energy field consists of pockets of light energy that aren't uniform nor evenly distributed throughout space. The electromagnetic field of space is made up of these pockets of light energy called photons, which are located at different points, stretched across the vastness of space. The concept of the instantaneous emergence of random assemblies has been applied to developing system theories in psychoanalysis, moving further away from a reductive approach toward focusing on relational process. The theory of particles and waves in quantum theory parallels the following description of the spontaneous manifestation of unpredictable new arrangements arising in time after an infusion of energy. Thelen and Smith's following statement, derived from physics, outlines the dynamic systems involving psychic material in psychoanalysis:

> *When sufficient energy is pumped into these systems, new, ordered structures may spontaneously appear that were not formerly apparent. What started out as an aggregation of … individual parts with no particular or privileged relations may suddenly produce patterns in space and regularities in time. The system may behave in highly complex, although ordered, ways, shifting from one pattern to another, clocking time, resisting perturbations, and generating elaborate structures. These emergent organizations are totally different from the elements that constitute the system, and the patterns cannot be predicted solely from the characteristics of the individual elements.* (Thelen and Smith, 1994, p. 54)

This approach, aligned with the paqos' orientation of being an integral part of the living cosmos, creates greater opportunity for attunement through connection in each moment in time as it is happening rather than being attached to a preconceived notion focused on the past. This brings spontaneity and aliveness into the analytic dyad because it centers on energetic movement rather than becoming reified through being wedded to preconceived constructs. From a psychoanalytic intersubjectivity theory perspective, Stolorow and Atwood have described psychoanalytic intersubjectivity as a field or systems theory that views psychological phenomenon as developing at the intersection of reciprocal points of shared experience that are not the result of permanent and separate intrapsychic configurations and processes (Stolorow and Atwood, 1992b, pp. 43–55).

Dynamic systems theory has also focused on understanding the developmental process of "emergent order and complexity: how structure and patterns arise from the cooperation of many individual parts" (Thelan and Smith, 1994, p. xiii). This is based upon the same tenants that physicists such as Rovelli (2017) have been proposing that emphasize the intersubjective context and interaction that create meaning and outcome.

> *These emergent organizations are totally different from the elements that constitute the system, and the patterns cannot be predicted solely from the characteristics of the individual elements.* (Thelan and Smith, 1994, p. 54)

The Nature of Energy: The Energetic Encounter

Within the space field, energy particles of electrons take on certain values caus-ing them to jump between atomic orbits—and release or absorb a photon of light energy as they jump.[12] This jump is referred to as a quantum leap.

The release of light that occurs through a quantum leap causes the energy particles of electrons to become visible and observable. Physicists such as Rovelli (2014b) (who credits Werner Heisenberg with this theory) say that energy electrons only exist when they are observable.[13] Because they are only seen when light is emitted, energy electrons only exist when they are colliding with other atomic structures, causing them to materialize in physical reality. "Quantum leaps" refers to the phe-nomenon of light energy manifesting in physical reality. Physicists frequently tie the concept of existence to the capacity to be observed—which implies consciousness.[14]

In tying quantum theory back to psychic states from a perspective based in tem-poral physical reality based upon the activity of electrons, it seems reasonable then that existence—or consciousness—is manifestation that occurs through contact, with atemporal states remaining as unobservable, unconscious states of discon-nection. The duality of existence that occurs in quantum physics and between conscious and unconscious states in psychology can be understood to be the rela-tionship between two phases of the same material, dependent upon state and per-spective (observable versus unobservable).

In Andean medicine, *tupay* ("spiritual meeting"), is an energetic exchange of disclosure between sentient beings involving confrontation. This engagement cre-ates the opportunity for deeper connection and spiritual development. Likewise, in dynamic systems theory, the lack of stability caused by states of attraction between electrons ebbing and flowing in relationships causes "collision"—or confrontation, bringing about the manifestation and evolution of new ways of being. This emer-gence results in a shift from atemporality into temporality.

From a dynamic systems perspective, development is viewed as "the con-tinual stabilization and destabilization, over time, of preferred attractor states" (Thelen & Smith, 1994, p. 61), as "evolving and dissolving attractors" (Thelen & Smith, 1994, p. 85). From this vantage point, change is defined as "the transi-tion from one stable state or attracto-to another" (Thelen & Smith, 1994, p. 63). Such a conception of change holds profound implications for conceptualizing the therapeutic process because it posits that change requires disorganization of the developing system. It is the loss of stability and coherence that "provides the bumps that allow the system to discover its new stable patterns. ... Developing systems must be in this unstable or quasi-stable mode to explore new coopera-tive patterns" (Thelen & Smith, 1994, p. 65), to "assemble new adaptive forms" (Thelen & Smith, 1994, p. 68). (Stolorow, 1997, p. 339)

In alchemy, this contact with undifferentiated, unconscious material of the *prima materia* (first matter), or "soul of the body," is worked with so that it is transformed into the "gold" of consciousness.

In quantum physics, Andean medicine, dynamic systems theory, and alchemy, direct encounter through contact creates a relationship that results in the emergence of a new form coming into being in temporal reality. In alchemy, this is the process of *coagulatio*, the result of action, symbolized by the element of earth (Edinger, 1985, p. 83), the process of creation. This process of creation in temporal reality is the energetic transformation of spirit into matter based upon an active relationship between conscious and unconscious, and soma and psyche, moving from atemporality into temporality. It corresponds with the paqos' concept of psychic levels of engagement in understanding experiential states, and the concept of unity, moving from the literal to the energetic. It also fits with the ideas presented by Von Franz (1992), Jung (1970), Rolland (1929), and Bohm (1990) that psyche and matter, and the unconscious and conscious, exist on a range in an energetic field that is state-dependent.

Psychoanalytic complexity theory (Stolorow and Atwood, 1992a; 1992b) has also proposed the existence of a complex interconnected system with elements being interdependent and changing within the system. This aligns with Thelen and Smith's (1994) dynamic systems approach that change within the analytic setting is uncertain and intermittent due to the lack of contextual constancy that exists in the emerging and developing patterns in the open configuration of elements. This system creates a freedom in the interaction of many different elements that "are nonlinear and capable of remarkable properties" (Thelen and Smith, 1994, p. 54).

Existence, Connection, and Temporal States

Rovelli's (2014a; 2014b) description of the information contained in space as a network of correlations between groupings of atoms, a system of actual shared information between physical atomic structures speaks to the comprehensiveness of the energetic field in space. In quantum physics, the network of atoms interacting with one another is a web of correlated connections existing between groups of atoms that provide reciprocal information (Rovelli, 2014a).[15] Rovelli's explanation also suggests potential for the emergence of psychic material to occur through association within the network of space.

The paqos' concept of the cosmos existing in a state of connection and reciprocity—or *ayni*—supports Rovelli's statement, "The way in which atoms arrange themselves is correlated with the way other atoms arrange themselves." According to Rovelli, "one grouping of atoms can have information, in the technical precise sense, about another group of atoms" (2014a).

Rovelli has written (2017, 2014a) that, materially, electrons only exist in relationship (interaction with other atomic structures). Electrons are discrete quanta of fluctuations of the field, which can pop in and out of physical existence, and consequent of this they can't be tracked in time, which causes them to be considered impermanent in physical reality. The field itself adheres to the first law of thermodynamics that states that although energy can change form, it cannot disappear altogether, nor be created or destroyed.[16] Based upon the concept that psychic energy cannot be destroyed, non-existence, or no longer existing in temporal reality doesn't infer annihilation—only a shift into an atemporal state.

Jung has written:

> *Energy is not to be observed in nature; it does not exist. What exists in nature is natural force, like a waterfall, or a light, or a fire, or a chemical process. There we apply the term energy, but energy does not exist ... Energy proper is an abstraction of a physical force, a certain amount of intensity.* (Jung, 1996, p. 8)

From a broader perspective that includes temporal and atemporal states, Andean cosmology, quantum physics, complexity theory, and depth psychology agree that there is permanence in the energetic essence of all things, and that an atemporal energy field holds the potential for physical manifestation and consciousness. Electrons moving in and out of existence are due to moving between states of temporality and atemporality. From a temporal perspective based in physical reality, particles disappearing is a function of moving from a temporal to an atemporal state.

Not only is energy permanent regardless of its state—temporal or atemporal, but everything also exists in relationship. Energy exists in space, in form through the interaction of electrons, and space itself is also energy (Rovelli, 2017). This aligns with the paqos' perspective that everything in the cosmos is made up of energy and is alive and connected.[17]

Space and Psyche Connected: Conscious Network of Energy

As mentioned in Chapter 2, according to Andean paqos the energetic realm referred to as *kausay pacha* is the substrate from which physical reality is created, as an atemporal fluid state of energy. Paqos move between realms in the meditative practice of *hamat'ay*.[18] For paqos who have entered a deep state of *hamat'ay*, psychic shifts are made by moving between different levels of psychic engagement, ranging from a physical state to an energetic state of connection.[19]

Kausay pacha resembles the energy field described in quantum physics that consists of pockets of light existing in a relationship of interaction (or connection) with other atomic structures. The Andean belief that we are part of an intricate cosmic system in which everything is alive and connected agrees with Rovelli's (2014) statements that space is a network of information. This understanding of the cosmos also aligns with current theories in intersubjective psychoanalysis.

In their application of quantum theory to psychoanalysis, in the dynamic systems approach they proposed that developed into complexity theory, Thelen and Smith have written:

> *Although behavior and development appear structured, there are no structures. Although behavior and development appear rule-driven, there are no rules.*

There is complexity. There is a multiple, parallel, and continuously dynamic interplay of perception and action, and a system that, by its thermodynamic nature, seeks certain stable solutions. These solutions emerge from relations, not from design. When the elements of such complex systems cooperate, they give rise to behavior with a unitary character, and thus to the illusion of structure. But the order is always executory, rather than rule-driven, allowing for the enormous sensitivity and flexibility of behavior to organize and regroup around task and context. … [Such organization is] emergent and not designed. (Thelen and Smith, 1994, p. xix)

The relational patterns of the world we exist in determine how we experience ourselves, one another, and how we live in and perceive our environment contextually. In physical reality we are living in a temporal interdependent state that takes place as a succession of events occurring moment to moment in the current *pacha* (allocation of energy at a point in time in space), which defines our consciousness.

This paradigm is also the basis of all our relationships including the transference process in psychoanalysis. Coburn has framed this notion of being embedded in a larger system within the context of the transference in complexity theory. He has written that all selfstates occurring in the analyst or analysand are dispersed across a wider relational shared experience in which they are both active participants (Coburn, 2006, p. 604). This intersubjective approach replaced one-person (intrapsychic) and two-person (interpsychic)[20] theories with the idea that the inner psychic world of an individual is embedded in other subsystems or networks with an ongoing, dynamic flow of reciprocity[21] and mutual influence in an intersubjective system (Stolorow and Atwood, 1992a, p. 18).

Stephen Seligman has written about the relevancy of complexity theory in its relevance and application to psychoanalysis, stating:

Although nonlinear dynamic systems theory may appear esoteric and overly intricate, it can be approached in an intuitive, experience-near way so as to offer a language and an imagery that captures many of the basic assumptions that underlie our everyday clinical thinking, interacting, and experiencing. (Seligman, 2005, p. 286)

William Coburn has conceptualized suprasystems as levels of consciousness existing within a relational field:

I refer to the distinction between what is experienced, on a variety of levels of consciousness and the dynamic, unpredictable interplay of the multitude of interpenetrating adaptive relational systems that give rise to such experience. All by way of saying, it is useful to know on what level of discourse we are speaking from one moment to the next, or, perhaps, which side of the tapestry we are employing—the phenomenological or the explanatory. Explanatorily speaking, I understand a "selfstate" to be a dimension of experience that is emergent and always of a context and that it is always a product and a property of a larger relational/ historical system. (Coburn, 2006, p. 604)

Coburn's (2006) statement about identifying the specific level of discourse corresponds to the phases of re-entry. The phenomenological being close to the actual sensory experience and explanatory referring to a state where the experience has been metabolized enough to become integrated into a narrative, describing the selfstate within a historical context. This parallels the moving between levels of engagement in Andean medicine—from energetic experience into physical reality that can be described through language.

Seligman's (2005) psychoanalytic conceptualization also resembles the paqos' description of levels of psychic engagement. Like Coburn (2006), he has presented a model involving systems interacting. He has written:

Attention to the changing patterns of systems leads to a nonreductionistic, nonlinear approach. It focuses attention away from causes and effects and toward a complex and shifting terrain in which causes and effects cannot be easily parsed—in which effects and causes are, in fact always being transformed into each other. Systems—organized in multiple levels—reorganize one another rather than simply responding to new events in easily predictable, linear ways. Contexts decisively affect outcomes, and the whole is greater than the sum of its parts. (Seligman, 2005, p. 287)

Seligman (2005) is describing a fluid intersubjective process that is inclusive of atemporal states that, by their nature, do not fit into a delineated structure. This conceptualization creates the possibility for openness within the analytic container that facilitates the opportunity for the analytic dyad to exist in nonverbal implicit states of connectivity—of being in the experience together rather than describing it—which results in creating states of separation. This perspective also allows for the emergence of different "time states" or *pachas* to exist in the analysis simultaneously, which can occur when working with cumulative traumatic experiences that have become confabulated in implicit memory. In these liminal states, existing on the edge of consciousness, the past and the present are intermingled, allowing for the ambiguity of uncertainty, staying closer to phenomenological experience. This analytic process is described in greater detail in Chapter 11.

The Psychoid, Synchronicity, and Supersymmetry

Jung (1960b) takes a more intrapsychic perspective, making room for different points in time to exist simultaneously within the individual psyche. He has written:

And the essential thing, psychologically, is that in dreams, fantasies, and other exceptional states of mind the most far-fetched mythological motifs and symbols can appear autochthonously[22] at any time ... These "primordial images" or "archetypes," as I have called them, belong to the basic stock of the unconscious psyche ... The collective unconscious comprises in itself the psychic life of our ancestors right back to the earliest beginnings. It is the matrix of all conscious psychic occurrences, and hence it exerts an influence that compromises the freedom of consciousness in the highest degree, since it is continually striving to lead all conscious processes back into the old paths. (Jung, 1960, p. 112, pars 229–30)

Jung's orientation, which includes both collective and individual experience, illustrates the fullness of information contained in what he refers to as the "psychoidal realm," the atemporal fluid state between soma and psyche. His conceptualization is inclusive of a collective history that is alive in the present experientially (Jung, 1954a).

These nonlinear analytic attitudes open the door for seemingly unpredictable cosmic relationships to exist. Einstein (1954) first proposed the concept that later became referred to as "entanglement theory," which states that something that occurs in one place can instantaneously link to something happening in a different location, regardless of distance. This indicates that spatial separation does not imply physical independence, and two objects that are far apart in space can function as a single entity, giving support to the premise that everything is connected (Greene, 2004).

Bohm has built on this theory, stating:

(This) implies that elements that are separated in space are generally non-casually and non-locally related projections of a higher-dimensional reality, it follows that moments separated in time are also such projections in reality... Interrelated time orders ... are all dependent on a multi-dimensional reality that cannot be comprehended fully in terms of any time order or set of orders. (Bohm, 1980, p. 268)

Jung's (1954a) and Von Franz's (1978) theoretical conceptualization of an objective psyche and a psychoid supports the premise that consciousness exists in the energy field of space, in which things transform into different states, and everything is connected. Rather than using a model of levels they have described a continuum ranging between soma and psyche. Their description of the psychoid, the intersection of soma and psyche, or matter (which is observable) and energy (which is invisible) again parallels the paqos' perception of different levels of psychic engagement. It also aligns with the paqos' idea of the existence of an essential form of consciousness—regardless of where something is located on the spectrum between soma and psyche.

Jung (1954a) has described a psychic continuum where at one end the invisible (ultra-violet) archetypal structure (archetype-as-such) occurs, and at the other end the visible (infra-red) symbol (archetypal image) exists. This idea is congruent with the paqos' explanation of shifting perception from an energetic collective (an energetic state of oneness) into physical reality.

Psychoidal material may arise in the personal psyche that corresponds with its existence in the objective psyche at the same time. Jung called this phenomenon synchronicity, describing it as the coinciding occurrences of meaningful similarities in casually unrelated events. Because of the occurrence of synchronicities, Jung (1960b) concluded that the psyche wasn't limited to a particular point in time and space (*pacha*). He has written, "I consider synchronicity as a psychically conditioned relativity of time and space" (Jung, 1960, p. 19). Jaynes (1996, p. 60) has stated, "You cannot, absolutely cannot think about time except by spatializing it. Consciousness is always a spatialization in which the diachronic is turned into the synchronic, in which what has happened in time is excerpted and seen as side-by-sideness."

Sacco has written about "one's subjective experience that coincidences between events in one's mind and the outside world [which] may be causally unrelated to each other yet have some other unknown connection" (2019, pp. 46–62). In the psychoidal archetypal realm that exists at the deepest layer of the unconscious, where psyche and matter become indistinguishable (Pauli, 1994), is the domain in which synchronistic phenomena arise and become activated (Atmanspacher and Fuchs, 2014).

Von Franz described synchronicity as the mirroring of psyche and matter, saying, "material events in the outer world would have to be regarded as statements in the objective psyche" (1980, p. 190). An essential feature of synchronistic events is that they carry energy with an emotional or psychic charge making the experience meaningful and numinous. A synchronistic connection is *felt*, not just understood intellectually.

String theory also involves the energetic linking of two seemingly separate domains, concentrating on the behavioral properties in the potential range particles, or strings, applied to higher dimensions with the implication that all known particles have undiscovered pairs. Also consistent with entanglement theory, the idea that there are undiscovered pairs for the particles is called supersymmetry. Superstring theory is based on the premise that matter and force in a sense are the same. As energies are increased, or distances reduced, the distinction between matter and force disappears.[23]

The occurrence of synchronicity—or supersymmetry—indicates that the oceanic experience of oneness is potentially bidirectional, and interpsychic as well as intrapsychic due to an energetic connection among living things and the natural world. Fundamentally, string theory, entanglement theory, supersymmetry, and superstring theory—like synchronicity—are all grounded in the understanding that there is a fluid relationship between essential particles that make up the cosmos based upon a network of energetic connection that is constantly changing and transforming between states of existence and nonexistence, or temporality and atemporality respectively.

This description of an archetypal reality, a reality based upon universal templates or patterns through which everything emerges in the psychoidal realm (Kerr, 2013), corresponds with the paqos' description of the mythic level of psychic engagement. This is the realm of the collective Andean cosmic beings and relates to an experience I had early in my training with the paqos.

Before visiting Peru for the first time, I had a dream about a numinous figure surrounded by a radiant white light in the form of a birdman who spoke to me. The figure had a bird's head with penetrating eyes, with wings and legs. Weeks later after arriving in Peru, I was walking through a market for the first time with the *altomesayoq* who would later become my teacher. During our stroll down one of the isles, he suddenly stopped and pointed to a painting of a birdman that was hanging in a stall of one of the vendors and said to me, using a combination of motion-gestures, Quechua, and Spanish, "There is the figure that appears in your visions." After spending some time in Peru, I later learned about the significance of the mythic condor *Apucheen* in Andean cosmology. For me, this early experience in Peru was an example of an intersection between soma and psyche.

Main has written:

> *The psychoid archetype ….is inaccessible to consciousness… located in the meeting place between the psychological and the physiological, it combines or transcends both. It can show up therefore in the relationship between a person's psyche and their body. Its … most significant aspect refers, in Roderick Main's words, "to the relationship between a person's psyche and the physical world beyond that person's body." (Main, 2004, p.26.*

As described, synchronicity, or supersymmetry, occurs in the temporal domain, between two seemingly unrelated events that are connected in an atemporal state, in which there is no conscious awareness in physical reality. These phenomena also occur intrapsychically when there is no apparent (ego-based) conscious awareness. This supports the paqos' premise that there is an atemporal consciousness in the energy body of the *manos wasi* that is not a function of the ego or dependent on the use of language for processing.

Clinical Data and the Space/Psyche Connection

Even Jung who thought the ego was the center of consciousness in his later years through his work with patients who had sustained a head injury or were in a state of coma admitted that there seemed to be a form of consciousness that was not ego-based. He has written:

> *These experiences seem to show that in swoon states whereby all standards there is every guarantee that conscious activity and sense perception are suspended,*

consciousness, reproducible ideas, acts of judgement, and perception can still continue to exist. The accompanying feeling of levitation, alteration of the angle of vision, and the extinction of hearing and of coenesthetic perceptions indicate a shift in the localization of perceptions from the body, from the cerebral cortex or cerebrum which is conjectured to be the seat of conscious phenomenon. If we are correct in this assumption then we must ask ourselves whether there is some other nervous substrate in us, apart from the cerebrum, that can think and perceive, or whether the psychic processes that go on in us during loss of consciousness are synchronistic phenomena, i.e. which have no casual connection with organic processes ... perceptions independent of space and time which cannot be explained as processes in the biological substrate. (Jung, 1960b, p. 93)

After sustaining a massive stroke in the left side of her brain, forcing her to "live" in the right side of her brain until her left brain regained the capacity to function, neuropsychologist Jill Bolte Taylor wrote about her experience: `

I wondered how much of my newly found right hemisphere consciousness, set of values, and resultant personality I would have to sacrifice in order to recover the skills of my left mind. I didn't want to lose my connection to the universe. I didn't want to experience myself as a solid, separate from everything. I didn't want my mind to spin so fast that I was no longer in touch with my authentic self. Frankly, I didn't want to give up nirvana. What price would my right hemisphere have to pay so I could once again be judged as normal? (Bolte Taylor, 2009, p. 139)

Bolte Taylor appears to be referring to the implicit, atemporal states of connectivity that the paqos experience. Shotter (1993) and Schore (2005) have explained that in shared nonverbal states of implicit experience, people can connect in deeper, more profound levels. Daniel Siegel and Daniela Sieff (2015) have also written about experiencing a holistic connection in the body with relational possibilities in connecting with the natural world. They have used the term interoception, meaning "perceiving within" (Siegal and Sieff, 2015, p. 140) to describe the exchange of information that can happen in implicit states of body awareness, leading to the formation of a mental map of felt states of experience that can be accessed cognitively. According to Schore and Sieff (2015), these states are not only a psychological process. They use the term high positive arousal to refer to the positive implicit nonverbal states that paqos describe occurring in states of *munay*. These subjective states of connection are felt to be unlimited and timeless, without the sense of temporal limitation.

The Illusion of Time

While the concept of time as "flowing" within a temporal time and space paradigm is assumed to be true because it feels like what is experienced, paqos, psychoanalysts, and theoretical physicists understand temporality as a series of isolated events that become woven together in a narrative. Rovelli (2017, p. 58) has written, "Physicists and philosophers have currently concluded that the idea of a present that is common to the whole universe is an illusion, and that the universal 'flow' of time is a generalization that doesn't work." Rovelli (2017, p. 58) has quoted Einstein as saying, "People like us who believe in physics, know that the distinction made between past, present, and future, is nothing more than a persistent, stubborn, illusion."

Einstein (1954) first proposed that time is not universal. Our experience in temporal reality of the "present" only exists as a bubble that surrounds us with a diameter determined by our ability to perceive milliseconds (Rovelli, 2017). In the energy field of space, at each point time is different so that time exists as a "spiderweb of times" (Rovelli, 2017, p. 15). Because time is a series of discrete instances, time does not flow. Although temporal reality is experienced as sequential, it is discontinuous. This phenomenon makes sense when considered as a microcosm of the timeline of our life history. This becomes a succession of separate events in the process of remembering.[24] According to Rovelli's (2017) theory, the world as we know it is a set of events *not* ordered in time. The events create relationships between variables that are (based upon theoretical deduction), at the same level. Everything that exists in the world exists as a subset of the whole—as parts, or certain variables interact with other variables that are also a part of that specific collection of events. The value of these parts determines the state of the world in reference to the particular subsystem, within the context of variables that they are exposed to (Rovelli, 2019, p. 136). The subsystem—or context that they are existing in—does not differentiate the minutiae of the rest of the universe because the subsystem is only interacting with a limited number of variables. Based upon this process, as humans we can only observe the particular variables we are exposed to, within the vastness of the universe. The indistinguishable configuration of variables—due to our lack of exposure—causes entropy, and the phenomenon of blurring (Rovelli, 2019).

Stern (2004) has approached this topic in his discussion of the "present moment." He has written, "the span of time in which psychological processes group together very small units of perception into the smallest global unit (a gestalt) that has a sense or meaning in the context of a relationship. Objectively, present moments last from 1 to 10 seconds with an average of around 3 to 4 seconds. ... The present moment is structured as a micro-lived story with a minimal plot and a line of dramatic tension. ... It is a conscious phenomenon, but need not be reflectively conscious, verbalized or narrated" (Stern, 2004, p. 245).

Marc Whitmann (2017) has estimated the experience of the "present moment" to be slightly shorter than Daniel Stern, lasting up to maximum of three seconds. The experience of stream of consciousness, which requires the creation of a narrative to conceptualize it, is based upon a feeling of now that expands beyond three seconds. Whitmann has suggested that in living from one moment to the next, we are experiencing a "moving frame of nowness" with a specific duration that expands beyond sensory or iconic memory and includes short-term and working memory (Whitmann, 2017, p. 50). This is possible because our working memory provides a temporal bridge that expands the frame of "now," due to the capacity to hold and manipulate multiple pieces of information at the same time being stored in short-term memory (Cowan, 2008), creating a fluid sense of being in the world.

The word "reality" is from the Latin word *res* referring to becoming a "thing" (Bohm, 1980, p. 67). The experience of "now" involves processing experiences that happened from a few seconds to a few minutes ago, based upon a "sliding window within the context of working memory" (p. 77). The "now" experienced as present is actually several moments, and temporal duration is dependent upon short-term memory capacity (Whitmann, 2017).

The Relationship between Time and Space as a Function of Heat

Rovelli (2017) has postulated that the experience of temporality, with a discernable difference between past and future, is the result of heat. "Heat is the only basic law of physics that distinguishes the past from the future. … Every time a difference is manifested between the past and the future, heat is involved" (Rovelli, 2017, pp. 22–3). This is because there are a couple of changes that happen when shifts from hot to cold occur and these changes cause the phenomenon of temporality. Thermodynamic theory provides an explanation of temporality that takes place in the context of the phenomenon of heat.

According to Rovelli (2014a), in thermodynamics, in addition to the law that energy is conserved and cannot be destroyed, there is another law that states that information diminishes if entropy increases. Entropy is chaos, and a measure of the amount of disorder in a physical system. According to quantum mechanics, information cannot increase by itself, and information in physical reality—or nature—is finite (Rovelli, 2014b). The two basic postulates in quantum mechanics are:

1) The relevant information—or information available—about any given system based upon past interactions that allows for the prediction of the result of future interactions is finite. (The chaos of entropy reduces the capacity to predict because less information is available.)
2) It is always possible to obtain new information on a given physical system and when new information is obtained, part of the previous information becomes irrelevant.

The number of possible distinct states (or amount of information) depends on temperature. Rather than being a substance itself, heat is basically the condition of the microscopic agitation of molecules. The difference between a past and a future is due to the entropy that occurs as the result of changes in temperature.

The fact that molecules (made up of one or more atoms) move more quickly in heated matter than cold, and that things that are heated (as in the case of a cup of warm tea) cool down is because it is more likely that a faster moving molecule (in a hot substance) will collide with a cooler, more slowly moving molecule, than vice versa. Because there are more possible states for molecules[25] in heated substances to move than cool ones—due to the faster rate at which they are moving—there are more possible trajectories and configurations. Because each configuration is singular, there are more details, with more information—and more "particularity" (Rovelli, 2017, p. 30).

According to Boltzmann's theory (Rovelli, 2017), the phenomenon of hot becoming cold, based on probability, is an (almost) irreversible phenomenon.[26] This concept also applies to the direction of time moving forward not backward. If a complete description of a system is available to all systems, time is not a variable, as there is no irreversible phenomenon. Once one system has less information about the potential states of all systems, the system with less information is experienced as existing in the past and a sense of temporality is created. Information is gained when time moves forward. In other words, a loss of universal access to information causes temporality.[27]

When an interaction (a collision between molecules) causes the state, or position of a molecule to become concrete (that is, defined temporally in physical reality), the state of the molecule is altered, and it loses information. Not only are the number of configurations reduced, the speed and position also become more limited.[28] Rovelli (2019) has explained that if speed is apparent before the position of the molecule emerges, then the state of the molecule changes in a different way than if the order was reversed. This is called "noncommutativity" (Rovelli, 2017, pp. 121–2) because the order of materialization in the speed and position of a molecule are not interchangeable.

In creating order, noncommutativity creates temporality. Rovelli has credited Alain Connes with discovering the mathematical formula that temporal flow (the existence of a past and future) "is implicitly defined by the noncommutativity of the physical variables" (Rovelli, 2019, p. 122).

In the irreversible process of heat moving into what has been cold, entropy increases, and activity slows down. If the process becomes arrested and stops, traces are left. Traces are what create reminders of what has been and memories of the past. This phenomenon creates the sense that the past is determined and that the future is open (Rovelli, 2017, p. 145).

"Blurring" and Temporality

In addition to the irreversible phenomenon of heated substances cooling and the order that is established that alters molecules, due to noncommutativity occurring, these states of increased entropy can also be caused by another factor. A third phenomenon takes place that causes entropy to increase and the amount of information to decrease (Rovelli, 2014a, 2017). The activity of heat passing to cold creates thermal agitation (disorder) in the cold molecules, after colliding with the heated molecules, which increases disorder.

This process creates additional entropy because there is a decrease in particularity, referred to as "course graining"—or potential outcomes in predicting the configuration of the movement of molecules because they are moving slower, due to cooling, based upon probabilities.[29] The difference between the past and the future in the experience of temporality is the result of entropy increasing. These phenomena together cause a "blurring" effect to happen (Rovelli, 2017, p. 31).

The physicist Boltzman (Cercignani, 1998) arrived at a formulation that showed that the ability to see the world becomes blurred because entropy exists. The lack of particularity causes the blurring and is a function of temporal experience.

An example that resembles the phenomenon of blurring occurred in an old *Star Trek* episode, in which Dr. McCoy finds himself in a situation of needing to transplant Spock's brain. He is temporarily given access to information on how to accomplish this. During the surgery, he comments on how amazed he is that the operation is so easy. When the surgical procedure is complete and he returns to his normal state, he is unable to retain the valuable information he acquired. He remembers the sense of clarity he had performing what had seemed simple in his altered state and that it became more complex when he returned to his previous state of awareness. Shifting from atemporal energetic experience to atemporal physical reality resembles Dr. McCoy's predicament of futilely trying to hold on to irretrievable information.

Temporality is a state where the present moment exists, along with traces of the past. In temporal states the future is unknown and greater degrees of entropy are associated with more course-grained states, in which less specific information is available. Ismael (2016) has given the analogy of trying to locate a person in space. In a high-grained state it might be possible to locate the city they are in, and in an even higher-grained state the specific building that they are in might be known. In a more course-grained state, the country where they are located might be identified but the precise coordinates of their location would be missing. This indicates that lower entropy is associated with higher states of consciousness, with very high states of consciousness being atemporal.

When the exact details of the microscopic state of the world are not available, temporality and blurring take place, resulting in temporal asymmetry. It is possible to find traces of the past, which cannot be changed. The future has no traces and can be altered. Increased entropy results in asymmetry of causes and traces related to the past. Because of the fixed past and open future, entropy is a process that is asymmetrical *in* time.

With entropy, the observer is unable to predict the specific movement of elections. These changes in the capacity to perceive create the temporal experience of past and future. Thelen and Smith (1994) have linked this phenomenon to human development, which takes place in temporal reality.

[D]evelopment does not "know" where it is going from the start. ... There is no end-state other than the end of life itself. ... Development is the outcome of

the self-organizing processes of continuously active living systems. (Thelen and Smith, 1994, p. 44)

A lack of information available regarding all aspects of the world creates temporality.

If we could perceive the microscopic state of things (with low entropy) completely, the experience of temporality would disappear. The phenomenon of blurring creates the perception of cause and effect, but it is acausal. This occurrence explains the experience of synchronicity—the appearance of a relationship between two acausal events that occur in an atemporal domain outside of noncommutativity. The dynamic of human interaction takes place in temporal reality. The analytic process is based upon the nonlinearity in human interaction.

All living systems are thermodynamically open systems in that order and pattern continue to emerge and evolve—that is, to "self-organize"—so long as there is a continual influx of energy. Dynamic systems theory is concerned with "how complex systems ... produce patterns that evolve in time." (Thelen and Smith, 1994, p. 51)

Because we cannot predict the exact movement and patterning of living systems and human behavior it is important to maintain an open analytic attitude to observe what emerges in the analytic dyad and the analysand's individual experience of temporal reality. Betty Joseph has written, according to Spillius and Feldman (1989) in Bromberg (1996, p. 513):

[I]f one wishes to foster long-term psychic change, it is important that the analyst eschew value judgements about whether the shifts and changes in a session are positive or negative. ... Nor should we be concerned with change as an achieved state; it is a process, not a state, and is a continuation and development from the 'constant minute shifts' in the session. (Spillius and Feldman, 1989, p. 5)

Bergson (2001 [1913]) has described how consciousness can conceptualize spaces beyond three dimensions, but entering these dimensions is a process of engagement different from a three-dimensional perspective. Bergson believes that an atemporal understanding develops in time, through intuitive contact, without a process reasoning.

Human interaction is an open-ended, multi-dimensional process. Our experience of the world is a function of our specific *pacha*, how we are located in time and space at any moment. Complexity theory, depth psychology, Andean medicine, and quantum theory understand that our perception and way of being in the world is determined by our relationship to time and our current energetic state. These factors create an interdependent relationship of connection that we are all part of, creating a context that must be considered in understanding individual experience, essential in the analytic process. We are all part of an intricate energetic system of connection. Because there are endless emerging possibilities moving in existence, keeping an open mind to what is being experienced in each moment is essential to grasp a deeper awareness of the layer of potential engagement. The shared understanding of the experience, according to shamans, is called consensual reality. This will be explored further in the next chapter.

Notes

1 Jungian depth psychology and complexity theory based upon the intersubjective psychoanalytic theory.
2 Conversation with physicist Dean Rickles, April 14, 2023.
3 The American Psychological Association (APA) has defined complexity theory as, "A field that studies nonlinear systems with very large numbers of interacting variables using mathematical modeling and computer simulation. In general, it proposes that such systems are too complex to be accurately predicted but are nevertheless organized and nonrandom."
4 Complexity theory includes dynamic systems theory (Thelen and Smith, 1994).
5 Rate of motion can only be determined based upon a specific point in space that measures where clocks separate and when they get back together on a straight line. Speed is determined relative to distance moved on the line in a specific interval (Rovelli, 2017, pp. 36–7).
6 In Andean cosmology, *teqsi muyu* refers to the consciousness of the universe on a collective level.
7 *Pacha-wan kausay* are inherent essential properties of the universe (*Wira Cocha)* that transcend everything that exists both physically and energetically—temporally and atemporally.
8 The paqos' definition of a *pacha*.
9 Email exchange with Dean Rickles on June 20, 2023.
10 Conversation with physicist Dean Rickles, April 14, 2023.
11 With the emergence of loop quantum gravity (LQG) theory (Rovelli, 2008). LQG studies space while string theory emphasizes the behavioral properties of the particles of the strings. String theory can be applied to higher dimensions with the implication that all known particles have undiscovered pairs.
12 Rovelli recognizes Dane Niels Bohr as the physicist who established the theory that the energy of electrons takes on specific values.
13 Rovelli attributes this conceptualization of something existing when it is observable to Werner Heisenberg's theory.
14 According to Dean Rickles (personal conversation, April 14, 2023) in addition to referring to the phenomenon of light energy manifesting in physical reality, quantum leaps refer to any jump between a pair of discrete levels—energy levels, amount of volume of space, and so on.
15 These are called *ceke* lines.
16 https://en.wikiversity.org/w/index.php?title=Thermodynamics/The_First_Law_Of_The rmodynamics&oldid=2137727. Conversation with Dean Rickles, April 14, 2023.
17 Rovelli (2017, p. 32) has explored the theory of "The Standard Model of Elementary Particles," which states that a particular quantity of fields exists interacting among themselves, with certain values and forces. Rovelli's explanation of The Standard Model of Elementary Particles resembles the paqos' conceptualization of psychic levels of

engagement. In the Andean cosmos, although unified and connected, the cosmos is also made up of different levels of vibrational frequencies beyond human comprehension, which also potentially could align with "supersymmetric" (Rovelli, 2017, p. 35) theories that forecast the probability of the presence of a new type of particles in space that have yet to be discovered.

18 See p. 63 of this text.
19 *Misawan kuasay* refers to bringing different states/energetic levels together. See pp. 66 and 71 of this text.
20 One-person approaches focused on the inner psychic experience of the individual while two-person approaches focused primarily on relationship with others in the external world. A dynamic systems approach says that the distinction between one- and two-person psychologies is outdated because the intrapsychic world is a subsystem within the larger intersubjective system.
21 Paqos refer to this state of receptivity as *ayni.*
22 Indigenous rather than descended from migrants or colonists.
23 Conversation with Dean Rickles, April 14, 2023.
24 Although according to Rovelli (2019) changes are not organized in a linear sequence; temporality is more complex. *Hatunmesayoqs* (the most evolved paqos) say that experience is multi-dimensional rather than linear.
25 A molecule is two or more atoms. An atom is the smallest particle of any element, whereas a molecule is the smallest particle of the compound. Atoms may or may not present independently whereas molecules exist independently.
26 According to Dean Rickles (personal conversation, April 14, 2023), this result only holds statistically— in terms of lower probability for the process to reverse and go into a more ordered configuration. This was Ludwig Boltzmann's discovery (Cercignani, 1998). Ludwig Boltzmann, *The Man Who Trusted Atoms*. Oxford University Press.
27 Perhaps access to all the information existing in the universe could be conceptualized as a universal consciousness.
28 Andean paqos call this a *pachacuti.*
29 According to Dean Rickles (personal conversation, April 14, 2023, "Certain changes of the microscopic particles don't change the overall macroscopic configuration, so you can bundle them together as the same state."

References

Ackerman, S. (2017) 'Exploring Freud's resistance to the oceanic feeling', *Journal of the American Psychoanalytic Association* 65: 9–31.

Atmanspacher, H. and Fuchs, C., eds (2014) *The Pauli Jung Dialogue*, Exeter: Imprint Academic.

Bergson, H. (2001 [1913]) *Time and Free Will. An essay on the immediate data of consciousness*, Mineola, NY: Dover.

Bohm, David (1980) *Wholeness and the Implicate Order,* New York, NY: Routledge & Kegan Paul.

Bohm, David (1990) 'A new theory of the relationship of mind and matter', *Philosophical Psychology* 3(2): 271–86.

Bolte Taylor, Jill (2009) *My Stroke of Insight: A brain scientist's personal journey*, London: Yellow Kite Books.

Bromberg, P. M. (1996) 'Standing in the spaces: The multiplicity of self and the psychoanalytic relationship', *Contemporary Psychoanalysis* 32: 509–35.

Bromberg, P. M. (2009) 'Multiple selfstates, the relational mind, and dissociation: A psycho-analytic perspective', in P. F. Dell and J. A. O'Neil (eds) *Dissociation and the Dissociative Disorders: DSM-V and beyond*, Abingdon, Oxfordshire: Routledge/Taylor & Francis Group, pp. 637–52.

Coburn, W. J. (2002) 'A world of systems: The role of systemic patterns of experience in the therapeutic process', *Psychoanal. Inq.* 22: 655–77.

Coburn, W. J. (2006) 'Terminations, selfstates, and complexity in psychoanalysis: Commentary on paper by Jody Messler Davies', *Psychoanalytic Dialogues* 16: 603–10.

Cowan, N. (2008) 'What are the differences between long-term, short-term, and working memory?', *Progress in Brain Research* 169: 323–38.

Edinger, E. F. (1985) *Anatomy of the Psyche: Alchemical symbolism in psychotherapy,* Peru, IL: Open Court Publishing.

Einstein, A. (1954) *Relativity: The special and general theory*, London: Methuen & Co. Ltd.

Galatzer-Levy, R. M. (1978) 'Qualitative change from quantitative change: Mathematical catastrophe theory in relation to psychoanalysis', *Journal of the American Psychoanalytic Association* 26: 921–35.

Ghent, E. (2002) 'Wish, need, drive: Motive in the light of dynamic systems theory and Edelman's selectionist theory', *Psychoanal. Dial.* 12: 763–808.

Greene, Brian (2004) *The Fabric of the Cosmos*, New York, NY: Random House.

Heisenberg, W. (1962) *Physics and Philosophy: The revolution in modern science,* New York, NY: Harper and Row.

Ismael, J. T. (2016) *How Physics Makes Us Free*, New York, NY: Oxford University Press.

Jaynes, J. (1996) *The Origins of Consciousness and the Breakdown of the Bicameral Mind,* London: Allen Lane.

Jung, C. G. (1954a) *On the Nature of the Psyche* (Collected Works, vol. 8).

Jung, C. G. (1954b) *The Practice of Psychotherapy* (Collected Works, vol. 16).

Jung, C. G. (1960a) *Structure & Dynamics of the Psyche* (Collected Works, vol. 8).

Jung, C.G. (1960b) 'Synchronicity: An acausal connecting principal' (Collected Works, vol. 8), in *The Structure and Dynamics of the Psyche Princeton*, Princeton, NJ: Princeton University Press.

Jung, C. G. (1970) *Psychological Reflections*, Princeton, NJ: Princeton University Press.

Kerr, Laura K. (2013) 'Synchronicity', in T. Teo (ed.) *Encyclopedia of Critical Psychology*, Berlin, Heidelberg: Springer-Verlag.

Kohut, H. and Wolf, E. S. (1978) 'The disorders of the self and their treatment: An outline', *International Journal of Psychoanalysis* 59: 413–25.

Main, R. (2004) *The Rupture of Time: Synchronicity and Jung's critique of modern Western culture*, New York, NY: Routledge.

Pauli, W. (1994) *Writings on Physics and Philosophy,* Berlin: Springer-Verlag.

Rickles, Dean (2023) personal conversation, April 14.

Rickles, Dean (2023) personal conversation, June 20.

Rolland, R. (1929) *The Life of Ramakrishna* [Essai sur la mystique et l'action de l'Inde vivante. La vie de Ramakrishna], 20th edn, trans. E. F. Malcolm-Smith, Kolkata: Swami Bodhasarananda.

Rovelli, Carlo (2008) 'Quantum gravity', *Scholarpedia* 3(5): 7,117.

Rovelli, C. (2014a) *Reality is Not What it Seems: The journey to quantum gravity,* London: Penguin Random House.

Rovelli, C. (2014b) *Seven Brief Lessons on Physics*, London: Penguin Random House.

Rovelli, C. (2017) *The Order of Time*, London: Penguin Random House.

Rovelli, C. (2019) *The Order of the Universe*, London: Penguin Books.

Saarinen, J. A. (2012) 'The oceanic state: A conceptual elucidation in terms of modal contact', *Int J Psychoanal* 93: 939–61.

Sacco, Robert G. (2019) 'The predictability of synchronicity experience: Results from a survey of Jungian analysts', *International Journal of Psychological Studies* 11(3): 46–62.

Sander, L. (2002) 'Thinking differently: Principles of process in living systems and the specificity of being known', *Psychoanal. Dial.* 12: 11–42.

Sashin, J. I. and Callahan, J. (1990) 'A model of affect using dynamical systems', *Annual of Psychoanalysis* 18: 213–31.

Schore, A. N. (2005) 'Attachment, affect regulation, and the developing right brain: Linking developmental neuroscience to pediatrics', *Pediatrics in Review* 26(6): 1–14.

Schore, A. N. and Sieff, D. F. (2015) 'On the same wave-length', in *Understanding and Healing Emotional Trauma*, Routledge.

Seligman, S. (2005) 'Dynamic systems theories as a metaframework for psychoanalysis', *Psychoanalytic Dialogues* 15(2): 285–319.

Shotter, J. (1993) *Conversational Realities*, Thousand Oaks, CA: Sage.

Siegal, D. J. and Sieff, D. F. (2015) 'Beyond the prison of implicit memory', in *Understanding and Healing Emotional Trauma*, London and New York, NY: Routledge.

Spillius, E. B. and Feldman, M., eds (1989) *Psychic Equilibrium and Psychic Change: Selected papers of Betty Joseph*, London: Tavistock/Routledge.

Spruiell, V. (1993) 'Deterministic chaos and the sciences of complexity: Psychoanalysis in the midst of a general scientific revolution', *J. Amer. Psychoanal. Assn.* 41: 3–44.

Stern, D. N. (2004) *The Present Moment in Psychotherapy and Everyday Life*, New York, NY: W.W. Norton.

Stolorow, R. D. (1997) 'Dynamic, dyadic, intersubjective systems: An evolving paradigm for psychoanalysis', *Psychoanal. Psychol.* 14: 337–64.

Stolorow, R. and Atwood, G. (1992a) *Contexts of Being: The intersubjective foundations of psychological life*, Hillsdale, NJ: The Analytic Press.

Stolorow, R. and Atwood, G. (1992b) *The Intersubjective Perspective*, Northvale, NJ: Aronson.

Thelen, E. and Smith, L. (1994) *A Dynamic Systems Approach to the Development of Cognition and Action*, Cambridge, MA: MIT Press.

Von Bertalanffy, L. (1968) *General Systems Theory*, New York, NY: Braziller.

von Franz, M-L. (1978) *Projection and Recollection in Jungian Psychology*, La Salle, IL: Open Court.

von Franz, M-L. (1980) *Projection and Re-collection*, La Salle, IL: Open Court.

von Franz, M-L. (1992) *Psyche and Matter*, Boston, MA: Shambhala.

Waddington, C. (1977) *Tools for Thought*, New York, NY: Basic Books.

Wittmann, M. (2017) *Felt Time: The Science of How We Experience Time*, Cambridge, MA: The MIT Press.

Chapter 11

Quantum Theory, Human Experience, and the Analytic Encounter

Context and Consensual Reality

Consensual reality is primarily based upon collective agreement and to a lesser extent upon individual perspective within the *pacha* being experienced in temporal reality. Our view of the world comes from a certain localized perspective that we share with others in a like set of circumstances. Again, this view is shared by physicists and psychoanalysts. The intersubjective psychoanalyst Adrienne Harris has written:

> *There is no single problem giving more worry, in every branch of psychoanalysis, than the question of how the system and the person co-mingle, co-construct, and evolve. ... Theorists are trying to establish the site or purview or habitation of the individual while living and practicing and theorizing in the full absorption of the porousness and intersubjective experience of any living beings.* (Harris, 2013, p. 700)

This creates a consensual reality as we understand it. The term "indexicality" refers to the phenomenon of how the meaning of a word may change every time it is spoken depending upon the context (that is, the condition and situation of the person using the word as well as when and where) (Rovelli, 2017, p. 133).

Indexicality and our view of the world are determined by the *pacha* we are experiencing. Rovelli (2017) has described (what I am referring to as re-entry) as a relative phenomenon based upon interaction rather than an arbitrary quantity. It is the property of an object in relation to another object. He has argued that in physical reality, entropy does not only depend on the configuration of elements in the physical world, but it also depends upon how we are subjectively blurring the world, based upon the interaction we have with the variables in the world.

Our own particular interaction with the world, based upon the limitations of temporality, determines the unique configuration of how we experience the world. In line with the paqos' belief that our experience of the world is made up of *pachas*, Rovelli has written:

DOI: 10.4324/9781003356448-15

Hence, we can think of spacetime as being as rigid as a table. The table has dimensions: the one that we call space, and the one along which entropy grows, called time. ... In the end, therefore, instead of many possible times we can speak only of a single time: the time of our experience: uniform, universal and ordered. This is the approximation of an approximation of an approximation of a description of the world made from our particular perspective as human beings who are dependent upon the growth of entropy, anchored to the flowing of time. (Rovelli, 2017, pp. 170–1)

Rovelli (2019) has argued that it is important to understand that the temporal structure of the universe that we experience depends upon our being part of the structure from within rather than viewing it from the outside (Ismael, 2007, 2016). David Stork has written:

Consensus reality therefore refers to the agreed-upon concepts of reality which people in the world, or a culture or group, believe are real (or treat as real), usually based upon their common experiences as they believe them to be. Anyone who does not agree with these is sometimes stated to be "in effect ... living in a different world." (Stork, 1998, p. 201)

When a description of the world is given, based upon the assumptions we make in consensual reality that doesn't consider the subjectivity of the view, we fail to see the world as it exists, only by what we think we know. I had a drawing instructor who used to say, "Draw what you see, not what you know."[1]

Castaneda described this process in his statement, "To change our idea of the world is the crux of shamanism and stopping the internal dialogue is the only way to accomplish it" (1998, p. 118).

In psychoanalysis, complexity theory's view of understanding our experience within the context of subsystems coincides with quantum theory. William Coburn has written:

[O]ur experiential worlds are not exactly ours, given how radically contextualized we are and given that each of us is the product and property of larger, complex systems. However, they often may feel like they are ours, that we own them, and that they are self-generated, phenomenologically speaking. And thus, this leads to one of our human conundrums—a most complex paradox: Each of us is quintessentially separate and individual and unique, but also systems generated, context dependent, and context embedded. (Coburn, 2019, p. 77)

In addition to the external limitations imposed by our lack of exposure in our current *pacha*, the subjective perspective is further developed by the occurrence of selective memory, only remembering certain aspects of an event, and then organizing the information and creating a narrative based upon these specific aspects of an event. The events that we witness and interact with, and the way we process the information internally, determine what we will perceive and remember.

The American Psychological Association (APA) has described the cognitive memory strategy "chunking" as "the process by which the mind divides large pieces of information into smaller units (chunks) that are easier to retain. ... As a result of this recoding, one item in memory (e.g., a keyword or key idea) can stand for multiple other items."[2]

Our memories, like time, exist as discrete intervals rather than as a fluid state. Although sometimes confabulated, memories of events are remembered in chunks. Clinicians working with clients who have trauma histories are aware of this phenomenon. Psychoanalyst Donna Orange has written:

> *The absence of temporality is a(n) ... important feature of Cartesian thinking. It results, sooner or later, in ... the idea of an individual isolated as a point in space from other human beings and from the natural world. Worst of all, such a point in space is atemporal, and thus has no developmental history, no story to tell ... [P]sychoanalysis, ... both manifests and challenges the atemporal Cartesian mind. Past penetrates and shapes the experience of the present, almost like a template, and past experience is always understood and reinterpreted.* (Orange, 2001, p. 293)

The task of the psychoanalyst is to work with our analysands in weaving these points in time together, to make meaning in connection with our experience. This corresponds with the conceptualization of time in quantum theory. Rovelli has written:

> *Thinking of the world as a collection of events, of processes, is the way that allows us to better grasp, comprehend, and describe it. It is the only way that is compatible with relativity. The world is not a collection of things, it is a collection of events. ... The difference between things and events is that things persist in time, events have a limited duration.* (Rovelli, 2019, p. 87)

Rovelli's (2019) perspective in seeing the world as events rather than things is useful in theorizing the way we understand the world, in that it enables us to be open to the possibility of what emerges. Susan Langer (1967) has written that ideas and thoughts are verbs, not nouns, because they do not exist outside of the context provided by time. The use of language offers the structure to understand time as a linear, sequential cognitive process, which defines the way in which time is experienced in temporal reality. The sense of a verbal self creates opportunities in interpersonal relations to observe the self from a separate vantage point, providing the capacity to be self-reflective using language. This type of cognitive operation involves mentation—the capacity to think about thinking.

Yet, using verbal language can also be limiting because it is a sequential temporal experience and if we are not cognizant of it, we may fall into the trap of reifying the experience. Once language is used, what we are describing becomes contextualized in the past because it is being reflected upon, and what is being referenced becomes a "thing." Even talking about the flow of time becomes a "thing" because it becomes an account of an experience, which is an event. Describing something a second later is another event.

Carlos Castaneda has stated:

Warriors say that we think there is a world of objects out there only because of our awareness. But what's really out there are the Eagle's emanations, fluid, forever in motion, and yet unchanged, eternal. (Castaneda, 1998, p. 236)

Castaneda (1998) appears to be referring to experience occurring at the mythic level of psychic engagement, —the realm in which transpersonal constellations of energy/matter are constantly fluctuating between form and energy, with the capacity to shift from atemporality into manifesting in temporal states. At the archetypal level, the psychic material that emerges often carries powerful feeling affect that shapes our interpretation of physical reality, existing within an interconnected matrix that we are all part of.

According to Rovelli (2019, p.89) the world exists as a "network of events." We do not experience time per se, we experience change and movement. An example of this is Rovelli's description of a family. He has written:

(A family is) not as a thing, it is a collection of relations, occurrences, feelings. And a human being? A knot of knots in a network of social relations, in a network of chemical processes, in a network of emotions exchanged with its own kind. (Rovelli, 2019, p. 89)

Castaneda's (1998) and Rovelli's (2019) statements can be applied to the paqos' conceptualization of *pachas*—the organization of energy at a specific point in space and time, existing in the living cosmos of *Wira Cocha*. The way the past relates to the present is carefully attended to in an emerging relationship of—as the paqos say—*ayni* (reciprocity in right relationship), not constrained by a preconceived narrative of history we have adopted that may have become comfortable because it is familiar.

As clinicians, our interpretation of our analysands' experience of the world may become less entrenched in the theoretical narratives we have come to accept, that have become reified from operating in a limiting paradigm of Self and Other. Approaching an understanding of human experience in this way may broaden our capacity to perceive and interpret what is occurring in the analytic setting at each moment in time as the process is unfolding.If we adopt the perspective physicists such as Rovelli (2019) are presenting, that our experience of the world is solely dependent upon our interactions in relationship (that is, things colliding, which occurs even at the microscopic level of electrons), this may help us help our clients (and ourselves) refrain from becoming "stuck" in attaching to the assumptions of a "closed-ended" that we and our clients create and continue to loop in. Engaging from a more open and contextual stance as it is unfolding may bring us closer to our analysand's immediate experience, deepening our capacity for connection.

Staying attuned to the immediacy of what is evolving in the analysis and alert to a common tendency to become attached to an interpretation of our analysands' subjective memories of events that have become arranged in a particular configuration may help to keep the analytic process alive and moving. Knowing that other interpretive configurations are possible, different from what we know we think we know, may help us to hold a more receptive stance to what may be emerging in the analytic process.Coburn (2019) has made a distinction between levels of conscious experience and the spontaneous interaction occurring between multiple interpenetrating systems of relating that are adaptive, facilitating these emerging experiences. The object relations psychoanalyst Phillip Bromberg has written:

> *Psychoanalysis is at its core a highly specialized communicative field, and what constitutes a psychoanalytically "meaningful" moment is constantly in motion with regard to one's experience of both reality and temporality. The shifting quality of time and meaning reflects the enactment of selfstates in both patient and analyst that define the multiplicity of relationships that go on between the patient's selves and the analyst's selves, only some of which are being focused on at any given moment. I would thus agree with Loewald (1972, p. 409) who wrote that "the individual not only has a history which an observer may unravel and describe, but he is history and makes his history by virtue of his memorial activity in which past-present-future are created as mutually interacting modes of time."* (Bromberg, 1996, p. 530)

From this perspective, our creation of the past, present, and future does not have a universal meaning because it can change depending on whether one is "here" or "there." Time is not uniform. It depends on variable exposure based upon specific location. The concept of a "now" does not exist as a totality only in the context of a "here"—because "there" time will be different—either past or future from here and now (Rovelli, 2019).

In moving from observing space at the level of atomic structures, into space at the minute, essential level—which paqos refer to as *qaway kusaq*, the perspective of time changes again. Quantum theory states that "atoms of space" that are a "billion, billion times smaller than the smallest atomic nuclei" are linked to one another, forming a network that creates a texture in space (Rovelli, 2017, p. 41). These smallest elements of space are not in the space—they *are* the space. Because space is continuous at this level, temporal time doesn't exist—as events or objects indicating separation no longer exist. With no separation, there is no potential for experiencing sequencing, and no temporality. James Grotstein (1978) has written that without separation between the self and the object, the experience of time does not exist, and that there is no capacity for perception and reflection to exist when there is no space for representation.

This is at the level of the energetic collective in the levels of psychic engagement in shamanism.

The quantum state of a system corresponds to the potentiality or "wave function" of a system. The complete autonomy of the system only exists when it is not being observed. Once it is being observed, another system has come into being that implies interaction, which introduces new possibilities of realizing probabilities—at the expense of others that cannot come into being at the same time.

Bromberg also has said:

> *Stein (1937, p. 298), commenting about the nature of life and the pursuit of goals, wrote that when you finally get there, "there is no there there." My patients frequently make the same comment. The direct experience of "self-change" seems to be gobbled up by the reality of "who you are" at a given moment, and evades the linear experience of beginning, middle, and end. But linear time does indeed have a presence of its own—like the background ticking of a clock that cannot be ignored for too long without great cost—and it is this paradox that seems to make psychoanalysis feel like a relationship between two people, each trying to keep one foot in the here and now and the other in the linear reality of past, present, and future.* (Bromberg, 1996, p. 508)

Building on Einstein's theory of relativity and a "unified field theory," Bohm (1980) proposed that quantum, the smallest discrete unit of a phenomenon, is indivisible. There is a natural order to the growth of all living things of undivided wholeness because, essentially, the "universe is an undivided and unbroken whole" (Bohm, 1980, p. 158). Particles are an abstraction of "corresponding intense singularities" (Bohm, 1980, p. 158). There is not a division between singularities, and the idea of particles is a rudimentary concept to describe the singularities or aspects of the energy field. These create patterns that are indicated by describing them, which loses meaning when it is perceived as separate parts rather than undivided wholeness (Bohm, 1980).

The phenomenon of hologram, a three-dimensional image formed by the projection of a light source, has introduced a new total order, which occurs implicitly in each area of time and space. "Implicit," based on the verb to "implicate," translates as "to fold inward" (Bohm, 1980, p. 188). The creates a "holomovement," which is a continuous entirety and is undefinable and unmeasurable. Holographic movement goes from three-dimensional to multi-dimensional implicate order, which according to Bohm (1980, p. 247) includes life force. Paqos call this *kausay*. Light energy functions by "enfolding and carrying" the implicate orders relevant to the whole structure. These events are happening at the same time, which is synchronicity—and the implicate order of the universe.[3]

Generative and Implicate Order

Based upon these ideas, David Bohm and David Peat (1987, p. 151) have proposed that there is a generative order in the universe not focused on an explicit external development through a sequence of events but on an inward order pertaining to creativity through which things manifest and emerge in nature and in consciousness. Shifting away from conceptualizing the process of time as occurring as a stream of events, movement that happens within implicate and generative order origins at a source in which everything is happening at the same time. It is timeless and atemporal. This is in alignment of the paqos' conceptualization of the movement from the energetic collective into physical reality.

This generative order—that paqos refer to as *kausay*—is common to all life and everything that exists that has matter. Consistent with the Andean premise that everything is connected, conceptualized in complexity theory as imbedded in a greater system, what emerges into physical existence is affected by the environment. At the deepest layers of generative and implicate order exists a consciousness that is transferred to electrons and particles. There is no discontinuity between consciousness, life, and matter, regardless of whether it is animate or inanimate.

Bohm and Peat (1987, p. 212) have defined the word "consciousness," based on its Latin root as "what is known together," or "the total state of knowingness of the individual." All facets of experience are affected by creative intelligence and, through action, acquire meaning. The creative action of intelligence begins in a deep level of generative order, while cognitive processes involving language are based solely upon intellect—and only occur in a temporal paradigm, which Bohm and Peat (1987, p. 216) have defined as "relatively fixed knowledge and skills of various kinds."[4]

In Grotstein's (1978) discussion of selfstates, he wrote that the "me" self must allow itself to be separated from the relational object or experience, to "re-present" it, and for the object representation to contain it. This separation allows for the creation of a dimensionality in inner psychic space. This inner space enables mental content to exist, with the ego experiencing autonomy from the object representation. The experience of separation can only occur within temporal time because it provides a progressive structure that enables differentiation to take place at different points in a perceived temporal space and time paradigm. In other words, the capacity for self-reflection requires a then and now, to stand outside of the original experience.

Since the construct of linear time is not experienced consistently in atemporal states, conceptualizing the existence of provisional inner psychic spaces, held as layers in the energy body of the *manos wasi* body, establishes a means for discerning ongoing inter and intrapsychic themes taking place within human experience. Generative orders in the quantum domain are currently "hidden to science." Heisenberg's statement corresponds with the theory of a generative principle proposed by David Bohm and David Peat (1987). He has written:

The existing scientific concepts cover always only a very limited part of reality, and the other part that has not yet been understood is infinite. Whenever we proceed from the known into the unknown, we may hope to understand, but we may have to learn at the same time a new meaning of the word "understanding". (Heisenberg, 1962, p. 201)

The idea of a generative principle that contains "the totality of structures and forms of a range of related species ... contains a totality of structures and forms a range of related species ... [and] may be called a 'protointelligence'" (Bohm and Peat, 1987, p. 202). Protointelligence involves a sensitive awareness of the creative element that exists, all at one within the cosmos, that is atemporal. According to Bohm and Peat (1987), the primary characteristic of protointelligence is that "totalities" are formed that are manifested from subtler levels of generative order, enfolded beyond the understanding of current physics and chemistry. Protointelligence aligns with the paqos' concept of sourcing from *Pachamama* and the different levels of psychic engagement, from physical reality to the energetic collective. Like the *manos wasi* and Jung's idea of a subtle body, Sheldrake (1982) has proposed that species contain a cumulative formative memory that determines individual development.

Karl Prigram (1976) has written that memory and information is also enfolded in the brain as a whole, rather than being localized, with memories connected by association and patterns, resembling functioning as a hologram. Through enfolded neural activity, a thought is grasped through an implicate order of associations, intermingling elements that exist together in relationship simultaneously in patterns.

Bohm has described reality as:

The relationship of different stages of enfoldment from what is to what is becoming in neural patterning. Each moment of consciousness has a certain explicit content, which is a foreground, and implicit content, which is a corresponding background. ... Consciousness is a series of moments ... experienced directly in the implicate order. ... The manifest content of consciousness is based essentially on memory, which is what allows such content to be held in a fairly constant form ... (The) mind enfolds the body. ... Similarly the body enfolds not only the mind but also in some sense the entire material universe. (Bohm, 1980, pp. 259–65)

The Complexity of Layering and Fractal Dynamics

Bohm's (1980) conceptualization of a generative/implicate order, both intersubjective and intrasubjective experience imbedded in temporal and atemporal states, can be conceptualized with greater specificity in a clinical setting through the model of fractal dynamics. Shapiro and Marks-Tarlow (2021a; 2021b) have proposed a model in which the inner and outer processes converge. They have written that their model is based on Mandelbrot's (1977) finding that fractal patterns exist within the nonreductive realm of nonlinear active human interaction, in a blurring of boundaries and interpenetration of realms that appear unrelated. This model allows for an inherent holistic structure to exist within the intersubjective experience of the transference in the analytic setting. The repetitive patterning that exists between the whole reoccurring in each of its parts, a phenomenon referred to by Marks-Tarlow and Shapiro (2021) as "self-similar" (a term originally introduced by Mandelbrot in 1967) holds intricate processes of information in the totality of the psychophysical experience occurring in humans. The complexity of this interconnected structure is like the paqos' description of the *manos wasi* energy body, a connected energetic network that holds all aspects of personal and the collective lineage of human experience, in the past, present, and future, in temporal and atemporal states. A fractal consciousness exists with a sensitivity in responding with immediacy to meaningful importance. This state of awareness has the capability to intuitively sense patterning of the whole within brief segment of exposure to human relational experience (Marks-Tarlow and Shapiro, 2021). The physicist Richard Feynman proposed, "Nature uses only the longest threads to weave her patterns, so that each small piece of her fabric reveals the organization of the entire tapestry" (2017 [1965], p. 28). Subjective awareness of interpsychic events and what is experienced in physical reality expands outward through our interaction in the world, and then this consciousness through experience returns into itself again, unfolding and re-enfolding (Bohm, 1980), as self-similar patterns at multiple levels of organization. This intersubjective matrix within the edges of fractal experience between the analyst and the analysand is porous and permeable. The transpersonal energetic network that is in a constant state of flux, is simultaneously separating and reconnecting, with synchronistic, or "uncanny," shared information being exchanged between them (Bass, 2001; de Peyer, 2016; Eshel, 2006; Farber, 2017; Kantrowitz, 2001; Mayer, 2007; Tennes, 2007) that is "transtemporal."

Shapiro and Scott have written:

> The challenge of "scientific mysticism" is to map a rigorous study of nonlocal/participatory knowing that would sift facts from imagination and construct empirically verifiable models of these phenomena (p. 151). … there are no "supernatural" phenomena in nature but only as yet unknown principles that will be incorporated within ever more encompassing naturalistic and trans-materialist paradigms. (Shapiro and Scott, 2019, p. 167)

They encourage looking beyond the binary paradigm, which would include the explicit/rational versus implicit/intuitive modalities of knowing, as well as and local-interactive versus "nonlocal participatory modes of consciousness" (Marks-Tarlow and Shapiro, 2021, p. 507).

Marks-Tarlow and Shapiro (2021, p. 504) have referred to this as a "dialectic synthesis," with a common underlying fractal patterning of a "prime substrate" representing a broader reality of information. Their work builds on Jung's conceptualization of an objective reality, in which soma and psyche are connected. Jung believed that synchronicities occur most frequently when people reach an internal impasse (Marks-Tarlow and Shapiro, 2021; Connolly, 2015). This suggests an accumulation of affect, as what generally occurs in dissociated trauma states that have been blocked off. A psychic environment is created, in which the boundaries bordering consensual, temporal reality soften, becoming more permeable, and a wider range of selfstates becomes accessible.

As has been reported in the analytic literature, more extraordinary forms of synchronicity often occur in working with psychotic and borderline patients due to the constellation of a strongly charged archetypal field that is not well regulated, because of a chronic high state of arousal and lack of ego resources. Synchronicities also tend to arise in highly traumatized states, which according to Jung occurs because these kinds of events appear in times when danger and serious risk is perceived (Cambray, 2002, p. 421).The experience of feeling is a nascent process related to transition in the brain's body mapping—where movement between phases can occur as a sudden, abrupt change in one area transfers and spreads. This resembles "the sharp melting points of many crystalline solids: as the temperature is slowly raised to being at or just over this point a rapid change of state from solid to liquid occurs" (Cambray, 2006, p. 7).

The Realms of Feeling—Collective and Personal in the Fractal Consciousness of Analysis

Cambray (2009, pp. 82–3) has said that empathy is the connecting, often unconscious psychoidal element between Self and Other that creates a meaning that breaks up symmetry when we self-reflect. This creates a patterning network of archetypes that is universal, with a synchronistic field dimension that is "affect charged" and transpersonal. Interior and exterior psychic spaces are included in this patterning that exists as an open system creating a field between individuals that is self-organizing.

Cambray's description of universal empathy as an agent of connection is what paqos refer to as *munay* (see Chapter 3, page 41). In Andean medicine, *munay* is an expression of a collective love between all living things in *ayni*, or a right relationship of reciprocity that is nonattached and experienced as an energetic current, or "flow state" at the level of the *energetic collective*. This state is often experienced as numinous and manifests in liminal spaces such as dreams and trance states. In analytic work, these feeling states most become embodied, to avoid dissociation through the defense of spiritual bypassing to avoid processing shadow material at the personal level.

At the personal level, relationally, attending to an analysand's vulnerable feeling states—experienced in attachment, is necessary because it provides a necessary mirroring component in healing trauma. However, Marks-Tarlow and Shapiro (2021) have also stressed the need to concentrate on transition points, moving in and out of feeling states, to the edges at points of constellation and of dissolution for a more dynamic focus. These are the moments when synchronicities are most likely to occur, generating openings with greater availability into deeper regions of the psyche. Working in these psychic spaces, when these selfstates have emerged closer to the surface, promotes active engagement with a more dynamic orientation that includes easier accessibility to potential entry points into sequestered areas that may affect change in the analysands' relational pattens. This happens within the immediacy of the transference. Marks-Tarlow (2008, 2011) has used the term "fractal consciousness" to describe the capability of intuitively detecting repetitive wholistic patterns that exist within brief "slivers" of relational experience. The edge-of-chaos dynamic provides an opening to work with feelings associated with trauma at the edge of their window of tolerance (Siegel, 1999). This often borders on the atemporal, psychoidal domains that Jung has described that carry potent archetypal energy. Synchronistically, in the middle of writing this section an analysand brought in the following dream that illustrates this phenomenon:

> *I was looking for a new house and I went into a magical forest with sentient mushroom trees that bordered a large house that I was going to live in. I took one of the mushroom trees and brought it inside of the house. I was looking for a pot to plant it in so that its roots would be in soil. There were men working on a desk in the entry area. There was a hole in the floor, and they wanted me to put the plant there and work at the desk, but I didn't like the space. I wanted to see the rest of the house. The man that owned the house was a pot maker. I went to look for a pot because I needed to plant the tree now. I went into the main room that was V-shaped, spacious, with a lot of windows. It was beautiful. In one corner of the V was a bedroom with a fireplace. There was a small room off the bedroom, where a powerful (positive) female politician lived. There was a picture of her in the room smiling. The room was compressed and only 2' tall. At the other end of the "V", was an office for creativity. It was the most important room in the house. I kept looking for the potmaker and a pot to plant the tree.*

In the dream there were a lot of edges in the V shape psychic configuration, with the woods surrounding the exterior a numinous source of fertility in the archetypal regions of the unconscious. The edges defining these spaces were visible, enfolding the exterior of the house into the interior, with the house representing the psychic spaces and resources my analysand was discovering lived within herself. My analysand's dream ego was curious about exploring the deeper regions of her psyche. In the dream her dream ego was moving beyond the surface layer, with the desk and the workers, which she felt represented being in a secretarial role, as "the dutiful good girl" in service of her own patriarch complex. A complex pattern that had lived inside of her since childhood had discouraged her from connecting to the creative writer living inside of her that was evolving. As my analysand moved into the deeper areas of her psyche, she found an environment that supported her creativity. She was moving into a comfortable living space where her own inner fire could reside—along with another aspect of the complex that constricted her ability to expand into her potential as a powerful woman out in the world. In the dream my analysand was moving into a realm that fostered a relationship with a positive inner masculine that she had not yet connected with, that would help her support her own root system, giving her access to the Self. Her dream ego's intent to plant the tree in the interior space might represent the "ego-Self axis" in her own individuation process. Overall, the dream landscape provided multiple transition points into and out of various affective and selfstates, providing windows into regions of my analysand's psychic structure. Her exploration of the different rooms of her psyche gave her a map of the fractal pattern at the liminal borders of consciousness and dream states, which supported her creative process and relationship with archetypal layers of the unconscious. These are the psychic spaces in which pertinent evolving patterns continually re-establish equilibrium in the analytic encounter (Shapiro and Marks-Tarlow, 2021a), and from which potential transference–countertransference undercurrents appear. These psychic domains are aspects of a psychic layering phenomenon that provides a way of conceptualizing the analytic experience that are self-similar and constantly changing. Marks-Tarlow and Shapiro (2021a, 2021b) have stated that because of the self-similar, the fully interpenetrating nature of "fractal seams" have boundaries with less rigidity in the outer limits, between selfstates, making it easier to experience more profound meta-patterns of reality that lie at the borders of chaos, closer to more implicit arousal states away from the equilibrium that exists in well-established ego states. Because analysts often engage with their analysands who are experiencing trauma states, moving into the paradigm of fractal consciousness during the analytic encounter is less difficult, because greater spontaneity and accessibility exists in the multi-layers of fragmentation and deeper spaces of psychic connection. Marks-Tarlow and Shapiro have encouraged shifting:

> *Intuitive knowing and "uncanny" experiences remind us that we live in an Unus Mundus where subjective worlds of meaning continually interpenetrate with each other and with their wider informational reality to form a tapestry of self-similar connections across apparent divides of inner/outer, mind/matter, psychological/physical, and micro/macro domains. ... We are all bound by the web of sensory local-interactive connections that underlie empathic and implicit relational knowing, and by extrasensory nonlocal-participatory sharing that manifests in "uncanny" and synchronistic experiences.* (Marks-Tarlow and Shapiro, 2021, p. 505)

The nonlinear nature of clinical intuition lives in the spaces between theory and practice (Marks-Tarlow, 2012, 2014a, 2014b, 2015), and the ways in which the analyst understands selfsimilar patterning in their perception of their analysand's experience of inner and external reality will influence their subjective and intersubjective perspective (Marks-Tarlow, 2008).

An interobjective zone emerges in the analytic dyad through the shared exploration of consensual reality based upon intersubjective interpretations that take place at the edges of the analysand's and analyst's perspective (or fractal boundaries). The interobjective zone is created by moving beyond the conceptualization of an objective external reality through acknowledging the influence of the unique subjective experience on the interpretation of reality.

A fractal theory of interpretation enables the development of an understanding of consensual reality that is transsubjective, beyond individual interpretation, through the selfsimilar informational patterns that join objective and intersubjective territories. Because in a fractal network system the pattern of the whole is present in each of the parts, it can never be extracted, requiring the existence of a multi-faceted paradigm of relatedness. This spans temporal and atemporal states, encompassed in an expansive informational reality that is inclusive of nonlocality (Marks-Tarlow, 2008).

Fractals also occur in the experience of time, across time intervals (Marks-Tarlow, 2008). Psychologists who conduct psychological assessments know that the best predictor of future behavior is past behavior. Infants learn to anchor themselves in physical reality through experiencing repetitive time intervals between need and satiation. The experience of temporal fractals is responsible for anticipation of an event from another, and acquiring the skill of waiting in the time occurs through developing a tolerance of the time intervals in between.

Because linear time intervals are often experienced as rhythmic and cyclical, certain points in the cycle repeat and carry different qualities of affect. Moments before a baby's hunger pains are satiated are experienced very different from the moments after. Cycles of experience often repeat, however the way we make meaning of a repeating event is dependent upon our current maturity and level of development.

Through having an awareness of different potential aspects of fractal consciousness, analysts will be more attuned to their analysand's experience moment to moment, with a greater sensitivity to the multi-dimensionality of the analytic encounter. This understanding can provide a foundation for greater recognition, and therefore responsiveness to the intricate complexities of the psychic material being constellated as it is emerging.

Psychic Layering in the Analytic Encounter

Psychoanalysis places an emphasis on making what is unconscious conscious by working through what is being held in the unconscious in a timeless state, often related to trauma. Boyd (2008) has dispelled the popular myth that we only use ten percent of our brains and asserts instead that we only *understand* about ten percent of how our brains operate. This suggests that the unconscious is active. Jung (1955) has written that the conscious falls behind the unconscious and that prospective dreams and synchronicities are possible because the unconscious has access to information not yet available consciously.

Jung has written:

> *"Meaning" is an anthropomorphic interpretation. … What the factor which appears to us as "meaning" may be in itself we have no possibility of knowing.*

(1955, par 916) … I had learned that all the greatest and most important prob-
lems of life are fundamentally insoluble. They must be so, for they express the
necessary polarity inherent in every self-regulating system. They can never be
solved, but only outgrown. I therefore asked myself whether this outgrowing,
this possibility of further psychic development, was not the normal thing, and
whether getting stuck in a conflict was pathological. Everyone must possess that
higher level, at least in embryonic form, and must under favourable circum-
stances be able to develop this potentiality. (Jung, 1967, par. 18)

Bright (1997, p. 618) proposed that Jung's theory of synchronicity allows for
an acausal perspective toward psychological experience in which it is understood
that links are formed through an interpretation of meanings rather than through a
narrow, reductive lens of cause and effect. He has written, "any *conscious* attribu-
tion of meaning, such as an analytic interpretation, must be seen as subjective and
provisional" (p. 618). This information spans temporal and atemporal dimensions,
and is responsible for a psychic layering, enfolding simultaneously that occurs
within the analytic encounter. The individuation process evolves when the unconscious and conscious are both allowed to participate. If limited only to a reductive
polarization (Bright, 1997) there is no potential for transcendence, *conjunctio*, or
individuation.

A method of conceptualization in alignment with the models described in complexity theory, implicate and generative order, and fractal dynamism create a
paradigm that takes the analytic process away from chronological limitation into
a domain where everything can exist and unfold simultaneously, in line with an
orientation of reality inclusive of levels of psychic engagement, existing simultaneously (Bryon, 2012).

Bachelard (1939) has described a temporal dimension in waking dreams, or reverie, which he describes as vertical because it appears that there are states that are
not limited to being bracketed in existing within the time continuum of consensual
reality. In the analytic process, it seems that, at times, not only is time experienced as vertical, but that the analytic field becomes "stacked" or layered with
psychic material from different selfstates—or *pachas* that are present and accessible simultaneously, congruent with Bohm's (1980) description of implicate order
and Marks-Tarlow and Shapiro's (2021) description of fractal dynamics, in which
the layers enfold upon themselves. Marks-Tarlow and Shapiro's (2021) model of
fractal dynamics is a way of conceptualizing the layering that occurs within the co-
created experience that develops between the analyst–analysand experience with
greater specificity.

The following descriptions are of aspects of the potential layering—of selfstates'
psychic functions that may contribute to the experience of the analytic encounter
simultaneously with nonlocality, not bound in a consensual time and space continuum. The system or field[5] that emerges is an activation of a composite of selfstates associated with different *pachas*, or contextual experiences that create the
richly textured interwoven tapestry of one's life, which evolves and emerges,

becoming alive and accessible in the analytic encounter. Potential aspects that may exist within the layering that folds and unfolds transference dynamic will be described.

The Analysand's Somatic Memory from Infancy

Implicit memories from infancy in reaction to past events remain held in the body. These include nonverbal memory generated from neural patterns that are the result of sensory-motor interactions with the environment (Leuzinger-Bohleber and Pfeifer, 2002). They stem from the personal unconscious linked to past experience that occurred in early infant development. At birth, psychic development originates in somatic experience, when the edges between oneself—or sense of having a "me"—and the outer world are undifferentiated. Ogden (1989a) has referred to this atemporal state as the autistic contiguous position. It is the most primitive state associated with personal experience, referenced as *being* feelings of pleasure, anger, and/or fear before the awareness of *having* a feeling has been identified. In this preverbal state, there is no sense of separation from the external world. Some analysands access feeling states linked to fragmented memories previously frozen by gradually "thawing" and feeling what was going on in their bodies.

The Analysand's Episodic and Somatic Memory

Szpunar and Tulving (2011) have written about two forms of temporal memory that involve cognition. The first involves being conscious of temporal existence through remembering what has happened. This is referred to as episodic memory or auto-noetic consciousness, which only occurs in humans. The second is sematic consciousness (Ekstrom, 2014), which has to do with recognition. Episodic memory begins in semantic memory and has the capacity to travel to a different point in time, in space to what has happened or to the future to imagine a potential world (Clayton et al., 2007).

These forms of memory, in the analysand—and the analyst—construct the framework for the analytic encounter that is the basis for psychoanalysis. They create the demarcation between the past and the present and the co-created field for reverie that holds psychic material and enables what has been unconscious to be made conscious—and temporal. They also generate the capacity for awareness of a *pacha*, an allocation of energy at a specific point in time and space.

Levels of Experiencing in Analysis Related to Selfstates

In the relational field of the analytic encounter perceptual shifts vacillating between *pachas* happen that involve different mental and emotional states that affect how time is experienced, through memory. When the analyst is aware of the psychic shifts occurring in the analysand between atemporal and temporal states during an analytic session, an understanding of the analysand's experience moment to moment deepens, and the analyst has a greater capacity to stay attuned to the subtle movements taking place between selfstates. This paradigm provides a means for developing greater awareness of ego functioning in temporal reality, in relation to various states residing in the personal unconscious.

Winnicott (1971) has described that through the analyst's process of listening to the emergence of trauma that has previously been split off from the analysand's consciousness and holding the previously repressed psychic material in working memory, movement happens between the analysand's past memory states involving earlier events and real time in the present.

In this process, the analyst's attention remains fluid, open to the shifting occurring between selfstates, ego-consciousness, and somatic memories held in the body. Flow itself is a mark of an emergent state. For past trauma to become conscious and worked through, it must be witnessed by the analyst, as it is being relived by the analysand and contained in the transference. The analytic container brings the experiences of then and now together, through a process Bohm (1980) refers to as enfolding, that Winnicott (1971) calls holding and interpretation in the transference—allowing for a new narrative to be constructed.

Paqos call this point of manifestation, of implicate order, a *ñawin*. Within a paradigm of time being layered, an awareness of a *ñawin* in the psychic space can provide a means for tracking critical moments of change occurring within the dynamic of the analytic encounter. The *ñawin* is the point of contact between psychic levels of ego-consciousness and atemporal selfstates that have previously been split off and frozen in the unconscious. It is a potential doorway where implicit material is emanating from the personal unconscious into conscious awareness.

Philip Bromberg (1996) and Donnel Stern (2003) have both presented a structure of psychic organization, which incorporates conscious and disassociated selfstates, existing in a frozen state of isolation, or in an arboreal relationship with the others. The subjective experience of time in the analytic encounter can be thought of as being comprised of spherical layers of overlapping and discrete selfstates within the energetic field that includes the *manos wasi* of the analyst and the analysand within the living energy field that surrounds us.

Selfstate levels are energetic—with the potential for boundaries to become blurred and superimposed upon each other. The individual selfstates contained within the *manos wasi* consist of energetic layers of psychic and somatic experience held together energetically—what paqos describe as the "luminous body onion". The energetic appearance of the luminous body has been described by Castaneda:

> *When they are seen as fields of energy, human beings appear to be like fibers of light, like white cobwebs, very fine threads that circulate from the head to the toes. Thus, to the eye of a seer, a man looks like an egg of circulating fibers…* (Castaneda, 1998, p. 31)

Using the paradigm of the paqos, the *manos wasi* of the analyst and analysand connect in *tupay*, creating a bi-directional transference dynamic. The possible composite of selfstate experiences held in the *manos wasi* generate the potential for awareness shifts to occur between temporal, extra-temporal, and atemporal states of reality, creating a complex phenomenon that Bohm (1980) refers to as enfolding, or implicate order.

During an analytic session, multiple selfstate layers are actively held in *tupay* within the co-created energetic field of the analytic dyad. Both the analyst and the analysand are each having their own relationship with time at every moment depending upon the subjective experience they are having, and as was previously described in complexity theory (Coburn, 2002) and, in addition, they can be influenced by material arising from and being carried in the energetic field. The theoretical construct of enfolding that Bohm (1980) has described is useful in differentiating latent variations of possible temporal, experiential themes taking place concurrently—that lack the sequencing structure of linear time.

Psychoanalysis is grounded in sequential time, with the existence of past, present, and future, and ego-consciousness centered the current *pacha* of the here and now. Freud (1930) acknowledged that the past lives on in the present, in extra-temporal psychic spaces. Later, Bromberg (1996) introduced the phenomenon of time condensation, to refer to perceiving the present and future based upon an enactment involving reliving a frozen replica of the past. Sometimes in reaction to traumatic events pieces may split off in different directions, a phenomenon shamans refer to as soul loss, as described in Chapter 5, creating discontinuous selfstates of temporal experience often in opposition.

Bromberg (1984) has said that primitive mental states are usually the result of having been "into oneself" for too long a time or not having adequate ego structure to get out of one's "self"—and back to the here and now. Bromberg (2009) has described how such an organizational structure within the psyche, holding traumatic memories and their corresponding selfstates becomes insulated, obscured from other explicit selfstates that are consciously retrievable. Paqos and psychoanalysts agree that in these states, memories are not worn by the effects of time.

Like the potential movement of electrons in wave theory, in physics, there are multiple levels of potential intrapsychic experience and interpsychic engagement imbedded in an analytic encounter. Although the term "interlaced" could be applied to levels of reality rather than time, without the construct of time as scaffolding, thoughts and ideas cease to exist—because they exist as a process, not independently.Bion (1994) said that the capacity for thinking develops out of the need to metabolize thoughts derived from upsetting emotional experience, and that two minds are needed to think one person's most disturbing thoughts. Stern (2002) added to this by saying that both the analyst and analysand are responsible agents in moments of change, dependent upon the capacity to self-reflect.

Laplanche (1997) suggests that there are "unconsciously transmitted messages" occurring in the analytic field between the analyst and the analysand that inadvertently affect the analysis. The analytic transference is a complex, multileveled interaction with a subjective experience of time that fluctuates in any given moment. There is a shifting that happens, alternating between different selfstates when moving between temporal and atemporal states. Temporal states are cognitive and require the use of language, while atemporal states are experienced and held in the body.

Atemporal somatic experience in shamanism and the tendency for unprocessed trauma to be held as implicit memory outside of ego-consciousness in the body also share commonalities with preverbal, nontemporal symbiotic preverbal states during infancy. Traumatic memories that become fragmented and locked away in implicit memory, shamanic states of ecstasy, and preverbal infancy states all exist outside of linear time.

According to Namnum (1972), the construction of the mind is based on temporal association. The psychoanalytic process removes the perception that time is linear, enabling an open exchange of projection between the past in the present (Valkonen-Korhonen, 2019). This occurs in a co-created "analytic third" (Ogden, 2009). The psychoanalytic encounter is dependent upon the analysand's current level of functioning, and the way they are experiencing and referencing their own internal states (Ogden, 1997).

Co-created Aspects of the Analytic Field in Real Time

The co-created "analytic third" refers to the implicit, transference/countertransference interaction created in the analytic field from material emanating from the personal unconscious of both the analysand and the analyst (that is, the ongoing, bi-directional, conscious transference/countertransference dynamic). Menninger (1958) has written that transference and countertransference are unconscious processes that are unknowable.

Barad has written:

The point is that it is the intra-play of continuity and discontinuity, determinacy and indeterminacy, possibility and impossibility that constitutes the spacetime-matterings of the world … the dynamic relationship between continuity and discontinuity is crucial to the open-ended becoming of the world which resist acausuality as much as determinism. (Barad, 2007, p. 182).

Entanglements are the phenomenon that develop and emerge through "intra-action" (Barad, 2007). Specific configurations of patterning that are entanglements change through each intra-action, an existence in which there is no separation between interior and exterior worlds of psychic experience, and analyst and analysand. This suggests that the transference connection is created and emerges through intra-action rather than as two separate entities coming together.

In quantum physics, theory entanglements happen in unpredictable quantum jumps, which involve a sudden leap from one energetic state to another (Gleick, 1986). This phenomenon also can be applied to psychoanalysis at "breakthrough" moments.

Entering a receptive state of nonlinear dimensionality, with the potential for intuitive jumps to occur, similar to quantum leaps—making the shift from an atemporal, undifferentiated psychic state into existing in physical reality enables a transition, from what has been implicit to become explicit, and what has been unconscious to become conscious. (Bryon, 2023)

At these crucial analytic moments, significant transformation can happen, deepening the analytic process and bringing energy into the analytic encounter. While I continue to refer to the shared analytic space as an intersubjective field, I acknowledge that what is emerging in the transference dynamic is the emergence of a new, fluid range of possibilities, existing contextually within a fractal organization at different moments of time—with no separation between interior and exterior spaces. In these moments of intra-action are the psychic spaces of constantly evolving repetitive patterns that create a sense of a stable intersubjective structure of change, from which the potential transference–countertransference dynamic occurs (Bryon, 2023).

The shared state of imaginal reverie that occurs in states of intra-action is often referred to as the "analytic third." In this dynamic process, implicit relational knowledge emerges from "shared moments" of corresponding fitted actions mutually created between the analysand and the analyst in the analytic dyad. In the analytic process, the analyst must hold multiple themes emerging in the analytic dyad from the analyst's and analysand's unconscious, internal states of reverie that emerge while tracking the interplay of the threads of developing themes. Potential layers of psychic experience occurring within the interactive field and transference—as a function of the *manos wasi*—include different states of temporal reality in the here and now. Components of the energetic field that become co-created (Ogden, 1989b, 2009) between the analyst and the analysand may potentially include the following selfstates:

Oceanic Experience

Nonverbal, somatic atemporal states of spiritual connection with what paqos refer to as the energetic collective are experienced energetically in the *manos wasi*. Schore and Seif (2015, p. 117) use the term high positive arousal to refer to positive implicit nonverbal states not restricted to a psychological process. Being in states of high positive arousal often elicit the feeling sensation of "coming home."

In his writing on early psychological development, Bollas (1987) has described that experiencing of the object comes before knowing the object. There is a linking of automatic nervous systems creating heightened moments of connection, which is essential for growth and healing. Like the paqos opening themselves in connection with the earth and the mountains, resonance requires entering a receptive state of vulnerability with trust. Paqos develop the capacity for profound implicit experience, in spiritual nonverbal states of connection.

The Introjected Parental Imago

The Introjected parental imago (Coen, 2003) refers to the selfstate of the analysand-as-child's perception of their parents' (or primary attachment figure's) unfulfilled needs and desires that were introjected into the analysand as a child, now living in the analysand's psyche in the present (LaPlanche and Potalis, 1973). LaPlanche (1997) proposed that a child's experience of desire is influenced by "unconsciously transmitted messages," emanating from the parent as unmetabolized, "coded" communications that may unconsciously become internalized by the child as their own. In a similar vein, Meltzer (1967) described a placenta mother, also referred to an "umbilical transference."

Ulanov (2017) has described an interpenetrating mode or matrix, which is a reciprocated relationship acting on the other's experience while remaining separate. This can apply to the mother–infant dyad and/or analysand–analyst dyad and involves an influential potency exchange that, unlike the concept of the analytic container, is bi-directional, similar to the premise in complexity theory.

Schore and Sieff (2015, p. 118) have described how inconsistent interactions with overpowering parental figures can limit an infant's ability to develop a sense of connection and trust in their ability to tolerate and engage in novel situations. Developing a sense of trust through experiencing being accurately understood by the analyst is necessary for healing relational trauma. Shore and Seif (2015, p. 128) have written that for analysands to feel understood they need to experience the feeling connection of being seen by their analyst, implicitly, while the same time, the analyst is actively listening to make objective evaluations.

The Analysand's Narrative Truth

Freud (1923, 1933, 1938) proposed that early memory is a function of current need and desire. Spence (1982) described the analysand's narrative truth, or—the analysand-as-child, as being created from preverbal states, predisposed needs, urges, feelings, and temperament influenced both by the analysand's childhood experience, and the resulting incorporation of memory based upon early experience. This selfstate from the past lives is an accumulation of the analysand's interpretation and assimilation of experiences starting in infancy that have formed the assumption creating the analysand's narrative of themselves and the world in the here and now. Ulanov (2017, p. 61) has described how the "matrix of the unconscious emerges in images, impulses, nub of imagination, fastening to fugitive thought a bit gleaming in a dream." The analysand's narrative truth can be a source of creativity arising from the unconscious that may manifest in the form of creative expression.

The Analyst's Narrative Truth

In the analytic process, the analyst's beliefs and personal historical narrative, theoretical orientation, and emotional needs—including both uncomfortable "hot spots" and unmet desires—become involuntarily projected onto—or introjected into—the analysand. This is similar to the introjected parental imago (Hansell, 2012), but it is not anchored in the past. It is an introjection into the analysand's psyche happening in the here and now. While previously undifferentiated psychic material in the analyst's narrative truth has been worked with and metabolized, it corresponds with the analysand's narrative truth.

Projective Trans-identification

Projective trans-identification refers to the imago created through projective identification by the analysand. The inner representation of the analyst is what becomes projected into—not the analyst themselves (Grotstein, 1978). In return, the analyst projects into their perception of what the analysand is projecting about them. An intersubjective third emerges from the analysand's transference projection and the analyst's countertransference projection in an "interimage resonance"—a bidirectional phenomenon occurring between the analyst and the analysand in the present.[6]

Grinberg's (1979) nonlocal neurodynamics model builds on the concept of an intersubjective third that includes a domain based upon a directly shared reality, with a mental representation built upon memories or beliefs, corresponding to the external experience of the other, within the analytic encounter. This form of "direct knowing" is a non-defensive type of projective counteridentification (Grinberg, 1979), an aspect of an implicitly shared intersubjective and interobjective reality. In both, repressed and non-repressed aspects of subjective experience are accessible through penetrable, semi-porous boundaries that exist between the analysand and the analyst.

Interpsychic Archetypal States and "Sourcing"

Psychic energy states formed through the archetypal templates[7] existing in the collective unconscious become conscious through processes involving reverie, dream imagery, and/or as somatic awareness (Stevens, 2006). In these states, synchronicities occur, and, in dreamtime, time is bidirectional, demonstrated in the phenomenon of precognitive dreaming (Dunne, 1927), which Gary Lachman (2022) has described in his book entitled *Dreaming Ahead of Time*.

In quantum theory, a two-state vector formalism (TSVF) exists, associated with the phenomenon of retro causality; that a causal relationship in the present can be influenced by quantum states linked to the past and of the future (Wheeler and Feynman, 1945). These atemporal states are an aspect of the greater inner transpersonal psychic reality of the objective psyche, which have been referred to as the energetic collective and the mythic level of engagement (Bryon, 2012).

The phenomenon of retro-causality is congruent with the paqos' premise that when the current *pacha* (an allocation of energy at a point in time and space) is healed, a corresponding healing takes place in the lineage—for the ancestors of the past and the trajectory of their future children. Paqos say that the past and future do not exist—only as an aspect of the present.

In their healing work, paqos "craft visions of the future," for themselves and their communities, which involves moving into deep states of connection, by shifting into an atemporal paradigm. Accessing a paradigm in which a "healed state" is created through a dream state of envisioning corresponds with the psychoidal realm, transcending time and space. Shapiro and Marks-Tarlow (2021b, p. 469) has used the term "transsubjective" to describe a dimension that expands beyond subjectivity and intersubjectivity, transcending internal experience to include elements of the external world, similar to Jung's description of the psychoidal realm.

For Jung, "psychoid" applies to the latent and unconscious meaning that exists in everything. Jung understood the psychoid nature of meaning to have an objective existence as well as a subjective creation, in both mind and matter, conceived as collective and unconscious, making it possible to explore meaning in an archetypal context (Bright, 1997).

In depth psychology, the deepest energetic psychic states originate in the psychoidal realm. According to Ulanov (2017, p. 24), "This psychoidal quality of unconscious processes is not the result of repression but is there anyway, beneath trauma, before repression." Ulanov (2017, p. 42) has written, "Recognizing the psychoidal experience as existing, coming to consciousness many ways, many different times, what effects does that have for our clinical work? It helps mend trauma."

At this level, according to Jung (1958, par. 851), "The psychoidal nature of the archetype contains very much more than can be included in an explanation. It points to the sphereof the *unus mundus*, the unitary world." In Andean medicine, this is the energetic collective and the realm of *Wira Cocha*, the living cosmos. Jung stressed the necessity of not ascribing magical causality because it is unconscious and unknowable (Bright, 1997). It requires curbing the potential urge to assign absolute meaning, as it must be understood to be subjective and provisional to avoid reification (Bryon, 2012; Bryon, 2023). He also said that it is important to abstain from a defense response of trying to put information in "order," by enduring the chaos or *prima materia* states as much as possible within the analysis. This is due to the potential that occurs in reductive acts of ordering and compartmentalizing (splitting) that can lead to dissociation—the basis of psychologically induced psychoses and neuroses (Jung, 1955, par. 494).

The model of fractal dynamism avoids this predicament by allowing for fluidity to exist between states of atemporal and temporality, and nonlocality and locality in interpsychic archetypal states, in which time and space become provisional constructs rather than absolutes. An analytic perspective operating at the mythic level of psychic engagement in Andean medicine perspective is compatible in that it is also transpsychic, existing in a fluctuating state between form and energy, while bridging a multitude of dimensions that include but are not limited to the subjective experience of a time and space paradigm, as well as atemporal oceanic states of oneness at the psychoidal level.

Holding a "nonreductive" stance and operating with the premise that connection with the living cosmos and the energetic collective can be "sourced" from the analytic encounter creates the potentiality for this to happen. I had a supervisor during my analytic training who once said, "We hold the analysand, and 'the great mother' holds both of us."By using the approach of a paqo and staying connected with *Pachamama*—or maintaining a fluid and open state through receptive mirroring, as the process is unfolding in the transference, can also create a sense of containment in the analysis. By staying anchored and embodied, through focusing on what is emerging in the analytic encounter, moment to moment, allows "the darkness" (*hucha*) associated with traumatic unprocessed memories to move through the analyst when an analysand is in a dissociated state. Holding a fluid position creates a channel to avoid psychic energy from staying held somatically in the analyst's body. While sitting with analysands in deadening states of depression, when the psychic energy in the analytic field feels heavy or "flattened," shifting into a self-state of connection (*hamutay*) with *Pachamama* is a way of bringing the life force of *kausay* into the analytic session. Similar to the practice of meditation, forming neural pathways and establishing a palpable memory of psychic connection that has become imbued with energy (that is, sourcing) in the moment infuses "aliveness" (*kausay*) into the analytic field that is being co-created. Sourcing connection is a means of energetically infusing the analytic encounter, which can strengthen the potential for effective mirroring, while increasing vitality and the accessibility of a greater range of selfstates. This can facilitate the action of "breaking out" of the restricted, repetitive, closed-ended loop that often happens in the narrative and somatic experience of people with depression.

The Atemporal Co-Created Field

In analysis, the conceptualization of the "time paradigm"—as being linear (that is, a sequential historical timeline), and/or multi-dimensional and simultaneously layered—accessed through dreams, implicit states, and reverie will influence how meaning is made and how a new narrative becomes constructed. Developing a conceptualization of potentially shared selfstates that may emerge in the co-created analytic field may foster an awareness and sensitivity that may provide the analyst with an opportunity to observe each of these levels as they enfold and emerge during a session and expand the analyst's perception to include more of what is happening in real time. This would involve shifting away from viewing the analytic encounter as a linear sequence toward developing greater openness in observing and tracking the interpsychic and intrapsychic enactments as they are taking place in the analytic process.

Attending to potential layers of temporal and atemporal experience that may be occurring simultaneously during an analytic encounter may provide an opportunity to—as Bromberg (1996) has said—stand between the spaces and deepen our understanding. Once the analyst has formed a loose, open-ended conceptualization of the analysand's psychology, it can be used as a provisional container that forms a working schema (Piaget, 1937) receptive to assimilating emerging psychic material in the present. If conceptualizations based solely upon "known" analytic theory are formed, the process becomes reified and the spontaneity in moving in time between selfstates that creates an aliveness in the field is no longer possible.

Only through an awareness that the analysand does not exist in only one self-state, requiring insight or the right relationship, will an analyst be sensitive to the multiple selfstates that exist within the analysand that influence the way in which they form relationships with the analyst within the transference, each uniquely separate (Bromberg, 1996, p. 506). Expanding our conceptualization of the time and space continuum can broaden our scope of awareness to perceive incoming information through a broader range of psychic channels in any given moment. This involves shifting away from the assumption that the analytic encounter can only occur as a linear progression, by listening for and being open to perceiving potential dynamics that may be occurring as atemporal experience.

In the co-created field between the analyst and analysand, the trauma related to the past is experienced in the here-and-now, and co-constructed meanings emerge. In dropping into the somatic nonverbal states within the analytic container, the analytic session becomes a fertile, multi-layered microcosm, with potential to access implicit, "timeless" material and together create an intersubjective field combining the past, present, and future in "real" time.

Healing occurs through retrieving repressed somatic traumatic memories, forming explicit narratives of the memories during psychic spaces of connection between the analyst and analysand. This understanding frequently develops through linking symbolic imagery with feeling states. The space that is created between our immediate experience and the symbol that emerges creates the ability to name feelings and formulate a narrative in temporal reality. The development of a personal narrative makes implicit feeling states more consciously accessible. Being able to work with an event within a context of past time and space provides a vantage point to step outside of the experience and reflect upon it. Anchoring the experience in this fashion is necessary for self-reflection and mentation to occur. Next, internal and external variables that influence our experience of temporality will be explored.

Notes

1 For example, the white of eyes aren't really white, and drawing a person from a fore-shortened perspective requires paying attention to the position of the person from the specific perspective of the person drawing the picture.
2 https://dictionary.apa.org/chunking
3 Interestingly, Rovelli (2019) has described how when there is more energy—such as the sun—there is less entropy. The sun provides heat radiating from the sky, which (when it isn't too extreme, as in the case of global warming) balances the energy being released. For the paqos, *Inti Titi*, or "Father Sun" is the powerful being that they "source" from or connect with in spiritual practice. Again, the paqos' perspective appears to be in alignment with physicists' understanding that the sun is the center of our solar system.
   Another interesting phenomenon that can be applied to understanding the psychological state of depression (*hucha* or "negative energy"—according to paqos) often caused by a

lack of exposure to sunlight is that in a global condition when entropy is high and energy is low the world falls into a state of "thermal equilibrium," with no distinction between past, present, and future, and nothing happens (p. 139). Frozen states experienced in trauma, when memories become stuck in time, and psychic and somatic blockage, when energy becomes stuck.

4 Intelligence on its own is explicit and limited to temporality, which is why it is not particularly relevant to the re-entry process after experiencing the energetic collective.

5 I am using the term "field" to apply to temporal and atemporal states, without the limitations of time or space.

6 Creating an "interimage resonance" is a progression, involving many steps, as projections are continually changed and revised, creating what Grotstein (1978) termed projective trans-identification. It seems that there is potential for both projective identification and projective trans-identification to occur—with projective identification involving affect, and projective trans-identification being a cognitive process.

7 Archetype means *original pattern* in ancient Greek. https://conorneill.com/2018/04/21/understanding-personality-the-12-jungian-archetypes/

References

Bachelard, G. (1939) *Instant poetique, instant metaphysique, in L'intution de l'instant* [The poetic instant and the metaphysical instant in *The Instant Intuition*], Paris: Gonthier.

Barad, K. (2007) *Meeting the Universe Halfway*, Durham, NC and London: Duke University Press.

Bass, A. (2001) "It takes one to know one; Or whose unconscious is it anyway?' *Psychoanalytic Dialogues* 11(5): 683–702.

Bion, W. R. (1994) *Learning from Experience*, Northvale, NJ: Aronson.

Bohm, David (1980) *Wholeness and the Implicate Order*, New York, NY: Routledge & Kegan Paul.

Bohm, D. and Peat, D. (1987) *Science, Order, and Creativity*, New York, NY: Routledge.

Bollas, C. (1987) *The Shadow of the Object*, New York, NY: Columbia University Press.

Boyd, R. (2008) 'Do people only use 10 percent of their brains? What's the matter with only exploiting a portion of our gray matter?', *Scientific American*, https://www.scientificamerican.com/article/do-people-only-use-10-percent-of-their-brains/#:~:text=Ultimately%2C%20it's%20not%20that%20we,percent%20of%20how%20it%20functions, February, accessed May 26, 2023.

Bright, G. (1997) 'Synchronicity as a basis of analytic attitude', *J. Anal. Psychol.* 42: 613–35.

Bromberg, P. M. (1984) 'Getting into oneself and out of one's self: On schizoid processes', *Contemporary Psychoanalysis* 20: 439–47.

Bromberg, P. M. (1996) 'Standing in the spaces: The multiplicity of self and the psychoanalytic relationship', *Contemporary Psychoanalysis* 32: 509–35.

Bromberg, P. M. (2009) 'Multiple selfstates, the relational mind, and dissociation: A psychoanalytic perspective', in P. F. Dell and J. A. O'Neil (eds) *Dissociation and the Dissociative Disorders: DSM-V and beyond*, Abingdon, Oxfordshire: Routledge/Taylor & Francis Group, pp. 637–52.

Bryon, D. (2012) *Lessons of the Inca Shamans, Part I: Piercing the veil*, Enumclaw, WA: Pine Winds Press.

Bryon. D. (2023) 'Implicit states of connectivity in the clinical practice of Jungian psychoanalysis and Andean shamanism', *Journal of Analytical Psychology* 68: 569–89.

Cambray, J. (2002) 'Synchronicity and emergence', *American Imago*, 59: 409–34.

Cambray, J. (2006) 'Towards the feeling of emergence', *Journal of Analytical Psychology* 51: 1–20.

Cambray, J. (2009) *Synchronicity: Nature and psyche in an interconnected universe*, College Station, TX: Texas A&M University Press.

Castaneda, C. (1998) *The Wheel of Time*, New York, NY: Simon and Schuster.

Clayton, N. S., Salwiczek, L. H., and Dickinson, A. (2007) 'Episodic memory', *Current Biology* 17(6): R189–91

Coburn, W. J. (2002) 'A world of systems: The role of systemic patterns of experience in the therapeutic process', *Psychoanal. Inq.* 22: 655–77.

Coburn, W. J. (2019) 'A most complex paradox: Rethinking the individual', *Psychoanalytic Inquiry* 39: 77–87.

Coen, S. J. (2003) 'The thrall of the negative and how to analyze it', *J. Amer. Psychoanal. Assn.* 51: 465–89.

Connolly, A. M. (2015) 'Bridging the reductive and the synthetic: Some reflections on the clinical implications of synchronicity', *The Journal of Analytical Psychology* 60(2): 159–68.

de Peyer, J. (2016) 'Uncanny communication and the porous mind', *Psychoanalytic Dialogues* 26(2): 156–74.

Dunne, J. W. (1927) *An Experiment with Time*, Charlotteville, VA: Hampton Roads Publishing Co.

Ekstrom, S. R. (2014) *Memory and Healing: Neurocognitive and psychodynamic perspectives on how patients and psychotherapists remember*, London: Karnac.

Eshel, O. (2006) 'Where are you, my beloved? On absence, loss, and the enigma of telepathic dreams', *The International Journal of Psychoanalysis* 87(6): 1603–27.

Farber, S. K. (2017) 'Becoming a telepathic tuning fork: Anomalous experience and the relational mind', *Psychoanalytic Dialogues* 27(6): 719–34.

Feynman, R. (2017 [1965]) *The Character of Physical Law*, Boston, MA: The MIT Press.

Freud, S. (1923) *The Ego and the Id* (Standard Edition, vol. 19).

Freud, S. (1930) *Civilization and Its Discontents* (Standard Edition, vol. 21).

Freud, S. (1933) *New Introductory Lectures on Psycho-Analysis* (Standard Edition, vol. 22).

Freud, S. (1938) *An Outline of Psycho-Analysis* (Standard Edition, vol. 23).

Gleick, J. (1986) 'Physicists finally get to see the quantum jump', *The New York Times*, October 21.

Grinberg, L. (1979) 'Countertransference and projective counteridentification', *Contemporary Psychoanalysis* 15: 226–47.

Grotstein, J. S. (1978) 'Inner space: Its dimensions and its coordinates', *Int. J. Psycho-Anal.* 59: 55–61.

Hansell, J. (2012) 'Integrating the intrapsychic and the interpersonal in psychoanalysis: Laplanche's contribution', *Psychoanalytic Psychology* 29(1): 99–108.

Harris, A. (2013) 'Discussion: Putting our heads together; mentalizing systems', *Psychoanal. Dial.* 23: 700-707.

Heisenberg, W. (1962) *Physics and Philosophy: The revolution in modern science*, New York, NY: Harper and Row.

Ismael, J. T. (2007) *The Situated Self*, New York, NY: Oxford University Press.

Ismael, J. T. (2016) *How Physics Makes Us Free*, New York, NY: Oxford University Press.

Jung, C. G. (1955). *Synchronicity: An acausal connecting principle* (Collected Works, vol. 16).

Jung, C. G. (1958) *Psychology and Religion* (Collected Works, vol. 18).

Jung, C.G. (1967) *Alchemical Studies* (Collected Works, vol. 13).

Kantrowitz, J. L. (2001) 'The analysis of preconscious phenomena and its communication', *Psychoanalytic Inquiry* 21(1): 24–39.

Lachman, G. (2022) *Dreaming Ahead of Time*, Edinburgh: Floris Books.

Langer, S. K. (1967) *Mind: An essay on human feeling* (Vol. 1), Charles Village, Baltimore, MD: John Hopkins Press.

Laplanche, J. (1997) 'The theory of seduction and the problem of the Other', *Int. J. Psycho-Anal.* 78: 653–66.

Laplanche, J. and Pontalis, J. B. (1973) *The Language of Psycho-Analysis*, London: Hogarth Press/Institute of Psycho-Analysis.

Leuzinger-Bohleber, M. and Pfeifer, R. (2002) 'Answer to letter concerning our paper: 'Remembering a depressive primary object', *International Journal of Psychoanalysis* 83:1186-1188

Mandelbrot, B. (1967) "How long is the coast of Britain? Statistical self-similarity and fractional dimension', *Science* 156(3775): 636–8.

Mandelbrot, B. (1977) *The Fractal Geometry of Nature*, New York, NY: W. H. Freeman.

Marks-Tarlow, T. (2008) *Psyche's veil: Psychotherapy, fractals and complexity*, New York, NY: Routledge.

Marks-Tarlow, T. (2011) 'Merging and emerging: A nonlinear portrait of intersubjectivity during psychotherapy', *Psychoanalytic Dialogues* 21(1): 110–27.

Marks-Tarlow, T. (2012) *Clinical Intuition in Psychotherapy: The neurobiology of embodied response*, New York, NY: W.W. Norton and Company.

Marks-Tarlow, T. (2014a) 'The interpersonal neurobiology of clinical intuition', *Smith College Studies in Social Work* 84(2–3): 219–36.

Marks-Tarlow, T. (2014b) *Awakening Clinical Intuition: An experiential workbook for clinicians*, New York, NY: W.W. Norton and Company.

Marks-Tarlow, T. (2015) 'The nonlinear dynamics of clinical intuition', *Chaos & Complexity Letters* 8 (2–3): 1–24.

Mayer, E. L. (2007) *Extraordinary Knowing: Science, skepticism, and the inexplicable powers of the human mind*, New York, NY: Bantam Books.

Meltzer, D. (1967) *The Psychoanalytic Process*, Portsmouth, NH: Heinemann Medical.

Menninger, K. (1958) *Theory of Psychoanalytic Technique*, London: Imago.

Namnum, A. (1972) 'Time in psychoanalytic technique', *J. Am. psychoanal. Ass.* 20: 736–50.

Ogden, T. H. (1989a) 'On the concept of an autistic-contiguous position', *International Journal of Psychoanalysis* 70: 127–40.

Ogden, T. H. (1989b) *The Primitive Edge of Experience*, Abingdon, Oxfordshire: Routledge.

Ogden, T. (1997) 'Reverie and metaphor: Some thoughts on how I work as a psychoanalyst', *Int. J. Psycho-Anal.* 78: 719–32.

Ogden, T. (2009) 'The analytic third: Working with intersubjective clinical facts', in A. Ferro and A. Basile (eds) *The Analytic Field*, London: Karnac Books, pp. 159–88.

Orange, D. M. (2001) 'From Cartesian minds to experiential worlds in psychoanalysis', *Psychoanal. Psych.* 18: 287–302.

Piaget, J. (1954 [1937]) *The Construction of Reality in the Child,* New York: Basic Books.

Prigram, K. (1976) *Consciousness and the Brain*, New York, NY: Plenum.

Rovelli, C. (2017) *The Order of Time*, London: Penguin Random House.

Rovelli, C. (2019) *The Order of the Universe*, London: Penguin Books.

Schore, A. N. and Sieff, D. F. (2015) 'On the same wave-length', in *Understanding and Healing Emotional Trauma*, Abingdon, Oxfordshire: Routledge.

Shapiro, Y. and Marks-Tarlow, T (2021a) 'Bridging the unbridgeable: Toward a meta-reductive science of experience: Response to Harris and Cartwright commentaries', *Psychoanalytic Dialogues* 31(4): 503–10.

Shapiro, Y. and Marks-Tarlow, T. (2021b) 'Varieties of clinical intuition: Implicit, explicit and nonlocal neurodynamics', *Psychoanalytic Dialogues* 31(3): 262–81.

Shapiro, Y. and Scott, J. R. (2019) 'Extraordinary knowing within the framework of natural science: Towards a theory of "scientific mysticism"', in P. F. Craffert, J. R. Baker, and M. J. Winkelman (eds) *The Supernatural after the Neuro-turn*, Abingdon, Oxfordshire: Routledge, pp. 148 –71.

Sheldrake, R. (1982) *A New Science of Life,* Los Angeles, CA: Tarcher.

Spence, D. P. (1982) *Narrative Truth and Historical Truth: Meaning and interpretation in psychoanalysis*, London and New York, NY: W.W Norton and Company.

Stern, D. B. (2002) 'Language and the nonverbal as a unity: Discussion of "where is the action in the 'Talking Cure'?"', *Contemporary Psychoanalysis* 38: 515–25.

Stern, D. (2003) *Unformulated Experience: From dissociation to imagination in psychoanalysis*, Hillsdale, NJ: The Analytic Press.

Stevens, A. (2006) 'The archetypes', in Renos Papadopoulos (ed.) *The Handbook of Jungian Psychology*, London and New York, NY: Routledge, Chapter 3.

Stork, David G., ed. (1998) *Hal's Legacy: 2001's computer as dream and reality*, Cambridge, MA: MIT Press.

Szpunar, K. K. and Tulving, E. (2011) 'Varieties of future experience', in M. Bar (ed.) *Predictions in the Brain: Using our past to generate a future*, New York, NY: Oxford University Press.

Tennes, M. (2007) 'Beyond intersubjectivity: The transpersonal dimension of the psychoanalytic Encounter', *Contemporary Psychoanalysis* 43(4) 505–25.

Valkonen-Korhonen, M. (2019) 'On experiencing time and timelessness', *IJP Open—Open Peer Review and Debate* 6: 1–23.

Wheeler, J. A. and Feynman, R. P. (1945) 'Interaction with the absorber as the mechanism of radiation', *Reviews of Modern Physics* 17(2–3): 157–81

Winnicott, D. W. (1971) *Playing and Reality*, New York, NY: Penguin Books.

Chapter 12

Navigating Temporal Reality

The Subjective Experience of Time

There are multiple factors that affect our experience of time. Maturity and state of development, mood and cognition, ego-strength, organizational style of psychological defenses, situational and environmental circumstances, mind-altering substances, and trauma and dream states are all influential factors that will be examined in this chapter.

Atemporal and Temporal States in Infancy

Infancy begins as an atemporal human experience before the development of a functioning ego. In childhood, the sense of time is highly subjective, corresponding to psychic reality rather than consensual, or objective reality. Rather than conforming to time in the external world, subjective time is influenced by the personal, dynamic experience of the psyche (Colarusso, 1979).

In early symbiotic states in infancy, before there is any sense of separation from instinctual urges of need and being, there is nothing to strive for or obtain. There is no demarcation between then and now. In the unconscious state of existence, no need to change to adapt to the environment exists to survive because one is in a state of being—complete as all as there is no sense of a separation between self and other. Existence occurs in a state of timelessness—or nonseparation because there is no experience of differentiation in the unconscious. Nothing is personal because a sense of an individual self does not exist. There are no attitudes or a sense of context to frame one's experience to reflect upon. There is no sense of "other" from one's experience of self—and there is no experience of self—only being because "other" does not exist. Because of this, in the unconscious, there is no urge to create. Creation only occurs within the context of temporal reality in which there is the capacity to imagine something emerging in the future—the vision of what is to become versus where one is. Bollas (1993) has described an "environmental mother" which provides a holding environment that does not impinge on the infant, allowing for it to be as the object of the infant's instinctual drives who takes care of the infant's needs, experienced through her lack of presence. This creates a cognitive image of the impulse being experienced, leading to a distinction between the inner and outer world, with temporality.

DOI: 10.4324/9781003356448-16

Winnicott has written about the experience of early infancy as a "non-reflective state of sensory going on being" (1971, p. 303). He has described the progression from the child's partially internalized symbiotic state of union with the mother, into a transitional space between the child and the world that functions as an inter-mediary between the emerging sense of self and the mother. This gives the child a means of anchoring their experience contextually in time.

Freud (1930) interpreted the atemporal, preverbal state of infancy involving feelings of eternity, as a timelessness state of oneness with the universe, with an indistinct preverbal memory of sensation after hunger needs have become satisfied. He said that the infant "does not as yet distinguish his ego from the external world as the source of the sensations flowing in upon him" (pp. 66–7).

Orgel (1965) has written, "The awareness of time arises when the pleasurable, in other words, 'timeless' satiation of the infant is interrupted by the first 'need' through the feeling of hunger. Thus, the feeling of hunger is an initiation into the experience of time" (p. 103). Erikson (1956) has identified the mother as the regu-lator of a sense of time, as she is the one who alleviates hunger pain and controls the time span between when hunger is first experienced and when it is relieved.

Anna Freud described the differences in the perception of time between children and adults. She has written:

> How a child will experience a given time period will depend therefore not on the actual duration, measured objectively by the adult, by the calendar and by the clock, but on the subjective inner relations of either id or ego dominance over his functioning. It is these latter factors which will decide whether the intervals set or feeding, the absence of the mother, the duration of nursery attendance, of hospitalization, etc., will seem to the child short or long, tolerable, or intoler-able, and as a result will prove harmless or harmful in their consequences. (Freud, 1965, pp. 60–1)

Freud's statement indicates that because children's sense of time is not deter-mined by external measures established in the consensual reality of the external world, but rather guided by their internal subjective experience—which at times may be under the influence of the unconscious id—the experience of time for chil-dren is more often atemporal. In early infancy, before ego development and lan-guage, the capacity for an organized sense of time does not exist and there is no demarcation between past, present, and future, or a sense of duration.

In early infancy, in an unformed ego state, a sense of time with distinction between past, present, or future, does not exist. Temporal time is initially expe-rienced physiologically as the interval between need and satiation (Seton, 1974; Fenichel, 1945). In addition, breathing and heart rate also creates a somatic sense of rhythm (Fenichel, 1945), and the distinction between day and night develops through maternal reaction to the infant (Gifford, 1960) increases the infant's sense of becoming anchored in temporal reality (Loewald, 1972).

According to Loewald (1972), because ego perspective is not fully developed, "the connectedness of experience—which is temporal—as yet is not, or not firmly established" and each moment is not distinctly linked to the next (p. 40). The ability to comprehend sequential time is dependent on duration, "the qualitative experience of the passage of time, to the experience of time as continuous flow characterized, not only by successive moments and multiple changes, a sense of unity that transcends the awareness of multiplicity, and something that gives from within a diversity of content" (Seton, 1974, p. 800). The ego in infancy does not understand the course of time because it lacks the faculty for reality testing, object relations, an autonomous sense of self, and memory.

Colarusso (1979) has proposed that the mother becomes "mother time," with the development of a mother complex, that can be positive or negative, based upon her receptivity. Erikson (1956) has said that the mother's responsiveness facilitates an awareness of temporality and atemporality. Mahler (1963) has written that extended separation intervals of time from the mother lead to the development of a sense of autonomy as time becomes an organizing factor in the emergence of a "self." When infants can recognize that intervals of negative experience will eventually end, interior psychic spaces are developed through experiencing intervals of rhythmic time. This helps establish the mental capability to shift between points in temporal time and making meaning of experience—or in other words, formulate a narrative through using language. The first words for the time express delay of gratification and anticipation (Schecter et al., 1955; Werner, 1948).

Our sense of agency and the way we interpret events is a nonlinear, multi-layered process of association that requires interior space to move around in (Bryon, 2012; Gentile, 2016). Winnicott (1971) has spoken about how traces of the infant's symbiotic maternal experience remain in the transitional intermediary space between the inner and outer world, an imaginal realm, that foster a time sense between memory and present experience and that enables the formation of a "stable intrapsychic representation of the mother" (Settlage, 1972, p. 76). Through symbolic representation, past and present are woven together, creating a sense of object constancy and the ability to hold connections that occurred in one's mind in the present. As Settlage (1972) has written, "the existing primitive memories of already past experiences are externalized into this in-between space where they are compared and correlated with the current and more consciously perceived experiences with the mother and the emerging self" (1972, p. 76). A sense of "mother" experienced in the past continues to exist in the present, even when she is absent.

Through creative play, the infant engages with past and present mental images of self, object, and the relationship between them, forming an infrastructure of an intrapsychic representation. In this transitional space, past and present experiences become integrated, no longer fragmented, as object constancy is established, and the mental image of the mother can be held in mind in conjunction with the external representation of mother and self. Being able to shift between memory and present experience through play where ideas can be expressed through physical activity, the child learns that they can shift in the imaginal realm between past, present, and future. According to Jacobson (1964) object constancy creates a sense of self with permanence and a sense of agency, along with the ability to experience the subtleties of time.

Sternschein (1973) has identified a relationship between a child's sense of time and separation tolerance. Because of their undeveloped sense of time, time seems to move more slowly for children than adults, which relates to an infant's ability to handle separation from the mother because of the absence of a mental representation of the mother they can hold in their mind. The ability to internalize and carry the maternal representation of a "need-satisfying object" leads to the development of a sense of object constancy creating an ability to be less dependent upon the physical presence of the mother, along with a sense of duration and capacity to experience a sense of past, present, and future (Seton, 1974, p. 796).

Colarusso (1979) has written that a sense of time is subjective depending on the stage in the life cycle. Eissler (1955) has described that in childhood, time is experienced as limitless, while when a sense of mortality in adulthood occurs, with the realization of the unavoidability of death, time is felt to be finite and uncontrollable.

Philosophy of Time

Hartocollis and (1972) has proposed that there are two ways of perceiving time: "thought time that is rational and measurable, and felt time that is lived". This coincides with the ancient Greeks who also believed that there are two principles of time. Chronos refers to linear time that is chronological and Kairos is the right or opportune moment, relating to the subjective experience of time.[1]

In Abraham's (1976) comprehensive survey on the development in philosophy of an understanding of time, starting with Chronos, he describes the human need to try to grasp the essence of time, to control it. Aristotle concerned himself with the concept of the moment and proposed that time is the measurement of change yet (as explained in Chapter 5) this rate of change is not constant.

Because of the subjective nature of Kairos—attending to certain details and omitting others, even at a specific point of time and space the experience is qualitative, determined by the psychological state, age, and situation of each individual. In other words, an awareness of the difference between temporality and atemporality has been around at least since ancient Greece. Subjective experience, based upon internal states and external context, determines how the duration of time is estimated. This chapter will focus on variables that influence the experience of time within the context of temporality.

Environmental Factors that Affect the Perception of Time

While moving between two points speeds up the experience of time, the kappa effect refers to perceptual time dilation (time slowing down) that tends to occur when the time between two stimuli becomes longer (Goldreich, 2007). When time intervals between flashes of light are the same but the distance in location between lights is greater, time duration will also be perceived as being longer than if the distance between the location of the flashes was shorter.

Perhaps there is an internal perceptual adjustment that occurs in the expectation of how long something will take from the psychological experience of waiting potentially increasing the anticipated duration of time between stimuli (Gibbon et al., 1984; Burle and Casini, 2001; Wearden, 2004; Ulrich et al., 2006). From experience, we are conditioned to believe that traversing the distance between two points that are farther apart from each other will take longer than points that are closer together. However, opposite to the kappa effect, Roy et al. in Strumillo (2011) found that increasing the distance between two sources of sound led to a decrease in the perception of the time interval. In another study, where subjects repeatedly engaged in the action of pushing a button that flashed a light after a slight delay, over time subjects perceived that less time had elapsed before the light flashed. When the light was shown immediately after they pressed the button, participants thought that the light had flashed before the button was pressed (Eagleman, 2008). Perhaps this phenomenon suggests that in actions with predictable outcomes, there is less focus on the experience, which accounts for the sense that time is speeding up, like what happens in the perception of time in older people. This might also parallel the sense of losing time in states of disassociation. Perhaps this is a defensive response to mitigate the experience of being in a painful situation. Interestingly, the ability to detect time sequencing was not found significantly correlate with IQ (Wittmann, 2017). The research findings associated with the time sequencing phenomenon suggests that there is a time distortion due to anticipation and the subjective tendency not to experience things as they are but to experience them based upon what is "known" from experience. This concurs with Rovelli's theory (2017) that the world is experienced as a group of events not structured in time, but as relationships formed by deducting what we think we know. This is also congruent with Piaget's (1936, 1937) theory of cognitive development, which proposes that we form a schema to make sense of the world. Often, if the information we are taking in is incongruent with our internal map, it is discarded because there is no place where it fits. If it is accepted, then there is an experience of disequilibrium before the material can be accommodated (fit into the schemata) through an adjustment of what is understood and accepted and assimilated—when it is incorporated into the overlying cognitive structure (Piaget, 1936, 1937).

Gravity, Movement, and Aging

As described in Chapter 5, Einstein discovered that gravity causes the experience of time to move more slowly. The trajectory is dependent upon the conditions of space, determined by place and speed (Rovelli, 2017). Gravity is caused by mass, and so, as a result, time is slowed down by mass. For example, time passes faster in the mountains than at sea level due to less gravitational pull, causing people who live at sea level to age more slowly than people living in the mountains (Rovelli, 2017).

In addition, time passes more slowly for people who keep moving and a person that moves more ages less rapidly (Rovelli, 1917, p. 34) than someone less mobile. It also implies that people age faster when they are older and don't move as quickly.

Einstein said this is because a moving object experiences less duration of time than a stationary one to get to the same point, because through movement in the direction of the point, ground is gained, and the distance becomes shorter. An example of this are the electric walkways at the airport people use to take them from security to the departure gates, which can reduce the length of time it takes for them to get to their gate (if they are walking) as compared to someone who is walking next to them without using the electric walkway. This is because time contracts for a moving object, that is moving in the direction of the end point.

Freud (1920) commented that there is a tendency for humans to move toward a state of atrophy. In older people, the temporal range of imagining and planning a future becomes shorter (Whitmann, 2017) probably because the expected remaining lifespan grows shorter and the amount of time lived, in the past, grows larger. In a study of women from the ages of 60 to 85, a fear of death was linked to a significant sense of losing time (Quinn and Reznikoff, 1985). Neugarten (1965) has observed a tendency in elders toward introversion, less relations with others in the world, and a reduced capacity to psychologically withstand and assimilate a diverse range of stimuli. Novel situations have been found to be linked with the sense of time slowing down (Gifford, 1980) and perhaps the tendency for people to do less in retirement when they are older contributes to the sense of time moving faster as one ages since people often tend to fall into routines and become more stationary. It is not uncommon to hear an aging person remark, "I'm too old for that!"

Other than potentially limiting physical conditions in older people, a decrease in activity level is voluntary. Aging more rapidly is also a condition that frequently occurs involuntarily with inmates. Gifford (1971) has found that mental and physical changes that happen to a person during a period of confinement result in a more rapid rate of aging. The psychophysiological changes in healthy young men during severe sensory deprivation conditions of isolation resembles the progressive aging process for individuals in their later years. Seniors experience time moving more rapidly than people in their younger years. Both prisoners in solitary confinement and seniors often settle into daily routines, reducing activity and exposure to novel situations that potentially could involve learning.

Waiting and Boredom in Relation to Duration

While the perception of time speeds up in the aging process when people are slowing down, and in established predictable routines, the reverse is also true. A period of waiting can seem to go on forever in young children. Bertrand Russell (1940) said that the importance of time is determined by our desires rather than our relationship to truth. The capacity to tolerate waiting states influences how time is experienced subjectively. Young children who have not developed a sense of how long something takes and live in a state of immediacy often become impatient waiting to "get there" on a long car ride, asking how many days to Christmas or their birthday, and learning how to count how many days until a beloved grandparent arrives for a visit. The space experienced in the interval between the present and when the anticipated event occurs seems extended.

Piaget (1966) was interested in the correlation between experiencing time and environmentally enforced delays, related to the infant experience of the duration of wishful waiting for need satiation. The ego develops resources to bracket time in intervals so that it is not experienced as limitless. By experiencing manageable amounts of frustration, the ability to delay gratification and self-regulate feelings grows stronger. Being able to reflect on this relationship adds perspective in contextualizing the experience of satisfaction and unsatiated urges by bracketing the experience in a time interval as to when the current state will change (Hartocollis, 1972).

In a longitudinal study connected by Walter Mischel and Ebbe Ebbesen (1970) that started with 500 children aged four or five, children were given a choice to receive a marshmallow that they could eat immediately or wait ten minutes to be given two marshmallows. The results of the study indicated that the children who waited created ways of entertaining themselves by singing songs, playing peek-a-boo alone, or talking out loud. Children who were able to wait for the second marshmallow performed better in school (Mischel et al., 1989) had more success in social interactions with peers and had a greater frustration tolerance ten years later—all measures of success in our culture (Benjamin et al., 2020).

Children who did not wait to receive the second marshmallow were more oriented to the present, with temporal myopia—geared toward what is closer in the temporal horizon. While there is a correlation between success in life and capacity to delay gratification, research has also found that the feeling of regret experienced after a decision in which exercising restraint was involved lasted longer than regrets from giving into temptation (Gilbert et al., 2004).

Another study based upon delayed gratification and money values found that depreciation occurred in time intervals with longer waiting periods. Subjects chose a lesser amount associated with shorter waiting periods—a phenomenon referred to as temporal discounting. Events in closer temporal proximity elicit stronger physical and emotional responses, which influence decision making (Frederick et al., 2002).

People who are present-oriented tend to be more impulsive, live more dangerously, and take more drugs. They are more attention seeking and less future-focused. Psychiatric and neurological patient groups, as well as children diagnosed with Attention Deficit Hyperactivity Disorder (ADHD), had more difficulty judging time duration, with a tendency to perceive temporal duration as longer (Wittmann, 2017; Csikszentmihalyi, 1990). In other studies, adults with ADHD demonstrated the tendency to become hyper-focused and, while in these states, lost track of time (Ozel-Kizil et al., 2016). In the study, White and Shah (2006) found that adults with ADHD scored lower on impulse control but higher on divergent thinking, associated with creativity. This is consistent with other research findings that the experience of waiting does not occur; in fact the opposite happens—there is a tendency to lose track of time when distracted, or when engrossed in a project (Kooji et al., 2019; Webb et al., 2005; White and Shah, 2006).

In a state of pleasure, time exists in the instant of the present. The future tension of waiting for satisfaction is defended against and the drive for change to satisfy an impulse does not exist. Abraham (1976) suggests that with the development to tolerate the capacity for waiting, the reality principle of not giving into impulses of immediate gratification in service of greater gratification in the future grows stronger. Abraham has suggested that Freud's concept of the "death instinct" is less about destruction and more related to wanting to return to a narcissistic state of complete satisfaction, regardless of consequences. This happens outside of the temporal experience of longing and becoming when instinctual drives are satiated and not experienced in the current state.

Like Piaget's (1966) research findings in children, bracketing time in intervals as a way of managing overwhelming affect in long periods of waiting beyond one's control has also been reported to be beneficial by prisoners in solitary confinement. In Burney's (1961 [1952]) account of his time spent in solitary confinement in a French prison during World War II, he describes the comfort he felt in maintaining an established routine. For prisoners, controlling the passage of time through ritual was essential, and when the routine became interrupted, they developed a fear of change and novelty (Kropotkin, 1971 [1899]; Berkman, 1912). It is interesting how this phenomenon corresponds with the needs of infants and young children for an established routine. Perhaps prisoners in solitary confinement experience a regression, through a forced withdrawal from the outside world, and, like infants, lack the ability to contextualize external events as a way of orienting.

Hartocollis (1972) believes the experience of trying to control time has to do with the experience of a challenging situation or adverse circumstances. In adults in solitary confinement, a common theme is a focus on trying to manage the experience of time through controlling the minutia (Gifford, 1980). A greater number of events in a given period is found to be positively correlated with the perception of time passing more quickly (Gibbon et al., 1984; Burle and Casini, 2001; Wearden, 2004; Ulrich et al., 2006).

Figner (1927) wrote about his prison experience of "deathly stillness" that "little by little overpowers you, envelops you, penetrates into all the pores of your body … In this stillness, the real becomes vague and unreal, and the imaginary seems real. The long grey day, wearying in its idleness resembles a sleep without dreams; and at night you have such bright and glowing dreams …" (p. 185).

While waiting is the experience of having time before achieving a desired outcome, boredom involves the feeling of being trapped in time. The feeling often involves a sense of acute self-awareness of being empty (Wittmann, 2017). Hartocollis (1972) has described boredom as "the result of the awareness of the instincts without the awareness of their meaning" (p. 97).

During his time of imprisonment, Figner (1927), found that daydreams were the most successful way of killing time. He reported getting lost in reverie about his past life until he lost track of the time and where he was. Perhaps finding methods of feeling in control of the passage of time and discovering ways of intentionally disorienting oneself from a sense of "the here and now," by shifting attention to imaginal dream states, are ways of avoiding feelings of powerlessness in the "stuckness" of solitary confinement.

MacLeod and Roff (1935–6) observed two subjects respectively alone in a soundproof room for periods of time, without any cues referencing time. They observed that the subjects underestimated elapsed time for intervals of 17 minutes to several hours. Vernon and McGill (1963) repeated the experiment and found an underestimation of time duration by about 20 percent on average. These research findings, which discovered the tendency to underestimate elapsed time under conditions of sensory isolation, were duplicated in simulated cockpit situations. A tendency to underestimate the passage of time during sleep and overestimate it during waking periods has also been found (Gifford, 1980).

Finding Meaning and the Effects on Time

Mindfulness is the learned capacity to be fully present, to have a singular focus without distraction. Intense experience is only possible with full attention. Novel events are experienced as lasting longer because they place greater demands on thinking and feeling to process what is being perceived. Events that require greater emotional and intellectual exertion are also perceived as taking longer. The expansive feeling of awe also transfers to a sense of time expanding so that temporal perception slows down in these states. Marc Whitmann (2017) has written that people who live meaningful lives with diversity live longer.

Research findings indicate that the perception of time duration is influenced by the number of events stored in memory along with the number of changes experienced in each period. There is a positive correlation between change and the experience of time duration. The greater degree of change during an interval of time, the longer the perception of the length of time that has passed (Zakay and Block, 1997).

More routine leads to less experiences with intensity, which requires less focused attention, and inevitably results in less clarity—and a sense that more time has passed. When recalling a week, one where time was spent on an exciting vacation involving interesting adventures, it is remembered as lasting longer than the same old routine work week (Wittmann, 2017).

It's interesting that time is experienced as moving faster when there are more activities—and more stimulation as a defense against boredom yet recalling a week with more intensity seems longer (Gibbon et al., 1984; Burle and Casini, 2001;

Wearden, 2004; Ulrich et al., 2006). A period with more activities is experienced as moving faster when counteracting the experience of waiting and boredom, yet remembered as moving more slowly when the events are intense and as a result become more meaningful. One study found that although there is a perception that the experience of time slows down during dangerous events, the estimation of time duration during a frightening event is only perceived as being longer when it is remembered—not during the actual event itself (Whitmann, 2017).

The phenomenon that time is remembered as moving more slowly than it is experienced in dangerous situations supports Rovelli's (2019) supposition that time does not flow because it is actually a series of isolated events. It takes longer to remember a series of different events than a long chain of constant events that do not change because there is more information in recall.

In experiments involving sensory deprivation isolation tanks, a sense of time does not disappear, yet during longer periods lasting several hours, participants underestimated the length of time that had passed. Again, this was attributed to the fact that there were no events to remember so there were fewer memories (Forgays and Belinson, 1986). This is consistent with the paqos' experience of deeply meditative states during which atemporality is experienced and time is felt to move more slowly. Perhaps in this situation, when the meditative states are "full" of a sense of connection, there is a sense of layering, with the feeling that the experience is not only moving horizontally on a timeline of a temporal time and space paradigm, but also moving vertically by dropping deeper into the experience.

In addition to the tendency to adhere to narratives based on what is known from the past because it fits with our internal schemata rather than what is happening, narratives are also organized to reduce discomfort and regret regarding past decisions. According to the theory of cognitive dissonance (Festinger, 1962), when facts about current experience that filter into awareness are too uncomfortable to assimilate into the way we see the world, there is a shift in the narrative so that the uncomfortable realizations can be rationalized—and anxiety can be reduced. Regretting the past is often tied to feelings of guilt and a sense of "stuckness." Developing a defensive strategy of rationalizing may justify why it was necessary to have stayed so long in a situation that wasn't satisfying or productive, to reduce the experience of guilt or regret. As a result, the memory of being "stuck" may become less predominant so that less regret is felt.

When a narrative about an experience of a past event is formed, the event becomes anchored in and space—and the capacity to hold on to the immediacy of experience in the actual moment decreases. Although in other (uncomfortable) situations the desire to "kill" time is experienced, as one reflects upon the past—particularly when it is associated with missing out on something, the need to grieve the loss of time often emerges (Gilbert et al., 2004).

In letting go of his attachment to the past, Carlos Castaneda has described his personal experience working with his shaman teacher Don Juan who explains erasing traces of his personal history. In the following passage, Castaneda has depicted what it might be like to let go of attachment and being defined by personal history. This practice resembles the practice of mindfulness. In *Journey to Ixilan*, Castaneda has written:

> *It is best to release personal history because that would make us free from the thoughts of other people ... Take yourself for instance, right now you don't know if you are coming or going. And that is so, because I have erased my personal history. I have, little by little, created a fog around me and my life. And no one knows for sure what I am or what I do.* (Castaneda, 1972, p. 32)

The Experience of Time and Mood

Hartocollis (1975) has written that feelings such as anxiety, depression, and boredom have a fundamental time dimension, with the experience being determined by the ego's orientation in temporality that influences the experiential features of the feeling. The feeling experienced may affect the perception of time duration. Gil and Droit-Volet (2011) found that the emotions of anger, fear, joy, and sadness cause time to be perceived as "dragging" whereas the feeling of shame creates the perception of time moving much faster. Feelings of disgust have no influence on the perception of time.

Studies have found that angry facial expressions have the greatest effect on the perception of time (Droit-Volet et al., 2004; Tipples, 2008). In addition, research has found (Doi and Shinohara, 2009; Kliegl et al., 2015) that time seems to move the slowest when an angry expression is presented directly to subjects, with the effect decreasing when the gaze is averted. LeDoux (2003) has proposed that this may be linked to a neuroanatomical pathway enabling the processing of affective stimuli in the amygdala to be prioritized, perhaps as a survival reaction.

Being in a state of depression can also slow down the experience of time and increase the tendency to focus on the past. In graduate school, one of my professors used to say that people who are depressed have no future and that people who are psychotic have no past. Less exposure to light energy—along with experiencing increased psychic entropy (lack of energy, difficulty concentrating, confusion, and so forth) can lead to depression without the capacity to imagine a potential future. When a sense of hope of hope is lost, there may be a restriction in cognition, limiting the capacity for creative thinking, and as a result imaging a future. Depression can serve as a deadening defense against the acute pain of experiencing the "aliveness" of sadness, which can feel timeless. This experience, referred to as a condition associated with "lead" by alchemists, is often symbolized by chains and imprisonment, portraying a psychic state in which one is "confined within the limits of one's personal reality" (Edinger, 1985, p .93). People dealing with psychosis struggle with disorganized thinking that prevents them from accurately recollecting past events. Both conditions can create a suspension of time and a timeless state of passivity associated with leading an unlived life.

While depression may feel like having too much time, phobias have been associated with the fear of not having enough time, a sense of purposelessness related to having too much time, and feeling unsettled in time (Fenichel, 1945). The estimation of length of time that has passed also speeds up in a state of anticipatory dread of an impending event. Subjectively it may feel like there is no sense of space between the now and the future. Through rumination, often a response to anxiety, the future event is experienced as if it's already happening (Hartocollis, 1972).

For some people, "breaking up" time into smaller increments can be a way of defending against being flooded by anxiety. Bracketing time in intervals by "over scheduling" activities consecutively, through a phenomenon called "stacking," can be a way of managing anxiety. Mentally compartmentalizing periods of time from the past that hold painful memories is another coping mechanism to manage anxiety, as past trauma can create anticipatory dread of the future and fear of the unknown.

The Future as a Defense

Paqos and physicists agree that there is no future. Therefore, everything we imagine about the future is a projection. Anticipating what will happen next can be a way of navigating the world. Imagining a future based upon knowledge derived from experience is wisdom. "Wisdom is the capacity to have foreknowledge of something, to know the consequences (both positive and negative) of all the available course of actions, and to yield or take the options with the most advantage either for present or future implication" (Meacham, 1990, pp. 181–211).

During my training to become a psychologist when I was learning about preparing psychological evaluation reports, while working on an inpatient unit in a psychiatric hospital, I had a supervisor who frequently said that the best predicter of future behavior is past behavior. He was referring to the tendency for humans to repeat behavior patterns. As Piaget first pointed out (Piaget, 1977) to make sense of the world, we build cognitive maps based upon categories of information and patterns of potentially repeating events to organize an understanding of the world based upon causal relationships.

Sometimes focusing on the future is a defense against living in the present. An imagined "provisional" future can create a sense of false hope that can be an optimistic defense of denial to stay "above" underlying depression. Existing in a timeless phantasy of an unrealistic future to avoid facing challenging or unpleasant events in present reality can be a way of mitigating pain. Focusing on future goals can also be a distraction against "sitting" in current anxiety states. This psychic phenomenon also may correspond with what can happen after undergoing a traumatic experience when memories become frozen in time and the person experiences a sense of "stuckness."

Erikson (1959) applied the term "time diffusion" in describing adolescents who were disturbed, saying "a loss of the ego's function of maintaining perspective and expectancy, [a condition in which] every delay appears to be a deceit, every wait an experience of impotence, every hope a danger, every plan a catastrophe, every potential provider a traitor. Therefore, time must be made to stand still ..." (p. 141).

People diagnosed with antisocial personality disorders[2] also demonstrate a limited capacity for perceiving a future or past, along with a limited range of affect. As inpatients, they were reported to be restless and bored, which they often tried to avoid through fast or violent actions (Hartocollis, 1972).

Bonaparte (1940) and Hartmann (1958 [1939]) have written that a lack of capacity for reality testing often leads to a limited awareness of time in relation to orienting one's actions in preparing for a foreseeable future. Barande (1965) reported that in cases of people diagnosed with hysteria, with repression as the primary defense mechanism, memories became frozen and undifferentiated in time. This has also been found in people with trauma histories (Bromberg, 1996).

Fuchs (1937) has described introjection[3] as a defense that happens within the context of atemporal time, while simultaneously being timeless. This is because it occurs somatically, outside ego-consciousness, where it remains unprocessed in the unconscious without form, space, and temporality (Matte-Blanco, 1988).

Each of these defenses are ways of avoiding feelings by sequestering them into atemporal states in the unconscious. The challenge in incorporating unconscious material often occurs because there is no internal system of organization in relation to ego functioning so that it can be consciously assimilated. Because of this, psychic material is ignored and remains unprocessed. This happens for two reasons: 1) there is no schemata to organize the material, so it is not assimilated, 2) it is incongruent with how reality is understood so it is dismissed. If there is no way to organize experience, it is not assimilated because it cannot be metabolized (Bromberg, 1996).

States of Timelessness and Ego Strength

The unconscious is acontextual and atemporal, without a beginning, middle, or end. Freud's (1925a, p. 291) theory of becoming conscious of time is based upon the perceptions of drives, first somatically in infancy, then as one matures, progressively through developing the capacity to imagine, and then forming a narrative. In somatic states, the feelings associated with need become "points of perception." The culmination of these points of experience—like Rovelli's (2017) description that temporal experience occurs as a series of events that become time intervals that are a way of linking sequential experiences that form narratives (Benedetti, 1969). Freud believed (1915) that contextualization of time and a sense of temporal reality occurs through ego-consciousness. He has written, "It creates the sense of 'me' and other, with the potential for establishing a historical narrative and a means of differentiating between the past and the present. Differentiation, necessary for reflection between one's experience and the external world, requires a way of delineating between then, now, and what may come to be" (1915, p. 187).

Consciousness is temporal through a functional, established ego that has capability for memory recall, self-reflection, mentation, and the ability to differentiate between past and present. In addition, using defense mechanisms, the ego also has the capability to avoid uncomfortable feelings in the present and to forget past trauma by storing the experience in implicit memories, frozen in time—removed from the past and present (Freud, 1925a). Freud's conceptualization of a preconscious and a conscious created a structure of compartmentalization that mitigated the experience of becoming overwhelmed and engulfed in incoming stimuli (Freud, 1940). The collection of experiences becomes grouped contextually and integrated and subsumed in an everchanging general fund of knowledge. With the establishment of a functioning ego, new experiences become assimilated and organized into a way of making sense of the world.

Cohn (1957) proposed that conscious time is measurable because it exists outside of oneself in the external world while the unconscious experience of time is "narcissistic" because it is an internal, subjective state without the constraints of a consensual reality.

Dream States

Ginzburg (2009) described three ways of experiencing time, which include serially ordered or asymmetrical time, symmetrical atemporal time, and a third that combines aspects of both. In dream states the boundaries of temporality become fluid with affect and the expression of what needs to be brought into conscious awareness taking precedence over temporal order.

Prospective dreams, according to Jung (1916), in which the dreamer is given an indication of future occurrences in the waking world, are a form of synchronicity not associated with linearity or causality. Jung believed that the dream has symbolic, dynamic dimensions in which an interplay between future influences on the past and the present may exist. Jung thought that the principle of teleology, the living meaning of events, aligns with the atemporal phenomenon of precognition, while causality applied to the sequential narrative of the way events unfolded. Both teleology—that extended beyond temporality, and casualty—the relationship between cause and effect contained within temporality, are necessary for the interpretation of reality and are processes that take place in dreams.

In dreams, the past is frequently not limited to a sequential chronological timeline. Both dreamtime and real time may involve sequential narratives, but dreamtime allows for condensation, often through symbolism. The metaphorical content that manifests in dreams may be a means of consolidating experience from different points of time in the present, bringing repetitive feeling patterns into awareness by weaving personal and collective experience from the past and present together. Memories from the past are often woven into current experience, combining the "then" with the "now."

In dreamtime, different time periods may exist simultaneously, allowing one to live in different time periods at the same time. The dreamer may have the capacity to draw distinctions between the two periods, making meaning by combining the past and the present together symbolically. This frequently takes place with the past merging contextually in the present, with selfstates being linked through related affect rather than by the logical course of events. Dreams can be an expression of that which has been forgotten, too painful to remember. The psyche's attempt to regulate and process suppressed psychic material dictates the chronology of dream content and determines how time is experienced. Dreams sometimes contextualize unanchored feelings that are split off implicit memory fragments from past events that have not been metabolized. If the intensity of unprocessed feeling related to a past event is high, the dream may be experienced as a nightmare. Dreamscapes often provide settings to work with previously unprocessed psychic material and to make meaning of the past and present and be ways of imagining a future beyond current life circumstances.

Before Covid, analysands' dreams were more often related to personal subjective and objective experience. During Covid, I noticed that analysands' dream content often had a collective overlay, that appeared to be an attempt to process the psychological and emotional stress of the ongoing collective experience. While meaningful connections between past and present experiences were being made by some analysands during Covid, many found it challenging to imagine a future; it was hard for them to imagine a contextual reality in time and space in the current collective conditions (Bryon, 2021).

The Effect of Trauma on the Experience of Time

The proverb "time can heal all wounds"[4] may be true in some cases if wounds become conscious and there is adequate ego strength to metabolize the feelings associated with the trauma. Rose Fitzgerald Kennedy, after losing multiple family members, disputed this statement in her famous quote, "It has been said, 'time heals all wounds.' I do not agree. The wounds remain. In time, the mind, protecting its sanity, covers them with scar tissue and the pain lessens. But it is never gone."[5]

Traumatic events that are intense and too painful to be remembered may become fragmented and split off from consciousness in the present and buried in implicit memory. As implicit memories, they become repressed in selfstates frozen in time and forgotten in a defensive response. The avoidance of working through fragmented memories of past painful traumatic events creates an impasse. Experience freezes when it exists outside of temporality in an "unlived" state. When memories are blocked off, they remain isolated as energy-charged, undifferentiated feeling-state fragments. In dissociated states there is no psychic energy flow between past, present, and future as memories remain detached and inaccessible. As implicit memories, they become repressed in selfstates, frozen in time and forgotten in a defensive response. In frozen trauma states, a distortion in the narrative of past experience occurs, awareness of time is missing, and a sense of agency to integrate experience into an explicit narrative framework is lost. In dissociated psychological states, periods of time disappear from conscious memory, indicated by memory lapses in the analysands' chronology. The capacity for reverie is also inhibited and the ability to imagine a future is blocked. Meaning of the experience cannot be made through forming a cohesive narrative because there is no capacity for mentation to integrate the experience into a contextual narrative framework. Repressed frozen memories can carry the same intensity of feeling as they did when the actual traumatic event was happening. When intense, implicit memories are blocked off, because they have become too much to hold consciously, they can bleed into the present and be re-experienced as if they are happening again or anticipated to reoccur in the future. Unprocessed fear from the past permeates into the present and is repeatedly relived until it is worked through and made consciousness. When repressed trauma is processed, memories that have previously been locked away in fragmented selfstates can become consciously integrated. To become present rather than remaining in an inner fantasy world, where the experience of time no longer exists, analysands must acutely feel the outside world.

Freud said that forgetting was a defense (1915) and believed that memories from the past kept in the unconscious remain timeless, unless activated when they may influence the present. He proposed that unconscious urges endeavor to repeat themselves within the timeless structure of the unconscious, in different organizational patterns of psychic defenses. Pent-up, repressed nonverbal feeling fragments from the past may be expressed as a re-enactment of destructive patterns of behavior. Acting out unmetabolized, past unresolved trauma held in implicit memory often becomes projected into an imagined future where past traumatic experiences are relived. In the healing process, forming explicit narratives that organize unprocessed psychic material stops pattern re-enactment. To become present—and not remain in a fantasy world where the experience of time no longer exists—the repressed memory must be felt to begin to experience the world again in real time.

The Influence of Drug States and Other Mind-Altering Conditions on Time

In recent years, there has been increased interest in exploring the effects of drug-induced states in relation to how the duration of time is experienced. Wood (1880) has described how, under the influence of cannabis, "Seconds seemed hours; minutes seemed days; hours seemed infinite... I would look at my watch, and then after an hour or two, as I thought, would look again and find that scarcely five minutes had elapsed" (p. 237).

More than a hundred years ago, it was discovered that hashish prolongs the experience of time. Bayard Taylor (1856) has described, while under the influence of hashish, "Though the whole vision was probably not more than five minutes in passing through my mind, years seemed to have elapsed" (p. 140). Abraham (1976) has also written that the experience of time is longer while under the influence of opium and hashish, and that time passes more quickly after ingesting psilocybin and mescaline.[6] Heroin has also been reported to speed up the experience of the passage of time (Zinberg, 1972). Alcohol and tobacco have a smaller but similar effect on time perception (Gifford, 1980).[7]

There are parallels between drug states and the mystical experiences stimulated without the use of drugs (Underhill, 1964). Under the influence of psychedelic drugs and in states of ecstasy a sense of temporality often fades, creating a feeling of timelessness (Hartocollis, 1972; Freedman, 1968).

During long periods of celibacy and fasting, sensory and sleep deprivation and disruption, self-inflicted pain, and deep meditative states are often experienced as non-linear and timeless (Gifford, 1980). Hartocollis (1972) has written that in states of ecstasy—like boredom, the present may be experienced as feeling like an eternity, the difference being in the former it is pleasurable and in later, uncomfortable.

Notes

1 Liddel, George and Scott, Robert (2022). "A Greek–English Lexicon." www.perseus. tufts.edu. Archived from the original on October 30.
2 The diagnosis was made based on the projective tests TAT (Thematic Aptitude Test) and the Rorschach.
3 "The American Psychological Association Dictionary of Psychology" www.apa.org. American Psychological Association. Retrieved October 30, 2021. Introjection has been defined as "a process in which an individual unconsciously incorporates ... the attitudes, values, and qualities of another person or a part of another person's personality. Introjection may occur, for example, in the mourning process for a loved one."
4 The Greek poet Menander, who lived in about 300 BC, first said *time heals all wounds* in the quote, "Time is the healer of all necessary evils." In the 1380s, Geoffrey Chaucer's poem, *Troilus and Criseyde*, contained the phrase: "As tyme hem hurt, a tyme doth hem cure." https://grammarist.com/proverb/time-heals-all-wounds/
5 https://www.goodreads.com/quotes/140515-it-has-been-said-time-heals-all-wounds-i-do#:~:text=Quote%20by%20Rose%20Fitzgerald%20Kennedy,%2C%20'time%20heals%20all%20wounds.
6 Perhaps this is because there is less mental activity in opioid states and increased mental activity in psychotropic drug-induced states. Perhaps more mental activity expands the experience of time and space as there are more thoughts that take up space.
7 Alcohol can be used to "numb out" from the demands and schedule of everyday life while tobacco for an addicted smoker may become a distraction and way of speeding up the experience of time during boredom.

References

Abraham, Z. (1976) 'The sense and concept of time in psychoanalysis', *Int. Rev. Psycho-Anal.* 3: 461–72.
Barande, R. (1965) 'L'inachèvement de l'homme comme structure de son temps', *Rev. Franc. Psychanal* 29: 281–303.
Benedetti, G. (1969) *Neuropsicologia*, Milan: Feltrinelli.
Benjamin, Daniel J., Laibson, David, Mischel, Walter, Peake, Philip K., Shoda, Yuichi, Wellsjo, Alexandra Steiny, and Wilson, Nicole L. (2020) 'Predicting mid-life capital formation with pre-school delay of gratification and life-course measures of self-regulation', *Journal of Economic Behavior & Organization* 179: 743–56.
Berkman, A. (1912) *Prison Memoirs of an Anarchist*, New York: SChocken,
Bollas, C. (1993) 'An interview with Christopher Bollas', *Psychoanal. Dial.* 3: 401–30.

Bonaparte, M. (1940) 'Time and the unconscious', *Int. J. Psycho-Anal.* 21: 427–68.

Bromberg, P. M. (1996) 'Standing in the spaces: The multiplicity of self and the psychoanalytic relationship', *Contemporary Psychoanalysis* 32: 509–35.

Bryon. D. (2021) 'Processing trauma in psychoanalysis in "real" time and in dreams: The convergence of past, present, and future during Covid-19', *Journal of Analytical Psychology* 66: 399–410.

Burle, B. and Casini, L. (2001) 'Dissociation between activation and attention effects in time estimation: Implications for internal clock models', *J. Exp. Psychol.* 27: 195–205.

Burney, C. (1961 [1952]) *Solitary Confinement*, London: Macmillan.

Castaneda, C. (1972) *Journey to Ixtlan,* New York, NY: Simon and Schuster.

Cohn, F. (1957). Time and the ego. Psychoanal. Q. 26, 168-189.

Colarusso, C. A. (1979) 'The development of time sense from birth to object constancy', *Int, J. Psycho-Anal* 60: 243.

Csikszentmihalyi, M. (1990) *Flow: The psychology of optimal experience*, New York, NY: Harper Perennial Modern Classics.

Doi, H. and Shinohara, K. (2009) 'The perceived duration of emotional face is influenced by the gaze direction', *Neurosci. Lett.* 457: 97–100.

Droit-Volet, S., Brunot, S., and Niedenthal, P. (2004) 'Perception of the duration of emotional events', *Cogn. Emot.* 18: 849–58.

Eagleman, D. M. (2008) 'Human time perception and its illusions', *Current Opinion in Neurobiology* 18(2): 131–6.

Edinger, E. F. (1985) *Anatomy of the Psyche: Alchemical symbolism in psychotherapy,* Peru, IL: Open Court Publishing.

Eissler, K. (1955) *The Psychiatrist and the Dying Patient*, New York, NY: International Universities Press.

Erikson, E. (1956) 'The problem of ego identity', *J. Am. psychoanal. Ass.* 4: 56–121.

Erikson, E. H. (1959) *Identity and the Life Cycle* [*Psychological Issues, Monogr. 1*], New York, NY: International Universities Press.

Fenichel, O. (1945) *The Psychoanalytic Theory of Neurosis*, New York, NY: Norton.

Festinger, L. (1962) 'Cognitive dissonance', *Scientific American* 207(4): 93–102.

Figner, V. (1927) *Memoirs of a Revolutionist*, New York, NY: International Publishers.

Forgays, D. G. and Belinson, M. J. (1986) 'Is flotation isolation a relaxing environment?', *Journal of Environmental Psychology* 6(1): 19–34.

Frederick, Shane, Loewenstein, George, and O'donoghue, Ted (2002) 'Time discounting and time preference: A critical review', *Journal of Economic Literature* 40(2): 351–401.

Freedman, D. X. (1968) 'On the use of abuse of LSD', *Arch. Gen. Psychiat.* 18: 330–47.

Freud, S. (1915) *The Unconscious* (Standard Edition, vol. 14).

Freud, S. (1920) *Beyond the pleasure principle.* Standard Edition, 18:7-64. London: Hogarth Press.

Freud, S. (1923–5) *The Ego and the Id and Other Works* (Standard Edition, vol. 19).

Freud, S. (1925a) *A Note Upon the 'Mystic Writing-Pad'* (Standard Edition, vol. 19).

Freud, S. (1930) *Civilization and Its Discontents* (Standard Edition, vol. 21).

Freud, S. (1940) *An Outline of Psycho-analysis* (Standard Edition, vol. 21).

Freud, A. (1965) *Normality and Pathology in Childhood*, New York, NY: International Universities Press.

Fuchs, S. H. (1937) 'On introjection', *Int. J. Psycho-Anal.* 18: 268–93.

Gentile, K. (2016) 'Generating subjectivity through the creation of time', *Psychoanalytic Psychology* 33(2): 264–83.

Gibbon, J., Church, R. M., and Meck, W. H. (1984) 'Scalar timing in memory', *Ann. N.Y. Acad. Sci.* 423: 52–77.

Gifford, S. (1960) 'Sleep, time, and the early ego—comments on the development of the 24-hour sleep–wakefulness patterns as a precursor of ego functioning', *J. Amer. Psychoanal. Assn.* 8: 5–42.

Gifford, S. (1971) *Time's Wingèd Chariot: The origins of time-experience and its fate in later life.* Paper presented at fall meeting of American Psychoanalytic Association, New York, December.

Gifford, S. (1980) '"The prisoner of time": Some developmental aspects of time perception in infancy, sensory isolation, and old age', *Annual of Psychoanalysis* 8: 131–54.

Gil, S. and Droit-Volet, S. (2011) '"Time flies in the presence of angry faces" ... depending on the temporal task used!', *Acta Psychol.* 136: 354–62.

Gilbert, D. T., Morewedge, C. K., Risen, J. L., and Wilson, T. D. (2004) 'Looking forward to looking backward: The misprediction of regret', *Psychological Science* 15(5): 346–50.

Ginzburg, A. (2009) 'Time and the unconscious', *Ital. Psychoanal. Annu.* 3: 217–23.

Goldreich, D. (2007) 'A Bayesian perceptual model replicates the cutaneous rabbit and other tactile spatiotemporal illusions', *PLOS ONE* 2(3): e333.

Hartmann, H. (1958 [1939]) *Ego Psychology and the Problem of Adaptation*, New York, NY: International Universities Press.

Hartocollis, P. (1972) 'Time as a dimension of affects', *Journal of the American Psychoanalytic Association* 20: 92–108.

Hartocollis, P. (1975) '"The Present of Things Future—Explorations of Time in Human Experience", by Thomas J. Cottle and Steven L. Klineberg. New York: The Free Press, 1974. Pp. 290', *Psychoanalytic Quarterly* 44: 484–7.

Jacobson, E. (1964) *The Self and the Object World*, New York, NY: International Universities Press.

Jung, C. G. (1916) 'Preface', in *Collected Works on Analytical Psychology* (Collected Works, vol. 4).

Kliegl, K. M., Limbrecht-Ecklundt, K., Dürr, L., Traue, H. C., and Huckauf, A. (2015) 'The complex duration perception of emotional faces: Effects of face direction', *Front. Psychol.* 6: 262.

Kooij, J. J. S., Bijlenga, D., Salerno, L., Jaeschke, R., Bitter, I., Balázs, J., Thome, J., Dom, G., and Kasper, S. (2019) 'Updated *European* consensus statement on diagnosis and treatment of adult ADHD', *European Psychiatry* 56: 14–34.

Kropotkin, P. (1971 [1899]) *Memoirs of a Revolutionist*, New York, NY: Dover.

LeDoux J. E. (2003) 'The emotional brain, fear and the amygdala', *Cell. Mol. Neurobiol.* 23: 727–38.

Loewald, H. W. (1972) 'The experience of time', *Psychoanalytic Study of the Child* 27: 401–10.

MacLeod, R. B. and Roff, M. F. (1935–6) 'An experiment in temporal disorientation', *Acta Psychol.* 1: 381–423.

Mahler, M. S. (1963) 'Thoughts about development and individuation', *Psychoanal. Study Child* 18: 307–24.

Matte-Blanco, I. (1988) *Thinking, Feeling, and Being: Clinical reflections on the fundamental antinomy of human beings and world*, Abingdon, Oxfordshire: Routledge.

Meacham, J. A. (1990) 'The loss of wisdom', in R. J. Sternberg (ed.) *Wisdom: Its nature, origins, and development*, Cambridge: Cambridge University Press.

Mischel, W. and Ebbesen, Ebbe B. (1970) 'Attention in delay of gratification', *Journal of Personality and Social Psychology* 16(2): 329–37.

Mischel, W., Shoda, Y., and Rodriguez, M. (1989) 'Delay of gratification in children', *Science* 244(4,907): 933–8.

Neugarten, B. L. (1965) 'Personality changes in the aged', *Catholic Psychological Record* 3: 9–17.

Orgel, S. (1965) 'On time and timelessness', *J. Am. psychoanal. Ass.* 13: 102–21.

Ozel-Kizil, E. T., Kokurcan, A., Aksoy, U. M., Kanat, B. B., Sakarya, D., Bastug, G., and Oncu, B. (2016) 'Hyperfocusing as a dimension of adult attention deficit hyperactivity disorder', *Research in Developmental Disabilities* 59: 351–8.

Piaget, J. (1954 [1937]) *The Construction of Reality in the Child,* New York, NY: Basic Books.

Piaget, J. (1952 [1936]) *The Origins of Intelligence in Children,* New York, NY: International Universities Press.

Piaget, J. (1954 [1937]) *The Construction of Reality in the Child,* New York, NY: Basic Books.

Piaget, J. (1966) 'Time perception in children', in J. T. Fraser (ed.) *The Voices of Time,* New York, NY: George Braziller.

Piaget, J. (1977) 'The role of action in the development of thinking', in W. F. Overton and J. M. Gallagher (eds) *The Role of Action in the Development of Thinking. Knowledge and Development,* Boston, MA: Springer US, pp. 17–42.

Quinn, P. K. and Reznikoff, M. (1985) 'The relationship between death anxiety and the subjective experience of time in the elderly', *The International Journal of Aging and Human Development* 21(3): 197–210.

Reichenbach, H. (1951) *The Rise of Scientific Philosophy,* Berkeley, CA and Los Angeles, CA: University of California.

Rovelli, C. (2017) *The Order of Time,* London: Penguin Random House.

Rovelli, C. (2019) *The Order of the Universe,* London: Penguin Books.

Russell, B. (1940) *An Inquiry into Meaning and Truth,* London: Allen & Unwin.

Schecter, D. E., Symonds, M., and Bernstein, I. (1955) 'Development of the concept of time in children', *J. Nerv. & Ment. Dis.* 121: 301–10.

Seton, P. H. (1974) 'The psychotemporal adaptation of late adolescence', *Journal of the American Psychoanalytic Association* 22: 795–819.

Settlage, C. F. (1972) 'Cultural values and the superego in late adolescence', *Psychoanal. Study Child* 27: 76.

Sternschein, I. (1973) 'The experience of separation-individuation in infancy and its reverberations through the course of life: Maturity, senescence, and sociological implications', *J. Am. psychoanal. Ass.* 21: 633–45.

Strumillo, Dr. Pawel, ed. (2011) 'Effect of space on auditory temporal processing with a single-stimulus method', *Advances in Sound Localization*: 95–104.

Taylor, B. (1856) *The Lands of the Saracen,* New York, NY: Putnam.

Tipples, J. (2008) 'Negative emotionality influences the effects of emotion on time perception', *Emotion* 8: 127.

Ulrich R., Nitschke J., and Rammsayer, T. (2006) 'Perceived duration of expected and unexpected stimuli', *Psychol. Res.* 70: 77–87.

Underhill, E. (1964) *The Mystics of the Church,* New York, NY: SChocken Books.

Wearden, J. H. (2004) 'Decision processes in models of timing', *Acta Neurobiol. Exp.* 64: 303–18.

Webb, James T., Amend, Edward R., Webb, Nadia E., Goerss, Jean, Beljan, Paul, and Olenchak, Richard F. (2005) *Misdiagnosis and Dual Diagnoses of Gifted Children and Adults: ADHD, bipolar, OCD, Asperger's, depression, and other disorders*, Scottsdale, AZ: Great Potential Press, Inc.

White, Holly A. and Shah, Priti (2006) 'Uninhibited imaginations: Creativity in adults with Attention-Deficit/Hyperactivity Disorder', *Personality and Individual Differences* 40(6): 1,121–31.

Winnicott, D. W. (1971) *Playing and Reality*, New York, NY: Penguin Books.

Wittmann, M. (2017) *Felt Time: The science of how we experience time*, Cambridge, MA: The MIT Press.

Wood, H. C., Jr. (1880) *A Treatise on Therapeutics, Comprising Materia Medica and Toxicology*, Philadelphia, PA: Lippincott.

Zakay, D. and Block, R. A. (1997) 'Temporal cognition', *Current Directions in Psychological Science* 6(1): 12–16.

Zinberg, N. E. (1972) 'Rehabilitation of heroin users in Vietnam', *Contemporary Drug Problems* 1: 263–394.

Chapter 13

Conclusion

As humans, we are born into an oceanic state of "oneness." We begin to root in the collective temporal paradigm starting during infancy as we begin to experience the passage of time through intervals, experiencing instinctual needs, and the period between feeling hunger pains and when the need is satiated.

Objectively, sequential time is standardized, based upon the position of the sun in relation to a specific geographic location. Subjectively, there are many factors that affect our sense of temporal time that include but are not limited to location and gravity, age, altered states due to substances and meditative practices, degree of activity, mood, and level of cognitive functioning.

Developing a sense of time is necessary for perceiving physical reality. In our modern Western culture, we live our lives primary in a state of temporality anchored on a specific *pacha*, an allocation of energy at a point in time and space that is affected by gravity. Consensual reality and ego-consciousness is based upon this temporal awareness, and collectively we experience time and aging based upon this sequential paradigm. If we were unable to participate in our shared temporal experience, we would be unable to use verbal language and would be diagnosed as psychotic due to an inability to function with others in the physical world.

Part of our psyches hold and remember atemporal experience through oceanic preverbal states in infancy, as well as in shamanic states of ecstasy and religious experience, dreams, and trauma states when experiences that are too overwhelming to process become split off and held in implicit memory and somatically in the body. Dream processes and atemporal defense structures as the result of trauma are involuntary. A primary goal of psychoanalysis is to make what is unconscious, conscious, or in other words, what is implicit, explicit, by bringing psychic material that has been suspended in timeless unconscious states into conscious awareness with context through forming narratives using language. According to Loewald (1972) temporality, necessary for reflective thinking, is fundamental to the practice of psychoanalysis. Shamans, in general, use temporality as a point of departure—and return from entering energetic states of oneness. Paqos learn intentional ways of shifting between temporal and atemporal selfstates, into dimensions of connectivity with the cosmos through disciplined practice and ritual, while at the same time maintaining a footing in physical reality. The techniques used by paqos

DOI: 10.4324/9781003356448-17

involve moving between levels of psychic engagement, from the temporal realm of physical reality into the energetic realms of atemporality. Initially, learning how to shift between these states can be challenging, especially in the re-entry phase of moving from the atemporal experience of connection into experiencing separation through form, existing in time and space. Re-entry experiences initially may be experienced as loss and alienation. Over time, it is possible to develop the ability to shift between temporal and atemporal states, when the capacity to transfer one's conscious awareness intentionally into experiencing atemporal connection with the cosmos is acquired.

The theories developed in quantum physics in many ways parallel the paqos' experience, and offer explanations for synchronicity, the relationship that exists between discrete events that appear unrelated in temporality. The quantum theory of blurring, moving from atemporal to temporal states, corresponds with the re-entry experience often experienced after shamanic states of ecstasy. The theories of quantum physics also have provided the foundation of complexity theory that developed in intersubjective psychoanalysis, moving away from intrapsychic and interpsychic conceptualization of psychological experience. The emergence of complexity theory in the intersubjective school of psychoanalysis has provided a more integrated conceptual structure in which patterns of human experience are understood to be imbedded in a larger system in which everything is occurring in a dynamic, interrelated process.

Developing an awareness of the relationship between temporality and atemporality, with the capacity to intentionally enter these (non-drug induced) psychic spaces, can expand our range of consciousness and as analysts advance our ability to understand the range of potential selfstates our analysands may be experiencing internally. In the practice of Andean medicine, I have referred to this as levels of psychic engagement, ranging from the temporal experience in physical reality to the atemporal realm of the energetic collective. Jung has referred to this as the psychoid realm of the objective psyche. He has written (Jung, 1934), that psychic processes act along a sliding continuum of consciousness between instinct and spirit.

The capability to shift between states in physical reality and other dimensions may inform our understanding of the experience of time beyond a reified conceptualization of a discrete past, present, and future. A perception of an atemporal cognizance, not limited to ego-consciousness, can open us to states of consciousness experienced in shamanic states of ecstasy and near-death experiences, as well as intuitive knowing. This may deepen our sense of meaning and connection with our world.

In *The Psychoid, Soul, and Psyche: Piercing space-time barriers*, Ulanov (2017, p. 7) has quoted Jung as saying, "Under certain conditions it (psyche) could even break through the barrier of space and time precisely because of a quality essential to it … its relatively trans-spatial and trans-personal nature … The possible transcendence of space-time … is of such incalculable import that it should spur the spirit of research to the greatest effort" (Jung 1934, par. 813).

References

Jung, C. G. (1934) *The Practical Use of Dream-Analysis* (Collected Works, vol. 16).

Loewald, H. W. (1972) 'The experience of time', *Psychoanalytic Study of the Child* 27: 401–10.

Ulanov, A.B. (2017) *The Psychoid, Soul and Psyche: Piercing Space/Time Barriers*, Einsiedeln, Switzerland: Daimon.

Appendix

List of *Despacho* Ingredients

alabaster man and woman figurines: represents duality, serving in reciprocal union.

alphabet noodles: for communication and the ability to use language.

bread: binds the family together. It is commonly used in soul retrievals.

candles: used for light and illumination.

candy: used for harmony and attraction. Harmony in an environment occurs through sweetness, especially in the form of flower-shaped candies. Candy represents germination, fulfillment, and fruition.

candy house or car: the metaphor for success, however you define it.

candy man and woman: harmony in a couple. The element of two is very important because it not only symbolizes the right relationship among humans, but also between humans and the collective.

Chocolate frog: harmony and the cycles of water.

corn (maize, or sara in *Quechua)*: symbolizes production and abundance.

cotton: symbolizes purity and clouds and can represent the cycles of water and rain. In a *despacho* for *Pachamama* it represents water. In a *despacho* for the *apus* it represents heaven and purity.

crackers/wafers: flour products represent the *anima* (spirit).

dough wafers with a picture of a cross: symbolizes health and is used in *despachos* created for health.

dough wafers with a picture of St. Nicholas: given in offerings to the *apu* spirits who bring good news.

incense: attracts Spirit.

lima beans: because of the color, they harmonize the *despacho*. Sometimes a positive or a negative ability is given depending on the intent in different *despachos*.

llama fat: (*untu* in *K'echua*) used in the act of manifestation through vision. Coca leaves and llama fat are combined and are fundamental in *despachos* as a way of calling the *apus*. The *apus* may not respond if both are not present.

loadston/magnetite: brings attraction. It is a favored item for business in *despachos*.

metal frog: symbolizes attraction. The frog is the messenger that calls the spirit world.

metal hand: represents friendship. The hand is flanked by symbols of winged beings representing the *apus* and is the dynamic nature of all relations that must be served.

metal moon (luna): the agricultural calendar.

metal star (chaska): for protection.

metal sun (sol): the social calendar; social interaction.

mica: represents silver, and maintaining the integrity of the soul as it grows stronger.

molasses candy: for harmony.

pewter horseshoes: for lucidity in business and good fortune through *ayni;* "right relationship" and reciprocity.

pewter left hand: represents the act of giving. To receive, you must give—a circular process.

pewter right hand: positive, receiving, welcoming.

qolqi: silver, symbolizing spiritual wealth and lunar energy.

qori: gold, symbolizing spiritual wealth and solar energy.

rods: amplify sound.

seeds: all the seeds are the basic complement that the land needs to bring abundance.

sequins: ornamental décor to provide decoration.

shell: the womb of the heavens and the container in which creation sits. Sometimes wine is poured inside the shell to attract the spirits. The shell is a metaphor for creation.

tacu (red clay): brings positive or negative outcomes. It is used in *cuti despacho*s to wash off negativity or repel what is sent to you, depending on your affinities.

thread: yellow and white, and/or gold and silver representing *Inti Titi* (Father Sun) and *Mama Quilla* (Grandmother Moon) respectively; thread binds and brings wholeness.

tobacco: attracts spirits of North America. Tobacco is also used to attract and direct the spirit of the plant in *ayahuasca* ceremonies.

wayruro: a small red and black seed, representing the masculine and feminine principles, which brings protection. Two of these seeds are often placed in the center shell for fertility and balance.

wine: red wine is an offering for *Pachamama*. White wine is an offering for *Wira Cocha*, the heavens, and the celestial realm of the *apus*.

winkiki seeds: a seed that grows underground that has a supernatural presence; used for attraction. It also can bring together the polarizing energies of *yanantan* (masculine and feminine; man and woman).

Adapted from Bryon (2012, pp. 246–9)

Reference

Bryon, D. (2012) *Lessons of the Inca Shamans, Part I: Piercing the Veil*, Enumclaw, WA: Pine Winds Press.

Index

For Product Safety Concerns and Information please contact our EU
representative GPSR@taylorandfrancis.com
Taylor & Francis Verlag GmbH, Kaufingerstraße 24, 80331 München, Germany